MW00561961

ADVANCE PRAISE FOR

Interrogating Racism in Qualitative Research Methodology

"Whites, whiteness, and white racism continue to dominate U.S. education and educational research. However, few educational leaders or leading educational researchers are willing to fully engage this white dominance. In contrast, critical race theory—an epistemology, a political movement, a wide range of voices—has emerged in educational research to address and counter, to critique and dismantle white racism. Led principally by scholars of color, the emergence of critical race theory is supremely important. This excellent collection is a valuable addition to the continuing work of critical race theory. Buy this book, learn this theory, teach it to others, practice it, and end white racism."

James J. Sheurich, Associate Professor, Department of Educational Administration, The University of Texas at Austin; Author, Research Method in the Postmodern *(1997) and* Anti-Racist Scholarship: An Advocacy *(2002)*

"The contributors in this book raise important questions about epistemological racism, call into question the frameworks that privilege certain perspectives over others, challenging the conventional wisdom we have all taken for granted. *Interrogating Racism in Qualitative Research Methodology* offers ways of seeing that have been historically excluded."

Ruben Donato, Associate Professor of Education, and Chair of Educational Foundations, Policy, and Practice, University of Colorado at Boulder

Interrogating Racism
in Qualitative Research
Methodology

Studies in the
Postmodern Theory of Education

Joe L. Kincheloe and Shirley R. Steinberg
General Editors

Vol. 195

PETER LANG
New York • Washington, D.C./Baltimore • Bern
Frankfurt am Main • Berlin • Brussels • Vienna • Oxford

Interrogating Racism in Qualitative Research Methodology

EDITED BY

Gerardo R. López
& Laurence Parker

PETER LANG
New York • Washington, D.C./Baltimore • Bern
Frankfurt am Main • Berlin • Brussels • Vienna • Oxford

Library of Congress Cataloging-in-Publication Data

Interrogating racism in qualitative research methodology /
edited by Gerardo R. López, Laurence Parker.
p. cm. — (Counterpoints; vol. 195)
Includes bibliographical references and index.
1. Discrimination in education—United States. 2. Minorities—
Education—United States. I. López, Gerardo R. II. Parker, Laurence.
III. Counterpoints (New York, N.Y.); vol. 195.
LC212.2 .I58 306.43—dc21 2001029035
ISBN 0-8204-5532-6
ISSN 1058-1634

Die Deutsche Bibliothek-CIP-Einheitsaufnahme

Interrogating racism in qualitative research methodology /
ed. by: Gerardo R. López; Laurence Parker.
–New York; Washington, D.C./Baltimore; Bern;
Frankfurt am Main; Berlin; Brussels; Vienna; Oxford: Lang.
(Counterpoints; Vol. 195)
ISBN 0-8204-5532-6

Cover design by Joni Holst

The paper in this book meets the guidelines for permanence and durability
of the Committee on Production Guidelines for Book Longevity
of the Council of Library Resources.

© 2003 Peter Lang Publishing, Inc., New York
275 Seventh Avenue, 28th Floor, New York, NY 10001
www.peterlangusa.com

All rights reserved.
Reprint or reproduction, even partially, in all forms such as microfilm,
xerography, microfiche, microcard, and offset strictly prohibited.

Printed in the United States of America

Table of Contents

Acknowledgments

We wish to express our gratitude to the many persons who assisted and encouraged us in the preparation of this book. First of all, we gratefully acknowledge Heidi Burns, senior editor at Peter Lang Publishing, Inc., Bernadette Alfaro and the production staff, copy editors, and others who worked with us toward its publication. We gratefully acknowledge the advice and suggestions of those who read portions of the manuscript chapters. Frank Margonis, Audrey Thompson, and Sofia Villenas gave generously their time and knowledge to our work and suggested new directions for our research. Jay D. Scribner, James J. Scheurich, and Michelle D. Young also provided feedback and encouragement in earlier drafts of this book. In addition, Marquita Walker, our graduate assistant at the University of Missouri-Columbia, provided critical editorial, technical, and formatting assistance when we needed it most.

A number of key individuals also played important roles in this process and steps leading up to this publication and their role needs to be acknowledged as well. The initial group of participants involved in an internet discussion list sponsored by the American Educational Research Association deserve special mention for providing us with the idea and encouragement to get started on this project. They include Marjorie Davis and Daa'Iyah Abdur-Rashid; they were key participants in initiating this discussion. Our conversations with Bob Donmoyer were very important in terms of the critical questions he posed and the encouragement he gave us to sharpen our focus and interests. Maricela Oliva, Alicia Paredes-Scribner, Stafford Hood, and Pedro Reyes also added much to the initial ideas discussed in this book.

The framework for this project began to take shape at a symposium on race and research held during an annual meeting of the American Educational Research Association. We really respect and appreciate the work and initial efforts of chapter contributors Cynthia Tyson, Melanie Carter, and paper presenters Marjorie Davis, Donna Deyhle, and Mary Hermes. Marjorie, Donna, and Mary each offered key insights into their work on race and research from critical perspectives and continued encouragement over the years which helps as much as anything. A number of key audience members at that interactive symposium should be thanked as well, including Gloria Ladson Billings, Christine Sleeter, and Patti Lather, as they asked insightful questions regarding critical race theory, researcher responsibility, the intersection of race/class/gender/sexual orientation, and issues of researcher reflexivity.

The participants of a recent interactive symposium also need to be acknowledged for continuing this process, and we want to thank Ed Buendía and Wanda Pillow for joining us as presenters and chapter contributors. Members of the audience were active participants in this session, and we want to thank all of them including, in particular, Joy Williams (who linked her narratives of historical research on black power movements to the discussions we had on race and research method, methodology, and epistemology), Barbara Sizemore (who shared her stories about segregation and racism in schooling), and Fernando Diniz and other international audience members (who shared their valuable insights regarding race and research from broader global perspectives).

Arisve Esquivel and Jennifer Ng also deserve a special thank you as they came through for us in the eleventh hour with excellent contributions. Further, we would like to acknowledge the Department of Educational Policy Studies at the University of Illinois at Urbana-Champaign and its department head, James D. Anderson. Dr. Anderson should be acknowledged in particular for his personal and departmental support of this book.

Finally, we want to especially acknowledge our families, friends, and colleagues who made this book possible with their support, understanding, and encouragement through the long hours of work that it took to see this book project to its fruition. We feel particularly privileged to have collaborated with all of the authors who contributed to this volume.

Introduction

Critical Race Theory in Education: Theory, Praxis, and Recommendations

Sylvia R. Lazos Vargas

At a time when racial and ethnic confrontations continue to make the headlines of both the national and international newspapers on an almost daily basis, Critical Race Theory is the one movement within academe that unapologetically and relentlessly makes the study of race its primary focus. When a theorist is faced with an issue in which racial attitudes play a role, the analyst responds by fully exploring how race functions in that particular context. For Critical Race Theory, race is just not an additional variable in the equation; instead, it is at the center of the research enterprise. Critical Race Theory comprises four premises. First, it posits that "race" is largely a social experience and that different racial groups experience and understand race in different ways. Second, it theorizes that the racial experiences of racial minority groups are subordinate relative to a White racial experience. Third, much of the work of Critical Race Theory applies insights of how race functions to critique rules, norms, standards, and assumptions that appear "neutral," but which systemically disadvantage or "subordinate" racial minorities. Finally, Critical Race Theory describes and theorizes about the causes that maintain racial minorities' relative subordination in a post-Civil Rights American culture that has come to embrace the equality norm (Crenshaw, Gotanda, Peller, & Thomas 1995; Davis, Johnson, & Martinez, 2001; Delgado & Stefancic, 2000).

Critical Race Theory has its roots in law, gaining visibility during the 1970s and popular currency during the 1980s and early 1990s with the success of "crossover" books such as Derrick Bell's (1987) *And We Are Not Saved*, Richard Delgado's (1995) *Critical Race Theory: The Cutting*

Edge, and Patricia Williams's (1995) *Alchemy of Race and Rights.* As Critical Race Theory (occasionally referred to as CRT) has become an established jurisprudential movement within legal academe, it spawned or influenced other movements such as Critical White Studies (focusing on White privilege), LatCrit (racial formation of Latina/os), Critical Race Feminism (focusing on the subordination of women of color), and Asian Pacific American Legal Studies (focusing on Asian and Asian Pacific Americans as a distinct ethnic/racial group). CRT and the fields that have developed from it, which I will refer to collectively as Critical Race Studies, have been greatly influenced by the humanities—in particular cultural studies, sociology, psychology, and history—in addition to the philosophical movements of postmodernism, poststructuralism, and post-colonialism. Because of their interdisciplinary roots, Critical Race Studies can be applied, in turn, to the very disciplines that influenced their creation.

Critical Race Studies' core thesis is that racism is much more endemic than the isolated one-on-one instances that can be easily named and understood, such as the dragging death of James Byrd Jr. in Texas in 1998. Rather, racism is rooted in American institutions, American culture, and concepts of self-identity and group identity. The power of race exists mainly at an unconscious level through practices of naming and labeling in dominant stereotypes about racial "others," in societal default rules that claim to be "neutral," and by the ability of majorities to ignore the many ongoing negative effects of America's racial past. The "color-blind" debate, for example, is a struggle to bring to the fore or render as inconsequential all the subtle ways in which racial assumptions continue to operate in modern society (Guinier & Torres, 2002). Time has made past racial practices and assumptions invisible to modern eyes. Thus, Critical Race Studies rejects Gunnar Myrdal's (1964) hopeful prediction that American society would eventually overcome racism because American character and Americans' legal and cultural commitment to equality, fair play, and individual merit would eventually erase past segregation practices. Instead, Critical Race Studies posits that time and good faith *alone* are not sufficient to cope with America's "race problem."

The roots of racism in American society run deep to the very founding of our nation (Bell, 1987). The U.S. Constitution of the Framers—Jefferson, Madison, Adams, and Hamilton—which Americans are taught to revere in high school civic lessons, protected that "peculiar institution" of slavery. Some devices were subtle, such as the method of election of the president by the Electoral College (U.S. Constitution, Art. II, §1), which protected the South from the possibility that a president would be elected by the popular support of the more numerous voters of the Northern states. Other provisions were more explicit, as was the Fugitive Slave clause (U.S. Constitution, Art. IV, §2, cl.2), which obligated Northern states to return escaped slaves, constitutionally enforcing Southern states' notions that Black human beings were property.

This past, it must be acknowledged, is just that, the past. However, for some Critical Race Studies theorists, White America has not yet shown that it is willing or able to abandon the many privileges that have accrued to Whites (Bell, 1992; Delgado, 1996). Neither has White America shown that it is committed in any consistent or sustained way to making the kind of systemic changes needed to eradicate racism "root and branch," as the Supreme Court famously commanded in *Brown v. Board of Education II* (Bell, 2000; Cha-Jua, 2001; Marable, 1983). Instead, empirical data show the very opposite. Almost all Americans of color feel that discrimination is something they must contend with and learn to confront on an almost daily basis, whereas a majority, but not all, of White Americans are unable to see discrimination as a significant social issue (Feagin & Sikes, 1994; Gallup Poll, 2001; Hochschild, 1995). This focus on the past may account for Critical Race Studies tendency toward pessimistic forecasts of race relations.

Professor Derrick Bell's (1992) "racial fatalism" thesis bluntly asserts that race relations in America will never improve. Bell's "interest convergence" collateral argument sets forth that social and legal conditions get better for Blacks only when the interests of Blacks converge with White interests. Thus, for example, Bell ascribes the willingness of the Supreme Court to overturn Jim Crow in primary education in *Brown v. Topeka Board of Education* to the interest of White elites to portray American society as racially just and as true followers of its democratic principles. Critiques of Jim Crow from communist nations during the Cold War, as well as the national interest in dominating global institutions, such as the United Nations, made it untenable for the United States to continue its forbearance of the blatant segregation practices and their violent enforcement, graphically depicted in newsreels (Bell, 2000).

Even though racial fatalism continues to be an important part of Critical Race Studies—mainly because it "keeps things real"—Critical Race Studies, nonetheless, embraces key liberal traditions. Predictably this creates tension, but it is this uneasy coexistence between critical fatalism and liberal optimism that distinguishes Critical Race Studies from countervailing postmodernist movements that drift toward a nihilistic bent (Harris, 1994). For example, much ink has been spilled by CRT scholars in "rights talk," arguing that courts should create remedies for discriminatory injuries that are not only clearly purposeful, but also cover unconscious and systemic discrimination (Freeman, 1978; Gotanda, 1991; Williams, 1995). More recently, Critical Race Studies scholarship has focused on the power of apology and restitution to foster racial reconciliation (Westley, 1998; Yamamoto, 1999; Yamamoto, Chon, Izumi, Kang, & Wu, 2001).

This more optimistic version of Critical Race Studies can be interpreted as holding that American society eventually can become more racially just and that Whites *can* overcome racism. This transformative message recalls the United Farm Workers' *"si, se puede"* ("yes, we can") chant, and it fits comfortably within the canons of the discipline of education. It is education, after all, that inherits the dictates of classical liberalism—i.e., the belief that education is transformative and that through schooling a knowledgeable and able citizenry is created in society (Mill, 1833/1984).

This volume and its earlier companion, *Race Is...Race Isn't: Critical Race Theory and Qualitative Studies in Education* (Parker, Deyhle & Villenas, 1999), fit within Critical Race Studies' transformative domain. One meaning of *Interrogating Racism*, used in this collection's title, is to uncover the myriad of ways in which race continues to operate in society and to sustain critiques of what is considered the norm. It is through knowledge and critique that individuals can come to understand what changes need to be made. Eventually such individual understandings can reach a critical mass sufficient to tip the scales. Thus, an academic discipline, such as education, could become less "racist," by which I mean *less biased* toward the White racial experience in its assumptions, norms, and established practices.

This volume fits within this transformative tradition. It presents a series of critiques that can lead educational practitioners to reconsider both their general assumptions of educational research practices and their discrete understandings of traditional assumptions. Laurence Parker's contribution, for example, fits neatly into the traditional CRT scholarship of "rights talk," arguing for a broader understanding of the impacts of segregation in fashioning court mandated remedies. For Parker, courts should broadly understand the present effects of past racial segregation practices to cover the entire educational track of K-12 and beyond. Past segregation and recalcitrant resistance to court ordered integration, as well as other political practices that have made de facto segregation the overriding reality of the American educational system, require radical remedies. Parker argues that these include not only adequate support for historically Black colleges, but also focusing on how Afro-American and other multicultural perspectives have been systematically excluded from the curriculum.

Jennifer Ng's chapter on multicultural education advocates for a better multicultural methodology and thus fits within CRT's transformative tradition. In her assessment of multicultural education as a training vehicle for preservice teachers who will be working in inner-city schools, she emphasizes that a properly understood multicultural methodology can be an avenue for promoting social justice. She proposes a multicultural method that critiques existing structural relationships of power and privilege, views racial identity development as part of the pedagogical mission within the classroom, and encourages teachers to constantly engage in self-critique and growth. She warns against a version of multicultural education that foments assimilationism and thus reaffirms White and class privilege in up-to-date garb. Ng's vision of multiculturalism is a *transformative educational* experience for both teacher and student.

Finally, Gerardo López's contribution seeks to inform educator's understanding of positive parental involvement in children's education. He uses the perspective of a Chicano migrant family to broadly assert that Chicano immigrant parents interpret parental involvement as providing their children with graphic life lessons (*"consejos"*) about the value of education. The prevalent assumptions about parental involvement, for López, must be inclusive of this kind of "life lesson" counseling and go beyond upper middle-class perspectives that view parental involvement more narrowly, such as helping their children with nightly homework tasks. Not only are these traditional assumptions biased toward the well-educated and affluent, they also assume all parents have the educational background to help with tasks such as algebra, and the luxury of spare

time in the evenings to work with their children. López argues that understanding why minority children fail in school might be a very complex phenomenon, and educational practitioners should resist easy
answers, such as minorities' lack of parental involvement, or facile labeling, such as "dysfunctional" family environments that may well rest on
dominant middle-class and White Anglo cultural perspectives.

At this interpretive plane Critical Race Studies might appear to be
domesticized; however, it remains radical because it cannot exist without
deep critique. Critical Race Studies works hard at "interrogating racism,"
as this volume announces, by communicating understandings of what
"race is...[and] race isn't" (Parker, Deyhle, & Villenas, 1999). How does
one "prove" that discrimination occurs in practices that educators of
good faith have established and fashioned generation after generation?
How does the traditional canon come to encompass the experience of
racial minorities, who experience and know that discrimination is part of
their daily lives, but who, because of our racial past, have also been excluded from the participatory process of formulating the academic canon
and academic management structures? Ultimately this task is also persuasive. What Professor Cheryl Harris (1993) has described as White
"property rights" can also be described as Whites' inherent comfort with
a status quo in which White perspectives dominate almost every aspect
of intellectual life. CRT practitioners must persuade those who benefit
the most from the status quo to abandon academic privilege. Audre
Lorde (1984) famously put this issue metaphorically: "shall the master's
tool dismantle the master's house?"

Such a critical project, within which this collection is also situated, is
as immense as it is profoundly ambitious. First, it challenges academics
to interrogate the familiar in the name of racial justice and a more inclusive social truth. This is an enterprise inherently subject to contestation,
and one fraught with personal risk for the researcher bearing a message
that some will inevitably interpret as noxious. Bourdieu (1988) teaches
that the enterprise of producing academic knowledge frames the parameters of what can be contested through dialogue and interrogation. Thus,
at one level, scholarship can be understood as an antecedent to setting
political and social agendas. However, the production of research is also
a social enterprise that creates academic power and privilege. Conversely, the critical enterprise aims to destabilize powerful edifices of
truth and knowledge. Thus, it inherently threatens those who preside in

self-appointed fashion over the preservation of the old truths and old canons (Gordon, 1990).

Melanie Carter's and Cynthia Tyson's contributions address these tensions at a personal level. Critical Race Studies practitioners must understand that, although their work may be valuable, their research may be marginalized and not given the recognition it may deserve by mainstream academia (Culp, 1999; Delgado, 1984, 1992). The question for individual researchers is how to proceed ethically in what they may perceive as a hostile environment for such research. For Carter the answer is "to resist the temptation to do 'hit and run' research, unconcerned about the consequences," and instead "pursue research that demonstrates concern for the collective good of our communities." Cynthia Tyson provocatively challenges those engaged in outsider research to maintain an ethic that does not take advantage of the subject of research and does not make the researcher complicit in research that tries to "hide" in neutral scientific pursuits, yet remains committed to a sustained critique of the pervasive assumptions that riddle academic research. She calls this ethic "liberatory or emancipatory" research in the fashion of Paulo Freire and argues that "research should become a conscious political, economic and personal conduit for empowerment."

Carter and Tyson underscore the inverted insider-outsider duality of Critical Race Studies. On the one hand, this research speaks to racial minority communities, as insiders; on the other hand, it seeks to inform the discipline, as racial outsiders, as to how race functions. Thus, Critical Race Studies researchers have a dual audience. The internal audience is the minority community and writings such as Carter's and Tyson's attempt to raise consciousness and solidify racial communities as healthy communities of resistance (Martinez, 1999). When Critical Race Studies addresses the external audience—i.e., all of the practitioners of the discipline—its aim is to seek a dialogue of how race functions within the discipline. This is the second central ambitious task of Critical Race Studies. At this level, Critical Race Studies carefully and methodically defines, describes and "evaluates" racism. This is the second meaning of "interrogating racism" to which the title of this collection alludes.

In this respect, Critical Race Studies methodology has been evolving. Race in American society today functions at both subtle and complex levels. For this reason, Critical Race Studies increasingly has come to study how race functions in discrete contexts. First-generation work was

more general and systemic, emphasizing the class and political components of racial discrimination and using materialist analyses of class conflict—as well as critiques of markets and their institutions—to help
depict and explain racial conflict in America. Some of these materialist
analyses lent themselves to damming interpretations of Whites' role in
the struggle for racial oppression (Marable, 1983; Omi & Winant, 1994).
Whites could be depicted as invested in continuing racial minorities' oppression (Bell, 1987). For these reasons, some in Critical White Studies
have made the remarkable call that Whites should abandon their race and
their racial privilege (Roediger, 1994). Such systemic analyses of racism,
not surprisingly, have attracted the greatest criticism (Austin, 1998; Farber & Sherry, 1997). In some contexts, these systemic arguments argua-
bly err in overstating the problem of racism (Lazos Vargas, In Press).
One response is to "interrogate racism" discretely, contextually, and
through deep analyses. Omi and Winant (1994) have described race as an
"unstable and 'decentered' complex of social meanings" (p. 55). As
Berta Hernández-Truyol (1999) explains:

> [Q]uestioning of race alone, or in isolation from other identity components,
> does not, and can not, explain or craft the setting for the inquiry into the inter-
> action of sex and race to effect gendered inequalities. Consequently, much
> work remains to be done in the areas of intersections of race, sex, and class
> with culture, language, and sexuality. (p. 813)

For this reason the second generation has evolved as a plural noun—
Critical Race Studies—which define "race" in context. For example,
Critical White Studies considers the variety of ways Whites see themselves, conceptualize race, handle racial privilege, and ignore the consequences of racial power (Delgado & Stefancic, 1997; Flagg, 1993;
Frankenberg, 1993; Wildman et al., 1996). Critical Race Feminism situates the dynamics of race and gender in the different contexts that
women of color live their lives—in the workplace, family, and reproduc-
tively (Montoya, 1994; Roberts 1997; Wing, 1997). LatCrit asserts that
the racial dynamic that affects Latinos/as is distinct from the familiar
Black/White dichotomy (Espinoza & Harris, 1998; Haney-López 1997;
Iglesias & Valdes 1998; Perea, 1998). Latinos/as contest a national cultural ideology of assimilation that would dictate that assimilation leads to
homogenization (Glazer & Moynihan, 1970) and instead assert a vision

of cultural pluralism and/or assimilation on their own cultural terms (Johnson, 1999; Martinez, 1994).

The "Critical-Race-Theory-In-Education" movement fits within the second generation of Critical Race Studies. This volume emphasizes the discrete and contextualized ways in which race affects the educational process. For example, the chapter by Wanda Pillow makes clear the understandings offered in this volume involve the formulation of a "new paradigm" that is both methodological and epistemological. The task is not simply about "doing data collection" in a different way, but it is also about producing a new kind of knowledge, outsider centered knowledge, that can systemically explain the discipline of education from a standpoint at which race is at the center.

Esquivel's chapter contributes to the study of the racial construction of Latinas/os in context. Esquivel's archival research on the struggle at the University of Illinois at Urbana-Champaign to establish a Latina/o studies program is a valuable historical lesson and documents how race influenced this administrative decision. Esquivel documents the "public dialogue" of key university administrators in which they supported Latina/o students. In their "private dialogue," which Esquivel has uncovered in the university's archives, these same administrators raise concerns based on stereotypes about "non-serious" Latina/o students who might be too "radical" but had to be appeased given the political climate of the early 1970s. Esquivel documents how the past has continued to impact the University of Illinois' Latina/o Studies program. The lack of initial commitment by key administrators led to systematic underfunding. Without this initial support, this program continues to struggle.

In addition to the epistemological concern, this volume takes on a methodological task, expanding the dominant paradigm of what kinds of research methodologies should be applied in the study of race. Quantitative research methods capture the *frequency* and *magnitude* of the impacts of various kinds of discriminations, such as stereotyping or how a dominant group may engage in preferential in-group behavior. Qualitative studies complete the picture as they capture *how* race operates.

All of the works in this collection deploy narrative to a greater or lesser extent. While narrative remains unfamiliar to the traditional methodological canon, it is an essential methodology of Critical Race Studies (Culp, 1996; Delgado, 1989), feminism (Abrams, 1991) and gay legal studies (Eskridge, 1994). Melanie Carter announces that "our stories are our theories and our method."

Why does outsider research require narrative? The reason lies in the nature of race itself. What we call "race" is a social phenomenon that is experienced *subjectively*. When theorists assert that race is "socially constructed" what they mean is that race is an objective phenomenon that has no positive or negative implication until cultural and social practices provide that social meaning. However, there is no uniform racial identity or universal racial experience (Butler, 1990; Grillo, 1995; Harris, 1990). Nonetheless, researchers can—and do—theorize about race because a series of individuals with a common racial characteristic can experience the social world *similarly*. As Patricia Hill Collins (1997) asserts, "it becomes plausible to generate arguments about working-class and/or Black culture that emerge from long standing shared experiences" (p. 378). To illustrate, Black men almost uniformly experience racial profiling, whether they are well-dressed, educated, business executives, or hip-hop teenagers. Even though police stop Black men individually, and each Black man reacts to being stopped by police based on his individual psychological makeup and the security/insecurity of his social and economic standing, Black men have come to understand these isolated experiences as common to them *as Black men*. In turn, the individual narratives of Black men, together with data capturing the frequency of this occurrence, have come to convince the American polity that "racial profiling" is an aspect of discrimination that needs to be addressed by both the legal and political systems. Thus, narratives are valuable in the study of race because narratives link the individual experience in all its subjectivity to the common experience that we quantitatively measure. The subjective and the objective cannot be separated; both are needed to forge a knowledge of race.

Nonetheless, the fact remains that narratives capture only a *single, subjective* racial experience. While no narrative attempts to universalize from a single experience, to be persuasive, narratives must also be able to show how singular insights improve disciplinary knowledge of the racial experience. Can any single subjective instance *ever* make such a claim? Let me suggest that narrative can claim relevance in three ways. First, the narrative itself might yield insights that are important to the dialogue of race. The contributions by Melanie Carter and Cynthia Tyson illustrate how narratives *per se* are helpful at a persuasive level. Second, narratives can capture an aspect of racial experiences that quantitative data have not yet documented as a relevant common experience. In other words, narratives capture subtlety that quantitative methods can only describe in broad strokes. The contributions by Gerardo López and Edward Buendía fall into this second modality. Third, narrative can anchor to qualitative analysis and critique. Jennifer Ng's assessment of multicultural education is based on her dual perspective, as an Asian American whose citizenship and belonging-ness as an American is questioned by her own students and as a middle-class suburbanite who "passed" as White in her youth. Ng's contribution interweaves personal narrative with a tough critical assessment of multicultural pedagogy.

Whatever the mode, the relevance of narratives must be judged on their own merit based on the context that the researcher presents and her ability to relate the personal insight she offers to the broader theoretical issues within the discipline (Lazos Vargas, 1999). As Edward Buendía offers, such research must "allow researchers to see, conceptualize or envision how particular social phenomenon fit or are at work in relationship to a social setting and context."

As to the first modality, how narrative might yield insights that are important to the dialogue of race, "outsider's" knowledge and perspective can help both racial minorities and non-minorities acquire deep understanding of how race functions in society (Anzaldúa, 1987; Matsuda, 1987). It is a truism that Whites and racial minorities experience their race differently in society. The key challenge in race relations is to create a reservoir of knowledge and good will that can bridge this experiential racial divide. Narratives help to bridge the cognitive racial divide by explaining the racial experience at a personal level. For example, Melanie Carter and Cynthia Tyson squarely address the theme of how race may affect the educational researcher. They ask what it means for a woman of color to be a researcher in a field dominated by Whites. W. E. B. DuBois (1903), in his landmark *The Souls of Black Folk,* described racial minorities as living in a dual world, and negotiating between divided selves: "The Negro…is…born with a veil and gifted with second-sight….[In] this double-consciousness…one ever feels his two-ness—American, and Negro; two souls, two thoughts, two unreconciled strivings; two warring ideals" (pp. 16–17). Thus, Carter and Tyson provide personal explorations of the problems of this duality in the context of being researchers of color in a field where the consequences of race have only begun to be explored. Therefore, their narratives have per se value (Lazos Vargas, 2000).

Buendía's contribution illustrates the second modality, how narrative can help the understanding of race at broader levels. A key question in race relations is why do minorities in this post-Civil Rights era continue to experience their race as "subordinate," while social, cultural, and legal practices claim to emerge from an ethic of equality? Charles Taylor's (1994) explanation is often quoted as the answer:

> [O]ur identity is partly shaped by recognition, or its absence, often by the mis-recognition of others, and so a person or a group of people can suffer real damage, real distortion, if the people or society around them mirror back to them a confining or demeaning or contemptible picture of themselves. (p. 26)

Subordination, however, merits being unpacked further. Buendía uses three narratives to make the case that racial "subordination" should be understood in more complex ways. Buendía illustrates how whimsy and humor are a foil to negative social images. By mocking rude stereotypes, making light of Whites' insensitivity, and depicting minorities, not as "victims" but rather as strategic players who understand the social dynamic of race better than Whites, racial minorities can preserve positive self-images and divert their anger into less confrontational avenues. The tradition of *basiladas* (elaborate joking) in the Chicano and Native American communities, similarly to minstrelsy in the antebellum South (Lhamon, 1996), meaningfully informs "subordination." Outsider experiences do not necessarily mean inferiority; rather these may be better understood as a mix of rejection of majority hostility, defiance, and adopting strategic behaviors for survival and health.

Finally, Jennifer Ng's contribution illustrates the third modality of narrative, how researchers benefit intellectually from being connected to their life experiences. By connecting her insight as to how her own racial privilege experienced as a youth could blind her to the salience of race, she is able to relate to well-meaning preservice teachers who suffer the same ailment. Thus, she brings to the table a deep critique of multicultural pedagogy.

In closing, allow me to underscore what I believe education practitioners already largely understand: The study of race in education is increasingly a core issue of this discipline. In the demographics of the 2000 Census, racial minorities increasingly populate the classroom, particularly at the elementary level and in the largest cities in the United States. In this new environment, understanding race is not just an interesting footnote; it is an integral challenge at the level of practice. In spite of ongoing efforts to diversify the profession, educator professionals remain mostly women, White, and middle-class. The inevitable confrontations of different racial experiences, social understandings, and identities could lead to "war in the classroom" as the motif of the future. The classroom—as a locus of clash of wills rife with misunderstandings—must be the exception; classrooms should be the locus of opportunities for learning how to bridge the racial, cultural, and class divides.

How do individual educators deal with this immense challenge? What Richard Delgado and Jean Stefancic (2000) have called "critical-race-theory-in-education" could lead the way in understanding how race affects the practice of education in ever-changing America. The response requires first, personal understanding, perhaps transformation, and, second, understanding, perhaps empathy, of the new minority pupil. It has been often stated abstractly, but it is worth repeating, that educators must overcome their own racial identities and develop the ability to be open-minded and sensitive toward other life experiences. *In practice,* how can this be accomplished? Cognitive psychologists are increasingly documenting that human beings understand at both abstract levels and emotional levels. The emotion of personal stories, similarly to the narratives in this collection, linked to the intellectual, the theoretical issues that education practitioners confront, can help educators intuit how racial differences impact their daily practices.

Educators must also understand the educational process from the perspective of their pupils. Given the rapid demographic shift in this society, this expectation increasingly refers to racial, religious, and cultural minorities. For these groups, the educational process involves coming to terms with their outsider identity. The new wave of children's stories poignantly capture the "it's not fair" feeling that minority children experience when they realize that life's opportunities and rewards will be meted out differently to them, solely because they are different. The struggle to find and become comfortable with racial identity may be the single most important socialization task that minority children confront. Insights into that process are particularly important. The range of qualitative studies presented in this collection is a starting point in that process.

Taken holistically, *Interrogating Racism* is not a "for members only" enterprise. The work in this collection is an important step toward improving intradisciplinary discourse. Research, such as this, that imparts intellectual and emotional authenticity, holds the promise of helping practitioners understand and engage previously unfamiliar realities.

References

Abrams, K. (1991). Hearing the call of stories. *79 California Law Review, 971.*

Anzaldúa, G. (1987). *Borderlands/la frontera/The new mestiza.* San Francisco, CA: Aunt Lute Books.

Austin, A. (1998). *The empire strikes back: Outsiders and the struggle over legal education.* New York: New York University Press.

Bell, D. A. (1987). *And we are not saved: The elusive quest for racial justice.* New York: Basic Books.

Bell, D. A. (1992). *Faces at the bottom of the well.* New York: Basic Books.

Bell, D. A. (2000). *Race, racism and American law* (4th ed). Gaithersburg, MD: Aspen Law & Business.

Bourdieu, P. (1988). *Homo academicus* (P. Collier, Trans.). Stanford, CA: Stanford University Press. (Original work published 1984).

Brown v. Topeka Board of Education, 347 U.S. 483 (1954).

Brown v. Board of Education II, 349 U.S. 294 (1955).

Butler, J. P. (1990). *Gender trouble: Feminism and the subversion of identity.* New York: Routledge.

Cha-Jua, S. K. (2001, February). *Racial formation and transformation: Toward a theory of Black racial oppression in structural racism and American democracy: Historical and theoretical perspectives.* Paper presented at the RAIN Conference on Racial Formation, Columbia, MO.

Collins, P. H. (1997). *Black feminist thought: Knowledge, consciousness and the politics of empowerment.* London: Harper Collins Academic.

Collins, P. H. (1991). Comment on Hekman's "Truth and method: Feminist standpoint theory revisited": Where's the power? 22 *Signs, 375,* 378.

Crenshaw, K., Gotanda, N., Peller, B., & Thomas, K. (Eds.). (1995). *Critical race theory: Key writing that formed the movement*. New York: The New Press.

Culp, J. M. (1996). Telling a Black legal story: Privilege, antiethnicity, "blunders," and transformation in outsider narratives. *82 Virginia Law Review* 69.

Culp, J. M. (1999). To the bone: Race and white privilege. *83 Minnesota Law Review* 1637.

Davis, T., Johnson, K. R., & Martinez, G. A. (2001). *A reader on race, civil rights, and American law: A multiracial approach*. Durham, NC: Carolina Academic Press.

Delgado, R. (1984). The imperial scholar: Reflections on a review of civil rights literature. *132 University of Pennsylvania Law Review* 561.

Delgado, R. (1989). Storytelling for oppositionists and others: A plea for narrative. *87 Michigan Law Review* 2411.

Delgado, R. (1992). The imperial scholar revisited: How to marginalize outsider writings, ten years later. *140 University of Pennsylvania Law Review* 1349.

Delgado, R. (Ed.). (1995). *Critical race theory: The cutting edge*. Philadelphia: Temple University Press.

Delgado, R. (1996). *The coming race war? And other apocalyptic tales of America after affirmative action and welfare*. New York: New York University Press.

Delgado, R., & Stefancic, J. (Eds.). (1997). *Critical white studies: Looking behind the mirror*. Philadelphia: Temple University Press.

Delgado, R., & Stefancic, J. (Eds.). (2000). *Critical race theory: The cutting edge* (2nd ed.). Philadelphia: Temple University Press.

DuBois, W. E. B. (1903). *The souls of Black folk*. Chicago: A.C. McClurg.

Eskridge, W. N. (1994). Gay legal narratives. *46 Stanford Law Review* 607.

Espinoza, L., & Harris, A. P. (1998). Afterword: Embracing the tar-baby—LatCrit theory and the sticky mess of race. *10 La Raza Law Journal* 499.

Farber, D. A., & Sherry, S. (1997). *Beyond all reason: The radical assault on truth in American law*. New York: Oxford University Press.

Feagin, J. R., & Sikes, M. P. (1994). *Living with racism: The Black middle-class experience*. Boston: Beacon Press.

Flagg, B. J. (1993). "Was blind, but now I see": White race consciousness and the requirement of discriminatory intent. *91 Michigan Law Review* 953.

Frankenberg, R. (1993). *White women, race matters: The social construction of whiteness.* Minneapolis, MN: University of Minnesota Press.

Freeman, A. D. (1978). Legitimizing racial discrimination through antidiscrimination law: A critical review of Supreme Court doctrine. *62 Minnesota Law Review* 1049.

Gallup Poll. (2001). *Black-white Relations in the United States 2001 Update.* Retrieved Aug. 15, 2001, from http://www.gallup.com/poll/indicators/indrace.asp

Glazer, N., & Moynihan, D. P. (1970). *Beyond the melting pot: The Negroes, Puerto Ricans, Jews, Italians, and Irish of New York City* (2nd ed.). Cambridge, MA: M.I.T. Press.

Gordon, B. (1990). The necessity of African American epistemology for educational theory and practice. *Journal of Education, 172*(3), 88–106.

Gotanda, N. (1991). A Critique of "Our constitution is color-blind." *44 Stanford Law Review* 1.

Grillo, T. (1995). Anti-essentialism and intersectionality: Tools to dismantle the master's house. *10 Berkeley Women's Law Journal* 16.

Guinier, L., & Torres, G. (2002). *The miner's canary: Enlisting race, resisting power, transforming democracy.* Cambridge, MA: Harvard University Press.

Haney-López, I. (1997). Race, ethnicity, erasure: The salience of race to LatCrit theory. *85 California Law Review* 1143.

Harris, A. P. (1990). Race and essentialism in feminist legal theory. *42 Stanford Law Review 581,* 610.

Harris, A. P. (1994). Foreword to the jurisprudence of reconstruction. *82 California Law Review* 741.

Harris, C. I. (1993). Whiteness as property. *106 Harvard Law Review* 1709.

Hernández-Truyol, B. E. (1999). Latina multidimensionality and LatCrit possibilities: Culture, gender, and sex. *53 Miami Law Review* 811.

Hochschild, J. L. (1995). *Facing up to the American dream: Race, class and the soul of the nation.* Princeton, NJ: Princeton University Press.

Iglesias, E. M., & Valdes, F. (1998). Afterword: Religion, gender, sexuality, race and class in coalitional theory: A critical and self-critical analysis of LatCrit social justice agendas. *19 U.C.L.A. Chicano-Latino Law Review* 503.

Johnson, K. R. (1999). *How did you get to be Mexican? A white/brown man's search for identity.* Philadelphia: Temple University Press.

Lazos Vargas, S. R. (1999). Democracy and inclusion: Reconceptualizing the role of the judge in a pluralist democracy. *58 Maryland Law Review* 152.

Lazos Vargas, S. R. (2000). Critical race theory and autobiography: Can a popular genre make a serious academic contribution? *18 Journal of Law & Inequality* 419.

Lazos Vargas, S. R. (In Press). History, legal scholarship, and LatCrit/critical race theory: The case of racial transformations circa the Spanish-American War, 1896–1900. *Denver U. Law Review.*

Lhamon, C. E. (1996). Mother as trope in feminist legal theory. *105 Yale Law Journal* 1421.

Lorde, A. (1984). *Sister outsider: Essays and speeches by Audre Lorde.* Freedom, CA: Crossing Press.

Marable, M. (1983). *How capitalism underdeveloped Black America: Problems in race, political economy and society.* Boston, MA: South End Press.

Martinez, G. (1994). Legal indeterminacy, judicial discretion and the Mexican-American litigation experience, 1930–80. *27 University of California-Davis Law Review* 555.

Martinez, G. (1999). Philosophical considerations and the use of narrative in law. *30 Rutgers Law Journal* 683.

Matsuda, M. J. (1987). Looking to the bottom: Critical legal studies and reparations. *22 Harvard Civil Rights–Civil Liberties Law Review* 323.

Mill, J. S. (1984). *Essays on equality, law and education.* (J. M. Robson, Ed.). London: Routledge & Kegan Paul. (Original work published 1833).

Montoya, M. E. (1994). Mascaras, trenzas y greñas: Un/masking the self while un/braiding Latina stories and legal discourse. *17 Harvard Women's Law Journal* 185.

Myrdal, G. (1964). *An American dilemma.* New York: McGraw-Hill.

Omi, M., & Winant, H. (1994). *Racial formation in the United States: From the 1960's to the 1990's* (2nd ed.). New York: Routledge.

Parker, L., Deyhle, D., & Villenas, S. (Eds.). (1999). *Race is...race isn't: Critical race theory and qualitative studies in education.* Boulder, CO: Westview Press.

Perea, J. F. (1998). *The black/white paradigm of race: The "normal science" of American racial thought. 10 La Raza Law Journal* 127.

Roberts, D. E. (1997). *Killing the Black body: Race, reproduction and the meaning of liberty.* New York: Pantheon Books.

Roediger, D. R. (1994). *Towards the abolition of whiteness: Essays on race, politics and working class history.* New York: Verso.

Taylor, C. (1994). *Multiculturalism: Examining the politics of recognition.* Princeton, NJ: Princeton University Press.

U.S. Bureau of the Census. (2001). *National population projections.* Retrieved January 18, 2001, from http://www.census.gov/population/www/pop-profile/natproj.html

U.S. Constitution, Article II, §1.

U.S. Constitution, Article IV, §2, cl.2.

Westley, R. (1998). Many billions gone: Is it time to reconsider the case for Black reparations? *40 Boston College Law Review* 429.

Wildman, S. M., Armstrong, M., Davis, A. D., & Grillo, T. (1996). *Privilege revealed: How invisible preference undermines America.* New York: New York University Press.

Williams, P. J. (1995). *The alchemy of race and rights: Diary of a law professor.* Cambridge, MA: Harvard University Press.

Wing, A. K. (Ed.). (1997). *Critical race feminism: A reader.* New York: New York University Press.

Yamamoto, E. K. (1999). *Interracial justice: Conflict and reconciliation in post-civil rights America.* New York: New York University Press.

Yamamoto, E. K., Chon, M., Izumi, C. L., Kang, J., & Wu, F. H. (2001). *Race, rights and reparation: Law and the Japanese American internment.* Gaithersburg, MD: Aspen Publishers.

1

Research, Race, and an Epistemology of Emancipation

Cynthia Tyson

As an African American female researcher, I address the topic of race-based epistemologies with a continuation of an earlier question I raised (Tyson, 1998) in response to the Scheurich and Young (1997) *Educational Researcher* article titled "Coloring Epistemologies: Are Our Research Epistemologies Racially Biased?" The question is: If a race-based epistemology can be African American (or feminist, or gay/lesbian, or First Nation, and so forth), what is it that makes this epistemology different when developing a formalized research methodology?

My answer was then, and is still rooted now, in the "specificity of oppression—the response to which is not based solely on victimization but on struggle and survival" (Tyson, 1998, p. 22). The specificity of oppression made it necessary for the creation of a specific theory of knowledge in response to distinctive kinds of nationally sanctioned inhumanity. To be Black in America, for example, specified historically, and continues to specify, the ways in which systemic forms of racism—from enslavement through Jim Crow laws and onto racial profiling—manifests themselves in our experience. Across these historical periods, what counts as knowledge about racism has changed as attempts to redress problems have yielded continued oppression. In other words, the ending of slavery drove racism and the disposition to enslave into different arenas.

For example, the legal and social addressing of Jim Crow laws and practices were deeply entrenched in the varieties of racism that characterized earlier times. Even challenges to the Constitution and later amendments were only yielding returns that were reflective of the legal system from which they grew. Critical Race Theory (Crenshaw, Gotanda Peller,

& Thomas, 1995; Delgado, 1995a; Matsuda, Lawrence, Delgado, & Crenshaw, 1993; Parker, 1998), a countertheory of critical legal studies, began to deconstruct the mainstream legal ideology, which ignores racial oppression, and placed at its center the endemic racism in law and society that is often devoid of contextual and historical examinations.

In other words, Critical Race Theory (CRT) involved the examination of external practices—such as laws and policies—that restricted African Americans from full participation and citizenship in society. It accomplished this through a series of counterstories that kept race as the center unit of analysis. In this regard, counterstories and storytelling functioned as a type of counterdiscourse, as a means of analysis to examine the epistemologies of racially oppressed peoples. Under this framework, the metanarrative shifts to identify and account for the continuing anguish of racism in the face of legal and social "fixes." It is this very ignoring of the role of race and racism that CRT aims to challenge, attempting to analyze the traditions, "presuppositions and perceived wisdoms that make up the common culture about race that invariably render African Americans" (Ladson-Billings & Tate, 1995) and other disenfranchised groups powerless.

During a discussion about racism, a friend once asked me, "Why do Black folks want something special?" I answered, in the words of Dr. King, "Because something special has been done to us." It is this specificity of oppression that has a collective and empirical impact on the epistemological backdrop of research. As I stated in my earlier work:

> I reflect on the experience of being Black in America, I weave together the African tribal and American familial, community, and religious traditions—folk tales, foods, medicine men, priests and priestesses, Black churches—but I must also weave in the thread or realism in the politics, economics and so-called intellectual thought that allowed for the atrocities perpetuated by the Nazis in the holocaust, for the Middle Passage and the enslavement of millions of Black Africans, for Japanese interment camps, and for the annihilation of indigenous peoples. (Tyson, 1998, p. 22)

My theory of knowledge connects with these accounts of the threads of racism in politics, economics, and so-called intellectual thought that allow and sustain a full range of oppressions.

It is the understanding of lived oppression—the struggle to make a way out of no way—which propels us to problematize dominant ideologies in which knowledge is constructed. Postcolonialism and the so-called "standpoint" positions highlight the role of racism in societal ideology as endemic to the theoretical frameworks that underpin research epistemologies. These research frameworks represent blindness to the ways of knowing that come from the specific experience of oppression.

It is my contention that such experiences set the stage for inquiry from a different plane. In other words, the experience of racism and oppression moves the oppressed "Other" into a paradigm of survival creating a view of the world that is not shared by those gatekeepers who legitimize academic discourse and research.

A new question then arises: How do we begin to analyze the pervasiveness of race and the need for it to move from the margin to the center of our research paradigms? In answering this question, the initial challenge is to understand the complexity of such epistemological moves— moves that will require a multifaceted lens, much like a kaleidoscope, in an attempt to understand the implications for inquiry. For example, a small ball, when viewed with the naked eye, has discernable elements— e.g., color, shape, and texture. The same ball, when viewed through a kaleidoscope, is no longer a single color but may take on a prism of colors. Moreover, the once smooth round edges may now be flat in places and appear to have different textual properties.

In like fashion, racism, when viewed through different lenses, may also have different properties from the one deeply established in the consciousness of American society. These different perspectives engender many possibilities, particularly opportunities to transform an ideology of enslavement and oppression, to one of economic, political, and social equality.

Such a transformation, however, requires work on two fronts. First, we must systematically and consciously resist the injustices of racism. Second, we must work constructively to improve the ways in which the racism surfaces in the vocalized assumptions of those in power—i.e., who have the power to make generalizations "stick." In essence, we simultaneously attack the causes and heal the effects. We must work at both the macro level and the micro level—with systems and with individuals—in order to have an impact on ideology.

Working at two levels, however, raises yet another question: What effect does this rhythmic alteration have on researchers of color? The unending "dual consciousness" that DuBois[1] (1903) spoke of, places enhanced demands on marginalized researchers—most often African

American, Chicanas(os), Latinas(os), Asian American/Pacific Islander, American Indian/First Nation, Gay/Lesbian/Transgender[2]—on the development of our research agendas with, and in relation to, our community responsibilities (see also Abu-Lughod, 1990; Behar, 1993; Behar & Gordon, 1995; Delgado Bernal, 1998; Nayaran, 1993; Trinh, 1990; Villenas, 1996).

To awaken this stance and enact racial realism, to move race from the margin to the center of our research paradigms, entails a deconstruction of the White racial ideology as the normative stance. In other words, the status of being "White" is not necessarily superior; rather, all "others" are measured against it in terms of their "differences." While Whiteness, on the surface, has politically shifted from a claim of supremacy to the role of victim (as in reverse affirmative action suits), it retains, and potentially gains, power through being the standard against which everything else is compared. Whiteness remains the center and retains its control through "othering," a process that demeans the efforts of "others."

In discussions among educational researchers (e.g., López, 1997), the question has been asked, "Shall the master's tools dismantle the master's house?" (Lorde, 1984). To accept the colonial codification of the master and his tools in relation to our work suggests that we are, in essence, workers on "data plantations" (Irvine, 1997): enslaved, and in need of emancipation. This metaphor, though, is not to suggest that the research machine traps scholars of color or that we can never transcend our subordinate position because we rely on the master's toolbox for our livelihood. Rather, as Ladson-Billings (1998) has pointed out, all we can do is "add different voices to the received wisdom or canon" (p. 23). By offering counterstories, and different ways of viewing the world, emancipatory research is generated.

Emancipatory Research

> The ways of White folks, I mean some White folks, is too much for me. I reckon they must be a few good ones, but most of em ain't good leastwise they don't treat me good and Lawd knows, I ain't never done nothing to em nothing a-tall. (Hughes, 1933/1990, p. 171)

In his 1933 book (republished in 1990) from which the above quote was taken, Langston Hughes reveals the protagonist's knowledge of race, while defining the dominant White ideology from a non-White perspective. This definition "from the outside" renders visible the thinking and actions that stem from assumptions made invisible by their pervasiveness within the ideology. In other words, these assumptions cannot be made visible from within the ideology itself. The invisibility of these principles arises from a blindness that fails to legitimate perspectives that are not beneficial to White society (Bell, 1995).

Visibility, when achieved, is therefore an optional matter. What remains invisible are the epistemologies and "ways of White folks"— mores and practices that have been institutionalized throughout our history. They continue to exist across a variety of venues regardless of place and space. As is commonly known, wherever there is a dominant truth or story that is widely unquestioned, such a truth is always accompanied by the need to set the proverbial record straight.

Such an act requires us to create emancipatory epistemologies from which liberatory research methodologies are born. If liberation achieved by individuals at the expense of others is an act of oppression, then, educational research achieved by individuals at the expense of others is also an act of oppression. It is incumbent upon researchers, therefore, to stop "trying to hide in…the neutrality of scientific pursuits, [or be] indifferent to how findings are used, [or]…uninterested in considering for whom or for what interest they are working" (Freire, 1998). In other words, if we are to engage in emancipatory research, we must stop trying to benefit ourselves, and engage in the process of researching for the greater good of our communities.

If our goal is to do emancipatory research, we must ask ourselves "Who really benefits?" The reward(s) of the academy can deceive us into believing that our work is emancipatory when it is not. Emancipatory research cannot be built on the "participants' backs," but must have a simultaneous commitment to radical social change as well as to those individuals most oppressed by social cultural subordination.

As long as liberatory research can be interpreted as methodologically distinct, but not critically different in its ability to improve, challenge, and alter traditional forms of academic research in general—or social and cultural consequences specifically—then it will continue to be "tolerated" as a "variation" and "alternative" research stance. It will continue to be an "other" within the larger educational research community.

Liberatory or emancipatory research is likely to be viewed this way by White researchers who tend to call into question all inquiry that provides researchers with the opportunity to use their own race-based reality as theoretical grounding for epistemological and methodological moves. Such questioning constitutes a paradigmatic "backlash" that leaves race-based research and scholarship in a proverbial abyss.

Conservative backlashes notwithstanding, emancipatory research has been accepted in educational circles—but only as a means to offer a sanitized and depoliticized "reading list" in graduate qualitative research courses and/or opening conversations to discuss epistemological considerations related to the intersections and/or conflicts with qualitative research methodology (Denzin & Lincoln, 1997). Too often, however, the role of race and racism becomes little more than a critique of the traditional research epistemologies, never questioning the "normality" of White research forms. In essence, academic research that is situated in raced-based, gender-based, social class-based, and postcolonially based ways of knowing tends to be blocked by empiricisms, scientisms, and normalisms that remains methodologically oppressive.

Epistemologies of Emancipation

Research is formalized curiosity. It is poking and prying with a purpose.
–Hurston, 1994, p. 687

If educational researchers are to operate from epistemologies of emancipation—with frameworks that are transformative (as opposed to accommodative) in nature—and engage in methodologies that encourage the participants to challenge and change the world, then the purpose of data collection in educational research would be fundamentally different. Rather than collect data for data's sake, research would become a conscious political, economic, and personal conduit for empowerment. Educational research could then be a catalyst to support and complement larger struggles for liberation. The very nature of radical thought and liberatory action is that it has far-reaching effects and comes with the heightened sense of responsibility for researchers whose work is based on a commitment to defy historical and contemporary racial oppression. For scholars of color who have experienced the specificity of oppression their entire lives, such a move provides the basis for research that unapologetically places discussions of race, gender, class, and sexuality as part of a larger political and epistemological struggle for a better and just future.

The Emancipatory Researcher

[W]e have to think seriously about linkages between research and activism, about cross—racial and transnational coalitional strategies, and abut the importance of linking our work to radical social agendas. (Davis, 1998, p. 231)

Emancipatory research is generally recognized as most effective when undertaken by—or in concert with—the community, organizations, or peoples that are most affected by its analysis and dissemination. As such, research born at the intersections of the specificity of oppression can become a catalyst to fundamentally change the conditions of oppression (Davis, 1998, Freire, 1970). There are, however, certain challenges that will continue to arise as we move forward with this effort.

As researchers of color, the ability to do emancipatory research potentially creates an alienated life. Indeed, the trauma of independence exacts much from those who build their research agendas outside dominant educational research circles. We survive on the margins and take pride in the uniqueness of our marginality. Without a doubt, though, such a position also exacts a cost—do we advance our own careers or do we serve our communities? Many times, we are often caught in the middle of two competing agendas (Tyson, 1998; see also Delgado Bernal, 1998; Villenas, 1996).

Moreover, as Critical Race Theorists suggest, racism is a permanent fixture in our society. Therefore, it does not take long for us, researchers of color, to face the reality that no matter how hard we work, we will probably not see the end of racism in our lifetimes. Such a realization can discourage us from aggressively moving forward.

Nevertheless, many of us hold on to the belief that all we can do in our lifetime is become agents for social change through our research practices. If we wait for racism to be obliterated before we begin to enact epistemologies of emancipation, then we will be wasting—and waiting— a long time.

Emancipatory research facilitates radical thought; radical thought supports radical action, and radical action can advance a transformative social agenda. In other words, research can provide a working model for resolving the problems of marginalized populations because it incorporates a more organic methodology, connects with the "grass roots," enhances data collection and collaborative analysis, and because the grounded theory that arises from the specificity of the day-to-day experiences of oppressed people can provide links with broader social and political solutions to educational problems. Its hope and promise lie in courageous action for change and the desire for critical understanding.

Historically, an increased desire for liberatory and courageous action has led to a revolution. The time for change is now, and the time for educational research to lead such a change is at hand. Academia, on the other hand, is not a place for fermenting a revolution. Oppositionally speaking, academia is conservatively maintaining the status quo: a status quo that maintains a context that confuses knowing and understanding. As a researcher who shares the intersections of specificity of institutional and historical oppression, as a researcher whose epistemologies and methodologies can set the stage for change, and as a researcher who wants to teach "liberating arts and sciences," I await, prepare, and will join the educational research revolution.

Notes

1. Du Bois's concept of "double consciousness," he described as "a peculiar sensation....One ever feels this twoness—an American, a Negro; two souls, two thoughts, two unreconciled strivings; two warring ideals in one dark body, whose dogged strength alone keeps it from being torn asunder."

2. Gays, lesbians, and transgenders are not minority groups based on race. However, the historical oppression is analogous, in some ways, to racial oppression.

References

Abu-Lughod, L. (1990). Can there be a feminist ethnography? *Women and Performance: A Journal of Feminist Theory, 5*, 7–27.

Behar, R. (1993). *Translated woman: Crossing the border with Esperanza's story.* Boston, MA: Beacon Press.

Behar, R., & Gordon, D. (Eds.). (1995). *Women writing culture*. Berkeley, CA: University of California Press.

Bell, D. (1995). Racial realism—After we're gone: Prudent speculations on America in a post-racial epoch. In R. Delgado (Ed.), *Critical race theory: The cutting edge* (pp. 2–8). Philadelphia: Temple University Press.

Crenshaw, K., Gotanda, N., Peller, B., & Thomas, K. (Eds.). (1995). *Critical race theory: Key writing that formed the movement*. New York: The New Press.

Davis, A. (1998). Black women in the academy. In J. James, (Ed.). *The Angela Y. Davis Reader* (pp. 222–231). Malden, MA: Blackwell.

Delgado, R. (Ed.). (1995a). *Critical race theory: The cutting edge*. Philadelphia: Temple University Press.

Delgado, R. (1995b). The imperial scholar. In K. Crenshaw, N. Gotanda, B. Peller, & K. Thomas, (Eds.), *Critical race theory: Key writings that formed the movement* (pp. 46–57). New York: The New Press.

Delgado Bernal, D. (1998). Using a Chicana feminist epistemology in educational research. *Harvard Educational Review, 68*(4), 555–582.

Denzin, N., & Lincoln, Y. (1997). *Handbook of qualitative research*. Thousand Oaks, CA: Sage.

DuBois, W. E. B. (1903). *The souls of black folk*. Chicago: A. C. McClurg

Freire, P. (1970). *Pedagogy of the oppressed*. New York: Continuum.

Freire, P. (1998). *Pedagogy of freedom: Ethics, democracy and civic courage*. Lanham, MD: Rowman & Littlefield.

Hughes, L. (1990). *The ways of white folks*. New York: Vintage Books. (Original work published 1933)

Hurston, Z. (1994). *Folklore, memoirs, & other writings*, C. Wall (Ed.). New York: The Library of American Literary Classics.

Irvine, J. (1997). *Critical knowledge for diverse teachers & learners*. Washington, DC: AACTE.

Ladson-Billings, G. (1998). Just what is critical race theory and what is it doing in a nice field like education? *International Journal of Qualitative Studies in Education, 11*(1), 7–24.

Ladson-Billings, G., & Tate, W. (1995). Toward a critical race theory of education. *Teachers College Record, 97*, 47–68.

López, G. R. (1997). Reflections on epistemology and standpoint theories: A response to "An indigenous approach to creating knowledge." *International Journal of Qualitative Studies in Education, 11*(2), 225–231.

Lorde, A. (1984). The master's tools will never dismantle the master's house. *Sister outsider: Essays & speeches.* Freedom, CA: Crossing Press.

Matsuda, M., Lawrence, C., Delgado, R., & Crenshaw, K. (Eds.). (1993). *Words that wound: Critical race theory, assaultive speech, and the first amendment.* Boulder, CO: Westview.

Narayan, K. (1993). How native is a "native" anthropologist? *American Anthropologist, 95*(3), 671–686.

Parker. L. (1998). Race is…race ain't: An exploration of the utility of critical race theory in qualitative research in education. *International Journal of Qualitative Studies in Education, 11*, 43–55.

Scheurich, J. J., & Young, M. D. (1997). Coloring epistemologies: Are our research epistemologies racially biased? *Educational Researcher, 26*(4), 4–17.

Trinh, T. M. (1990). Not you/like you: Post-colonial women and the interlocking questions of identity and difference. In G. Anzaldúa (Ed.). *Making face, making soul/Haciendo caras: Creative and critical perspectives by feminists of color* (pp. 371–375). San Francisco: Aunt Lute Books.

Tyson, C. (1998). Coloring epistemologies: A response. *Educational Researcher, 27*(9), 21–22.

Villenas, S. (1996). The colonizer/colonized Chicana ethnographer: Identity, marginalization, and co-optation in the field. *Harvard Educational Review, 66*(4), 711–731.

2

Telling Tales Out of School: "What's the Fate of a Black Story in a White World of White Stories?"

Melanie Carter

The exclusionary practices of academic social sciences along racial lines have maintained a cultural hegemony that has monopolized the construction and legitimation of methodological perspectives.

—Stanfield II, 1993, p. 13

Her stories exist because of their parts and each part is a story worth telling, worth examining to find the stories it contains. What seems to ramble begins to cohere when the listener understands the process, understands that the voice seeks to recover everything, that the voice proclaims nothing is lost, that the listener is not passive but lives like everything else within the story.

—Wideman, 1981/1998a, pp. 198–199

This chapter[1] is the culmination of a dialogue that began in 1997 and has resulted in three national presentations, at least three published articles (López, 2001; Parker, 1998; Tyson, 1998), and much informal conversation around the question "How does raced/race-based research intersect with qualitative research methodology?" This chapter reflects my effort to address two critical elements of this question. First, I challenge the rigidity of academically sanctioned research methods that hinder the illumination of experiences that trouble mainstream educational theories and practices. Second, I challenge researchers to view alternative methodological approaches and "publishing venues" as viable options for conducting and disseminating their work.

At a 1997 American Educational Research Association (AERA) symposium, I presented a paper entitled "In Search of a Methodology for

Me: Does Critical Race Theory Help?" (Carter, 1997). In that paper, I embraced Critical Race Theory (CRT) and argued that the strength of CRT was, and in fact is, its emphasis on perspective and context or what I call an "epistemology of specificity." According to William Tate (1997), CRT critiques both liberal and conservative legal ideologies by rejecting the notion that law or justice is colorblind. This refusal to build theory from an aberrant falsehood situates CRT outside of more traditionally acceptable alternative methodologies. Within the academy, theories that are race or gender specific, often called standpoint theories, are viewed as narrow or undeveloped interpretive approaches. Nonetheless, Critical Race Theory embraces specificity as necessary for grounded epistemologies—thereby relying upon personal storytelling and narratives to shape ways of knowing.

The use of CRT in educational research is appealing for at least three reasons. First, it encourages researchers to trouble methodological rules that stipulate a particular interpretation of the dominant narrative. Second, it is useful as a platform to name and interpret realities that cannot or have not been understood using other methodologies. Third, I am encouraged by CRT's intrinsic applicability as a methodological tool to change societal conceptions of truth and justice versus other analytical tools that are not linked to societal change.

At a second AERA symposium, I asked "Methodologically Speaking: How does a 'Race' Woman do Raced Research in the Academy?" (Carter, 1998). In that paper I explored my understanding of self as a Black woman scholar doing research for the greater good. I argued the necessity of resisting the temptation to privilege my needs in the academy over the needs of the community. Though the two are not mutually exclusive, this effort requires ongoing vigilance. This vigilance emerges from an ideological framework, informs the focus of my research, directs my inquiry, and stipulates the level of my commitment to and actions toward my community. How we treat our communities is dependent upon how we view them. If I assume a singular identity as a researcher—rather than embrace my multiple identities as researcher *and* African American *and* woman *and* working class—then I reinforce the legitimacy of the often fictive relationship between the researcher and the researched. This artificial relationship creates an attitude of benign benevolence toward the communities where we conduct our research. More specifically, this position, as Vanessa Siddle Walker (1999) observes, intends "to do no harm" to our communities "rather than make an overt attempt to do them good" (p. 226).

This oxymoric position is indeed troublesome. It invents an artificial distinction between indifference and malintention that conceals the grave danger that both pose. Our challenge, as conscientious researchers, is to call out researcher neglect and arrogance parading as neutrality. As scholars of color we have a responsibility to ourselves and our communities to critically examine research methods that foster such methodological attitudes.

Patricia Hill Collins (2000) discusses the way in which positivist research methods and epistemological stances mute Black women scholars. Collins argues that rules dictating object and subject distance, emotional detachment, ethics, values, and methods of ascertaining truth are at odds with their cultural frames of reference. As a result, "Black women are more likely to choose an alternative epistemology for assessing knowledge claims, one using standards that are consistent with black women's criteria for methodological adequacy" (p. 189). Collins's call for Black women to determine their own methodological parameters problematizes the "one size fits all" myth that protects mainstream methodology from critique. However, while we are aware of the limitations of imposed research methods, we continue to utilize them. This essay seeks to explore and confront this dilemma.

Questions are frequently raised about the intentions and responsibilities of researchers whose work focuses on women and people of color. Some argue that work that considers the perplexity of race and gender realities in a White male dominated society requires an especially grounded perspective (Anderson, 1993; Facio, 1993). Such a perspective must be cultivated by privileging and substantiating experiences and relationships that respect and encourage methods that illuminate—perhaps even parallel and intersect with—macronarratives and micronarratives. I believe that storytelling is an effective way to make the implicit explicit. It has an organizing function that helps us to code and categorize.

However, the ability to fully understand and interpret the story is linked to the relationship between the researcher and the researched. Their shared dialogue is not merely "soon to be interpreted data." Instead, it is the cultural cradle that protects and bonds the stories between the researched and the researcher. I, therefore, called for the utilization of multiple and even hybrid methods of inquiry to conduct and interpret our research. I identified both Critical Race Theory and Portraiture (Law-rence-Lightfoot & Davis, 1997)[2] as methodologically attractive. For most researchers, locating a way of knowing that is "in sync" with the experi-ences of the researched is imperative. For me, it is the scaffolding upon which this ongoing dialogue rests. These approaches engender a meth-odological environment in which the researcher and the researched co-construct meaning instead of relying upon processes that dictate analysis and interpretation. These hybrid methods are not static modes of inquiry but instead create a methodologically responsive and dynamic terrain—one that simultaneously accommodates and interrogates multiple concep-tions of truth.

In both papers, I troubled some of the traditional boundaries of quali-tative research by acknowledging the centrality of race in my research and thinking aloud about how that understanding informed—both con-sciously and unconsciously—my methodological approach. In contrast to other methodologies (perhaps, even some nontraditional ones), CRT does not allow race to be left untheorized. Instead theorizing race drives the research (Ladson-Billings, 1998; Ladson-Billings & Tate, 1995). While race is indeed a shifting signifier, it cannot be ignored. As John Stanfield (1993) makes clear "racelessness has no meaningful category in Ameri-can experience" (p. 18). In short to ignore the magnitude of race and cul-ture in my work is to silence me.

I Pledge Allegiance to…:
Researcher Double Consciousness

> My struggle over form, content, etc. has been informed by a desire to convey knowledge in ways that make it accessible to a wide range of readers. It is not a reflection of a longing to work in ways that will enable me to have institutional power or support. This is simply not the only form of power available to writers and thinkers. There is power in having a public audience for one's work that may not be particularly academic, power that comes from writing in ways that enable people to think critically in everyday life. (hooks, 1990, p. 130)

Both symposia focused upon naming—and then deconstructing—dominant epistemological and ideological truths that determine and vali-date traditional research paradigms. These societally sanctioned truths stifle alternative conceptions of truth, justice, responsibility, and ethics.

While those were, and still remain, important considerations, novelist John Edgar Wideman's (1990) profound question regarding the "fate of a Black story" elevates our discourse by bringing to the fore the responsibility that the narrator has for the narrative. In other words, it forces us to be still and reflect upon the purpose of our work. As researchers we do have an obligation to the experiences that we expose. We cannot be casual participants, curious onlookers, or disinterested scholars if our purpose is to conduct research that is grounded in truth telling that seeks to liberate rather than oppress. We must not be motivated or intoxicated by the extrinsic rewards of the academy. We have a responsibility to resist the temptation to do "hit and run" research that is unconcerned about the consequences of our work. Instead, as much as is possible, we must encourage a researcher sensibility and ethic that expresses and demonstrates concern for the collective good of our communities. We must facilitate a "rearticulated consciousness" (Collins, 2000, p. 186) in the academy that deconstructs the hierarchical relationship that often characterizes the relationship between researchers and their research participants. It is important to examine these relationships theoretically, but it is more important to consciously create a research culture that privileges people over process. All researchers share in this responsibility.

Communities of color have suffered greatly at the hands of indifferent and unresponsive researchers and are particularly vulnerable. A methodological approach alone will not protect our communities from harm. However, it is imperative that we think about our individual and collective research motivations by reflecting upon the purpose of our work. Who is likely to benefit? Who is likely to suffer? Are our efforts designed to direct attention to "our work" and to deflect attention from our communities? Marginalized communities are favorite sites for researchers primarily because the communities themselves represent the possibility to observe phenomena that cannot be found in mainstream communities. As a result, renditions of the experiences of "the other" abound. However, these renditions have the potential to do great harm by reinforcing stereotypic understandings. Research methods that focus on external perspectives do not offer much hope for counternarratives. Instead they validate what we seek to deconstruct in the first place.

This essay also reflects my effort to peel away the ideological, epistemological, and methodological layers that conceal—and often distort— accounts that convey the lived experiences of the focus of our research. It

simultaneously illuminates the illegitimacy of the academy as the validating site for race conscious research and brings to the fore the core of
our work: the narratives, the stories, the tales.

To be sure, it is important how we tell our tales, but where we tell
them is, at least, equally important. Rules of the academy, whether spoken or unspoken, govern academic discourse, and therefore the rules and
roles of inquiry. The internalization of these rules has led to "academe-
centric" research approaches that privilege process over context. Many
would argue these rules protect the academy's integrity and necessary
standards of rigor. Others argue that these are gatekeeping techniques
used to protect the dominant narrative from new interpretations that cannot be fully explored with traditional modes of inquiry.

Derrick Bell (1994) writes of how his use of storytelling was received by his colleagues: "My publications were looked upon warily by
faculty members who judged my area of civil rights peripheral to the
main body of law, and my style of storytelling to be less rigorous than
the doctrine-laden, citation-heavy law review process they favored" (p.
39). However, he persisted, and his work (1992, 1994) inspired the development of Critical Race Theory as a method of legal analysis
(Crenshaw, Gotanda, Peller, & Thomas, 1995). Bell's account illustrates
the inadequacy of traditional rules of legal analysis in civil rights law, the
refusal of academic gatekeepers to acknowledge this inadequacy, and the
importance of continued efforts to develop culturally grounded interpretive approaches. Static methodological rules render invisible (within the
academy) stories that do not or cannot conform. This interpretation is not
necessarily an indictment of the academy; instead it is an effort to explore our insistence that it is the best site for the cultivation and dissemination of our work. As researchers who engage in race conscious
research, our fate is the fate of our stories.

This dilemma is certainly not new. Researchers of color have used
traditional and nontraditional venues (popular presses, self-publishing) to
disseminate their work. In most instances scholars view their work as
moving beyond theoretical gymnastics toward righteous research: research that is representative of a critical telling and seeks to facilitate and
encourage individual change, collective transformation, and deep reflec-
tion. Consequently, scholars must be concerned with where their research is published, who has access to their work and how this
knowledge will be utilized. The conscious decision to disseminate their

work outside of the academy's gates challenges the institution's mythical monopoly on knowledge and knowledge production (Gordon, 1999). This paper explores how we, as scholars in the academy, decide where we place our work and what that decision potentially reveals about who we are, what the academy is, and ultimately the fate of our research. This line of thinking seeks to trouble the academy's stronghold on legitimizing scholarship and the underlying censorship, which it seeks to protect. Again, this thinking is not intended to minimize the necessity of meaningful participation in the academic arena by scholars of color. Instead it challenges all of us to consider issues of access and audience when considering where and how to disseminate our work.

Our Race or Our Research: Must We Choose?

From these narratives—these analyses of the heavens, nature and humanity—it is evident that black people are building theory on every conceivable level. An internally derived, representative impression of core black culture can serve as an anthropological link between private pain, indigenous communal expression and the national marketplace of issues and ideas. These people not only know the troubles they've seen, but have profound insight into the meaning of those vicissitudes. (Gwaltney, 1993, p. xxvi)

The paradigm of race authors one sad story, repeated far too often, that would reduce the complexity of our cultural heritage. Race preempts our right to situate our stories where we choose. It casts us as minor characters in somebody else's self-elevating melodrama. (Wideman, 1994, p. xxi)

I come to this work as an African American woman passionate about race. This passion, however, does not embrace a narrow and one-dimensional definition of race. It rejects essentialist notions of race that favor a consensus perspective and embraces multiple/polyphonic and highly textured definition. Even so, I am passionate about critically exploring the way in which race, and conceptions of race, shape educational theory and practices over time and space. I am passionate about creating safe spaces to share the rich and varied stories that give the term "race" meaning.

Traditional academic research practices, though, do not embrace passion as a necessary theoretical or analytical lens. Researchers must be

objective, their findings empirically defendable, their hypotheses accepted or rejected. This prescribed and constricted expectation of researchers and their work can discourage scholars of color from pursuing
research that considers race as a primary focus.

Nonetheless, many scholars of color have resisted the academy's
urging and have grounded their work in issues of race (e.g., Anderson,
1988; Delpit, 1995; Fordham, 1996; Gordon, 1994; Hilliard, 1997;
hooks, 1994; Irvine, 1990; Ladson-Billings, 1994; Shujaa, 1994; and
Walker, 1996, to name a few). This body of work is representative of
both the universality and the specificity of the lives of people of color
and has provided the weapons to counteract racist and stereotypical notions that inform White supremacy ideology. Clearly, the struggle for
scholars of color to read race, think race, research race and write race
into the academy is ongoing. My research (Carter, 1996) challenges the
dominant schooling narrative by illuminating the schooling experiences
of African Americans. This historical work deconstructs White suprema-
cist mythology by acknowledging what I call "Black active resistance" in
the face of lacking (and oftentimes nonexistent) schooling opportunities.

Contrary to mainstream understandings of educational trajectories,
Black people have actively sought, and courageously struggled, to be
educated (Anderson, 1988; Walker, 1996). This acknowledgment of
Black agency is not new. In fact, many scholars have written about the
social, political, educational, economic, and ideological shackles that we,
as African Americans, have had to overcome throughout history (Du
Bois, 1968/1997; Hilliard, 1997; Woodson, 1933/1977). Our challenge is
to constantly reconstruct our identity and resist dominant renderings that
negate the role of White racism in the larger social order. Indeed, our
challenge is to tell our version of the story within a cultural and conceptual framework that honors Africans in America and throughout the Diaspora.

Derrick Bell's (1992, 1994) and Patricia Williams's (1991) use of
personal narratives and allegorical tales humanizes the interpretation of
legal doctrine. South Africans' testimony before their Truth and Reconciliation Committee personalizes the atrocities of apartheid. These examples illustrate what we already know: "data" do not talk, people do. CRT
challenges the hegemonic framework that legitimizes mainstream worldviews and knowledge production by embracing organic knowledge cultivated by our experiences. Our stories often conceal the complexities of

our experiences to larger society. However, they seek to synthesize the essence of our individual and collective narratives. While contradicting the largely mythical American themes of fairness, democracy, and justice, they validate the truth as we know it.

Dysconscious Reverence:
Our Relationship with the Academy

The need for hierarchical ranking and the deep-seated racism shot through bourgeois humanistic scholarship cannot provide Black intellectuals with either the proper ethos or conceptual framework to overcome a defensive posture. And charges of intellectual inferiority can never be met upon the opponent's terrain—to try to do so only intensifies one's anxieties. Rather the terrain itself must be viewed as part and parcel of an antiquated form of life unworthy of setting the terms of contemporary discourse. (West, 1991, pp. 138–139)

Telling ourselves our own stories—interpreting the nature of our world to ourselves, asking and answering epistemological and ontological questions in our own voices and on our own terms—has as much as any single factor been responsible for the survival of African-Americans and their culture. (Gates, 1989, p. 17)

The academic terrain, as Cornel West (1991) suggests, must be included in our struggle against methodological dictatorship. He calls upon Black scholars to adopt what he calls an "insurgency" model (p. 143). This model, according to West, "privileges collective intellectual work that contributes to communal resistance and struggle" (p. 144). West further notes that the central task of postmodern Black intellectuals is to "stimulate, hasten, and enable alternative perceptions and practices by dislodging prevailing discourses and powers. This can be done only by intense intellectual work and engaged insurgent praxis" (p. 144). Such a model is ideologically and methodologically empowering because it provides us with a language to speak our truths in the academy and in our communities. It is unapologetically linked to social action and social change.

In her piece entitled "The fringe dwellers: African American women scholars in the postmodern era," Beverly M. Gordon (1995) discusses the location of African American scholars and our work in relation to the academy. She suggests our peripheral and fragile positionality as scholars of color within academia obfuscates our perception of the academy and the academy's perception of us. Nonetheless, escaping the fringes has become, for many researchers, the focus of their academic struggles and goals. All scholars want their research to be recognized and valued as worthy contributions to the larger academic discourse. However, scholars whose work focuses upon the historically marginalized have an obligation to protect their research from theoretical and epistemological frameworks that distort rather than illuminate (hooks, 1990).

Because this responsibility to protect is sometimes viewed as "advocacy" within academy, our work is sometimes viewed suspiciously and is often perceived as lacking rigor (Bell, 1994). This absence of respect for our work undermines our relationships to the academy as an institution and relegates us to the fringes. However, bell hooks (1990) reminds us that our peripheral location should be viewed "as a position and place of resistance...[and is] crucial for oppressed, exploited, colonized people" (p. 150).

Still the ideological tension that undergirds this uneasy relationship remains unnamed. In some instances, this quest to be "honest-to-goodness members" of the academy has not served us well. Instead, it has placed our research and us in alien hands. This confounded relationship with the academy is not unique for people of color. In the United States, the struggle to retain our cultural identity and protect the cultural markers that sustain us is an ongoing one. It is therefore incumbent upon researchers to guard against the appropriation and co-optation (Collins, 1998) of our research. While it is a respectable goal to encourage reader recognition and connection with experiences of the researched (Bullough & Pinnegar, 2001), our stories must not be diluted in order to achieve a false sense of agreement, or to avoid meaningful points of conflict. As researchers, our difficulty in naming the academy as a terrain of struggle for race-based research is perhaps a result of dysconscious racism (King, 1992).[3] Nonetheless, we must take control of our scholarship by working at redefining the academy in a way that is culturally engaged rather than culturally deterministic or disengaged.

I am a race woman, a race woman in the spirit of early nineteenth- and twentieth-century African American race women and men like Mary McLeod Bethune, W. E. B. Du Bois, Ida Wells Barnett, Carter G. Woodson, and countless others whose ideologies emerged from a particular consciousness. This consciousness acknowledged the everyday struggles that complicated the lives of African Americans and sought to transform those struggles into victories—individual and collective victories that chipped away at dominant society's parameters that fenced in the range of possibilities for their lives. So, methodologically speaking, I find myself in a strange place as a race woman doing (what some would call) "raced research" in the academy.

In response to this paradox, I find it necessary to remind myself that research is neither an intellectual endeavor designed to demonstrate my ability to understand and replicate specific practices and methods of inquiry nor is it a theoretical exercise that identifies but does not respond to racist and sexist epistemological perspectives. It is a call to illuminate and to act. Furthermore, I believe that research is not a solitary enterprise. Research is, and ought to be, a collective effort. Consequently, the approach or approaches we employ in our research must respect the collective nature of research and provide a space for multiple voices. Research does not need to be legitimated by the academy or justified through its regime of "acceptable" methodological practices. Instead, its legitimation and purpose must be determined by the researched and by its value to the community. How we decide what is of value to our communities should not be predicated upon whether or not the focus of our research can be measured by an academically sanctioned research method. Instead "what is to count as a unit of analysis is fundamentally an interpretive issue requiring judgment and choice. It is, however, a choice that cuts to the core of qualitative methods, where *meanings* rather than *frequencies* are important" (Facio, 1993, p. 76). However, this work encourages us to interrogate fixed meanings that emerge from dominant ideology. It seeks to move the methodological discourse from merely oppositional (quantitative versus qualitative) to deeply reflective (is this method appropriate for my research?). We must be willing to wrestle with these messy questions that challenge our work and us.

The Blurring of Context and Form:
Our Stories Are Our Methods

It is not that elites produce theory while everyone else produces mere thought. Rather, elites possess the power to legitimate the knowledge that they define as theory as being universal, normative, and ideal. Legitimated theory typically delivers tangible social rewards to those who possess it. Elites simultaneously derogate the social theory of less powerful groups who may express contrary standpoints on the same social issues by labeling subordinate groups' social theory as being folk wisdom, raw experience, or common sense. (Collins, 1998, p. xiii)

For people of color have always theorized—but in forms quite different from the Western form of abstract logic. And I am inclined to say that our theorizing (and I intentionally use the verb rather than the noun) is often in narrative forms, in the stories we create, in riddles and proverbs, in the play with language, since dynamic rather than fixed ideas seem more to our liking. (Christian, 2000, p. 12)

Our stories are our theories and our method. They carry ideological truths from one generation to the next (Gwaltney, 1993). They also provide direction and govern our analytic inquiry by interrogating our epistemological positions. Methodology is a process or a set of standardized practices that govern and direct inquiry. Because process is a critical part of the search for knowledge and understanding, it should emerge from the research itself.

As an African American woman whose research focus is African American educational history, my methodological approach should not be an approach that is conceived separately from the subject of my study. My search should begin where my subjects are situated: physically, geographically, intellectually, emotionally, spiritually, and epistemologically. Other research methods acknowledge the importance of epistemological groundedness (Denzin, 1989). Proverbially speaking, however, the devil is in the details. How do we become appropriately situated? The answer to this question is not fixed, nor does the researched or the researcher solely determine it. It is not a dilemma but an ongoing challenge. It is a necessary part of the research process—one that encourages an open mind and serious commitment. It requires that we respect, embrace, and work to cofacilitate a cultural context that can receive and explore the stories of the researched. This work is not restricted to any particular group, but it demands sensitivity to cultural ways of knowing and a commitment to mutual negotiation as a strategy for building trusting relationships.

As a researcher, then, methodology is not an individual matter. It is a collective matter that is derived by—and functions for—the collective "we." Our method—our research tools, practices, and approaches—are those modes of inquiry that gaze at, relay and interpret the research experience. The utility of nontraditional theoretical approaches—whether labeled Critical Race Theory, Black Feminist Theory, postmodernism, or postcolonialism—cannot be considered outside of the research itself. While they can and should be stored in our methodological toolbox, our use of these theoretical tools should be directed and shaped from the belly of our research. This is not a new call for an "improved" research methodology. In fact, there is a rich history of narrative, which speaks about grounding our knowledge in a more truthful and accurate narrative historiography (Du Bois 1903/1990; Washington, 1908/1967). As V.P. Franklin (1995) points out, the autobiographical or narrative model has been widely used by African Americans and others to "clarify the reasons they adopted particular ideological positions during their lives," (p. 16) or "to present what they perceived as the missing chapters in the study of the collective experience of African Americans in the United States" (p. 16). It is instead a call to encourage the utilization of multiple tools that have presented our lives to ourselves, to each other, and to the world. These indigenous tools include oral and written forms of storytelling and testimony that acknowledge the interdependence of the researched to the stories they share.

What Is the Fate of Our Research?

Human problems considered and resolved in the absence of context are often misperceived, misinterpreted, and mishandled. Yet the hazards and liabilities of noncontextual interpretation and decision-making are not experienced randomly. Blacks and others whose stories have been and are excluded from the dominant discourse are more likely to be injured by the error of noncontextual methodology. (Lawrence, 1995, p. 345)

We are coauthors of the stories we tell. Our responsibility to the researched, to ourselves, and to our communities is to "document the intricate relationship between experience and ideology" (Franklin, 1995, p. 9). This is extremely important because the academy renders invisible paradigmatic discourse in which race is used as an analytic tool. For researchers of color, our challenge is to insist that race is an appropriate lens for exploration and analysis.

To illustrate how inadequate or inappropriate some research approaches are, as well as to highlight the centralities of race in the larger social order, I draw upon a methodological strategy I term "family tales"

(Carter, 1996, 2000). As a child I quickly realized that stories were the preferred mechanisms used to share knowledge that would eventually protect and sustain my siblings, my cousins, and me. These stories, whether my grandfather's sometimes humorous recollections of his boyhood and young adult life, or my grandmother's often angry personal tales, taught me much. While I was not reared on an Alabama farm in the segregated South or have worked as a "sleep-in" domestic in the segregated North, those images and their accompanying experiences are engraved in my memory. These family tales relayed not only specific information about particular occasions and circumstances but lessons about power, privilege, and Jim Crow also permeated these narratives at every level. In every instance, the "truth" to be interpreted is, on one level, visible and on another invisible. While this is generally the case with personal narratives as a whole (Bell-Scott, 1994), as discussed earlier, I argue that our ability to bring to the fore the invisible depends on a variety of factors. This critical discussion is necessary if our research is to endure.

What follows, then, is a "family tale" that I believe illuminates the challenges we face when telling our stories within the academy:

> While attending a cousin's wedding in 1990, my grandmother and I decided to watch a movie in our hotel room. *Driving Miss Daisy* was one of the available selections and I suggested to my grandmother that we watch it. She quickly told me—in a manner that was uniquely hers—"I've already seen it, and you don't want to see it. It's not what you think it is." Feeling curious about her remarks, I asked Granny: "you didn't like the movie?" She said "No. I didn't like the movie. In fact, I didn't need to see the movie, because I *lived* it. And there wasn't nothing about that movie that was the truth." On the surface, I found my grandmother's remarks to be somewhat humorous. She was after all quite a funny lady. But on a much deeper level, Granny was really saying that Miss Daisy's "story"—though accepted unconditionally by the larger public— was painfully incomplete.
>
> Perhaps this is due to the fact that my grandmother had worked for several years as a domestic before becoming a self-employed seamstress. During those years as a young wife and mother, she had endured much at the hands of women who looked like Miss Daisy. Clearly, she was angered—and resentful—by what she viewed as a sanitized version of her lived experiences. She was adamant in her refusal to permit me to watch the movie. She didn't want me to accept as truth the Hollywood rendition of the relationship between Miss Daisy and her chauffeur, Hoke.

As this example illuminates, the fate of our stories is linked to the context in which they are told, conveyed, and interpreted. Their fate, in other words, is dependent on who tells the story, how those stories are told, and who the intended audience is. Our challenge—and my responsibility to my grandmother—is to rescue our stories from those contexts, which silence and distorts, rather than honors and respects them.

Conclusion

While an oppressed group's experiences may put them in a position to see things differently, their lack of control over the apparatuses of society that sustain ideology hegemony makes the articulation of their self-defined standpoint difficult. (Collins, 2000)

And the shape of the story is the shape of my mother's voice. (Wideman, 1981/1998b, p. 94).

Our stories, and the research which aims to capture them, transcend time and space but are specifically tied to a circumstance, time period, place, or person. While it is necessary to share our stories with others, how do we simultaneously protect them from misinterpretation, abuse, and ill-usage? For me, this is a profound dilemma. Elsewhere (Carter, 2000), I have argued that our personal recollections—including our accounts of resistance and resilience—serve as sources of strength and motivation for the researcher, the research, and our audience. However, each time our stories are told, they move further away from the specificity from which they were borne (Lawrence-Lightfoot & Davis, 1997). Sharing these stories with others, therefore, moves them from the safety of our individual recollections and unencumbered interpretation and places them "at risk." While this may be part of the scholarly endeavor, our stories were never intended to endure such noncontextual critique. If our stories are to endure, we must be willing to direct their fate by creating and seeking physical, theoretical, and methodolgical sites that honor them.

Notes

1. The subtitle of this chapter is borrowed from a phrase by novelist John Edgar Wideman (1990). He used this phrase to describe the process by which cultural con-

text offers a "safe home" for the lived experiences of Black people. He argues that "this does not mean defining criteria for admitting stories into some ideologically sound, privileged category, but seeking conditions, mining territory that maximizes the possibility of free, original expression (pp. viii–ix).

2. Social Science portraiture is a method of qualitative research that acknowledges the importance of social and cultural context. "Portraitists seek to record and interpret the perspectives and experiences of the people they are studying, documenting their voices and their visions—their authority, knowledge and wisdom" (Lawrence-Lightfoot & Davis, p. xv).

3. Joyce E. King (1992) defines dysconsciousness as "one way ideological justification(s) of racial domination, that is, the status quo, shape(s) people's perceptions and ideas about themselves and society" (p. 321).

References

Anderson, J. D. (1988). The education of blacks in the South, 1860–1935. Chapel Hill, NC: University of North Carolina Press.

Anderson, M. L. (1993). Studying across difference: Race, class, and gender in qualitative research. In J. H. Stanfield II & R. M. Dennis (Eds.), *Race and ethnicity in research methods* (pp. 39–52). Newbury Park, CA: Sage.

Bell, D. (1992). *Faces at the bottom of the well: The permanence of racism.* New York: Basic Books.

Bell, D. (1994). *Confronting authority: Reflections of an ardent protestor.* Boston: Beacon Press.

Bell-Scott, P. (1994). *Life notes: Personal writings by contemporary black women.* New York: W. W. Norton & Family.

Bullough, R. V., Jr., & Pinnegar, S. (2001). Guidelines for quality in autobiographical forms of self-study research. *Educational Researcher, 30*(3), 13–21.

Carter, M. (1996). *From Jim Crow to inclusion: An historical analysis of the Association of Colleges and Secondary Schools for Negroes, 1934–1965.* Unpublished doctoral dissertation. Ohio State University, Columbus, OH.

Carter, M. (1997, April). *In search of a methodology for me: Does critical race theory help?* Paper presented at the meeting of the American Educational Research Association. Chicago, IL.

Carter, M. (1998, April). *Methodologically speaking: How does a "race" woman do raced research in the academy?* Paper presented at the meeting of the American Educational Research Association. San Diego, CA.

Carter, M. (2000). Race, jacks, and jump rope: Theorizing school through personal narratives. In R. O. Mabokela & A. L. Green (Eds.), *Sisters of the academy: Emergent Black women scholars in higher education* (pp. 151–159). Sterling, VA: Stylus Press.

Christian, B. (2000). The race for theory. In J. James & T. Denean Sharley-Whiting (Eds.), *The Black feminist reader* (pp. 11–23). Malden, MA: Blackwell.

Collins, P. H. (1998). *Fighting words: Black women and the search for justice.* Minneapolis, MN: University of Minnesota Press.

Collins, P. H. (2000). The social construction of black feminist thought. In J. James & T. Denean Sharley-Whiting (Eds.), *The black feminist reader* (pp. 183–207). Malden, MA: Blackwell.

Crenshaw, K. E., Gotanda, N. M., Peller, G., & Thomas, K. (Eds.). (1995). *Critical race theory: The key writings that formed the movement.* New York: The New Press.

Delpit, L. (1995). *Other people's children: Cultural conflict in the classroom.* New York: The New Press.

Denzin, N. (1989). *Interpretive biography.* Newbury Park, CA: Sage.

DuBois, W. E. B. (1990). *The souls of black folk.* New York: Vintage Books. (Original work published 1903).

DuBois, W. E. B. (1997). *Dusk of dawn: An essay toward an autobiography of a race concept.* New Brunswick, NJ: Transaction Publishers. (Original work published 1968).

Facio, E. (1993). Ethnography as personal experience. In J. H. Stanfield II & R. M. Dennis (Eds.), *Race and ethnicity in research methods* (pp. 75–91). Newbury Park, CA: Sage.

Fordham, S. (1996). *Blacked out: Dilemmas of race, identity, and success at Capital High.* Chicago: University of Chicago Press.

Franklin, V. P. (1995). *Living our stories, telling our truths: Autobiography and the making of the African-American intellectual tradition.* New York: Scribner.

Gates, H. L., Jr. (1989). Introduction. In L. Goss & M. E. Barnes (Eds.), *Talk that talk: An anthology of African-American storytelling* (pp. 15–19). New York: Simon & Schuster.

Gordon, B. M. (1994). African-American cultural knowledge and liberatory education: Dilemmas, problems and potentials in postmodern American society. In M. Shujaa (Ed.), *Too much schooling, too little education: A paradox of Black life in White societies* (pp. 57–78). Trenton, NJ: Africa World Press.

Gordon, B. M. (1995). The fringe dwellers: African American women scholars in the postmodern era. In B. Kampol & P. McLaren (Eds.), *Education, democracy and the voice of the other* (pp. 59–88). Westport, CT: Bergin & Garvey.

Gordon, B. M. (1999). Who do you believe—me or your eyes? Perceptions and issues in educational research: Reviews and the journals that validate them. *Review of Educational Research, 69*(4), 407–411.

Gwaltney, J. L. (1993). *Drysolong: A self-portrait of Black America.* New York: The New Press.

Hilliard, A. G., II (1997). *SBA: The Reawakening of the African mind.* Gainesville, FL: Makare Publishing.

hooks, b. (1990). *Yearning: Race, gender, and cultural politics.* Boston: South End Press.

hooks, b. (1994). *Teaching to transgress: Education as the practice of freedom.* New York: Routledge.

Irvine, J. J. (1990). *Black students and school failure: Politics, practices and prescriptions.* New York: Greenwood Press.

King, J. E. (1992). Diaspora, literacy, and consciousness in the struggle against miseducation in the Black community. *Journal of Negro Education, 61*(3), 317–340.

Ladson-Billings, G. (1994). *The dreamkeepers: Successful teachers of African American children.* San Francisco: Jossey-Bass.

Ladson-Billings, G. (1998). Just what is critical race theory and what's it doing in a nice field like education? *International Journal of Qualitative Studies in Education, 11*(1), 7–24.

Ladson-Billings, G., & Tate, W. F. (1995). Toward a critical race theory of education. *Teachers College Record, 97*, 47–68.

Lawrence, C. R., III. (1995). The word and the river: Pedagogy as scholarship as struggle. In K. E. Crenshaw, N. M. Gotanda, G. Peller, & K. Thomas (Eds.), *Critical race theory: The key writings that formed the movement* (pp. 336–351). New York: The New Press.

Lawrence-Lightfoot, S., & Davis, J. H. (1997). *The art and science of portraiture*. San Francisco: Jossey-Bass.

López. G. (2001). Re-visiting white racism in educational research: Critical race theory and the problem of method. *Educational Researcher, 30*(1), 29–33.

Parker, L. (1998). "Race is…race ain't:" An exploration of the utility of critical race theory in qualitative research in education. *International Journal of Qualitative Studies in Education, 11*(1), 43–55.

Shujaa, M. (Ed.). (1994). *Too much schooling, too little education: A paradox of black life in white societies*. Trenton, NJ: Africa World Press.

Stanfield, J. H., II. (1993). Methodological reflections: An introduction. In R. M. Dennis & J. H. Stanfield (Eds.), *Race and ethnicity in research methods* (pp. 3–15). Newbury Park, CA: Sage.

Tate, W. F., III. (1997). Critical race theory and education: History, theory and implications. In M. W. Apple (Ed.), *Review of research in education*. Washington, DC: American Educational Research Association.

Tyson, C. A. (1998). Coloring epistemologies: A response. *Educational Researcher, 27*(9), 21–22.

Walker, V. S. (1996). *Their highest potential: An African American school community in the segregated South*. Chapel Hill, NC: University of North Carolina Press.

Walker, V. S. (1999). Culture and commitment: Challenges for the future training of educational researchers. In E. C. Lagemann & L. S. Shulman (Eds.), *Issues in educational research: Problems and possibilities* (pp. 224–243). San Francisco: Jossey-Bass.

Washington, B. T. (1967). *Up from slavery*. New York: Airmont Books. (Original work published 1908).

West, C. (1991). Dilemma of the black intellectual. In b. hooks & C. West (Eds.), *Breaking bread: Insurgent black intellectual life* (pp. 131–146). Boston: South End Press.

Wideman, J. E. (1990). Preface. In T. McMillan (Ed.), *Breaking ice: An anthology of contemporary African American fiction*. New York: Penguin Books.

Wideman, J. E. (1994). *Fatheralong: A narrative on fathers and sons, race and ethnicity.* New York: Vintage Books.

Wideman, J. E. (1998a). The beginning of homewood. In *Damballah Stories* (pp. 193–205). Boston: Houghton Mifflin. (Original work published 1981).

Wideman, J. E. (1998b). Chinaman. In *Damballah Stories* (pp. 82–95). Boston: Houghton Mifflin. (Original work published 1981).

Williams, P. J. (1991). *The alchemy of race and rights: Diary of a law professor.* Cambridge: Harvard University Press.

Woodson, C. G. (1977). *The miseducation of the negro.* New York: AMS Press. (Original work published 1933).

3

Fashioning Research Stories: The Metaphoric and Narrative Structure of Writing Research About Race

Edward Buendía

A heap see, but only a few know.
—Carolyn Chase cited in Gwaltney, 1993

It is not a matter of looking harder or more closely, but of seeing what frames our seeing.
—Patti Lather, 1993

In my usual Sunday ritual of quickly perusing that behemoth of the *Sunday New York Times,* one of the articles that caught my attention described a newly installed photography exhibit at the Smithsonian depicting African American people throughout history. What drew me into the piece was not the picture that accompanied the story but the headline and the description of the conceptual framework underlying this exhibit. In contrast to story lines that might have framed this exhibit as one simply about Black inventors, scientists, or some other highly regarded professional group that had "made it," the headline read, "When asserting a self image is self-defense" (Goldberg, 2000, p. 39). The article proceeded to discuss the conceptual framework that organized this exhibit, which the curator, an African American woman, metaphorically framed "self-image *as* self-defense." After reading this, I wondered how this framing of the exhibit could be seen as an alternative narrative to what might have been rendered by someone else not connected to an African American community. The metaphoric and narrative structure underlying the organization of this collection of historical photos could have been something entirely different. Native American,

Black, and Chicana/o communities in the U.S. know all too well how the symbolic realm (i.e., the sphere of representation) has been a site of competing narratives.

The organization of this exhibit and others similar to this one have prompted me lately to ponder what it means to frame and write research stories about race.[1] More specifically, I have wondered how researchers, be they White or researchers of color, can frame their research narratives to be able to operationalize the epistemological standpoints of particular communities of color to "see" and write differently.[2] The quick response to my prompting is to say that researchers merely need to emphasize dimensions such as oppression, privilege, resistance, and/or struggle in their research focus. This may be one answer, but there may be something more to depicting the complexity of race in our research than merely embracing a specific focus in our inquiry. This chapter examines the subsequent questions:

1. What exactly are social scientists working with—theoretically, rhetorically, and discursively—when they set out to research and write about race?

2. What is it about the acts of seeing and writing race that create coherences that gel—even if only tentatively—into a politics of the text?

3. If seeing and writing have been repositioned from their natural and detached state, and recast as political acts (Clifford, 1986; Richardson, 1992; Rosaldo, 1989), how can researchers begin to conceptualize different frameworks of seeing and writing stories about race that untie the epistemological and narrative genres that circulate and have a hold in educational research?

This chapter analyzes the core units of conceptual systems that underlie writing stories about race. Specifically, it examines how metaphors of the self and the social have historically shaped the seeing and the narrative structure of racial stories. Furthermore, this chapter builds upon Critical Race Theory's (CRT) articulations of the power of narrative—or what Richard Delgado (1995) calls counterstories—and their ability to unmask, or name, the inherent racial character of society (Bell, 1994). While building upon CRT's notion of narrative, this chapter concomitantly expands upon the construct of "story" by analyzing how narratives about the social work their way into the epistemological positions and discursive practices of researchers. The chapter discusses the relationship between metaphor and the genres of narrative structure that work their way into researchers' ways of seeing and writing. The analysis merges CRT's analyses of "story" with other insights surrounding the implications of our conceptual frameworks to show how particular metaphors come to comprise researchers' conceptual systems and structures (Gordon, Miller, & Rollock, 1990; Scheurich & Young, 1997; Stanfield, 1994). Finally, this chapter identifies and describes alternative frameworks that researchers can align themselves for writing other types of research stories about race. It argues that the metaphors that guide the interpretations and survivance of working class people of color—or what Gerald Vizenor (1989) has defined as survival and surmounting—may provide researchers with alternative narrative structures for writing research stories about race.

The Role of Metaphor in the Seeing and the Writing of Race

Multiple theorists (e.g., Banks, 1995; Gordon, Miller, & Rollock, 1990; Scheurich & Young, 1997; Stanfield, 1994) have illuminated how the epistemologies that we use to engage in research are racially biased. These scholars have collectively argued that the conceptual systems that researchers bring to the enterprise of research bear the markings of a "civilizational racism" (Scheurich & Young, 1997) that privileges the White race. Moreover, they submit that the ways of seeing and naming the social have translated into the imposition of a logic that has created particular types of coherencies in categorizing and explaining the real. Gordon and his colleagues (1990), for example, have cogently identified how this logic functions to create a "communicentric bias" where the prevailing conceptual systems "tend to make one's own community the center of the universe and the conceptual frame that constrains all thought" (p. 15).

The process of writing has also been implicated as working from the same frameworks as seeing and naming race. Joining a host of writers of color such as James Baldwin (1955) and Zora Neale Hurston

(1937/1978), theorists such as Edward Said (1978) have institutionalized a critique that has called into question the manner in which symbolic representations (i.e., texts) inscribe a logic of hierarchical difference of the First and Third World. Contemporary theorists working within this tradition have further problematized the act of writing the social and the cultural by arguing that "scientific" texts need to be seen as social and political treaties imbued with literary processes and academic and literary genres (Lather, 1993; Clifford, 1986, 1988; Richardson, 1992). Expounding on this point, James Clifford (1986) states:

> Ethnographic writings can properly be called fictions in the sense of "something made or fashioned," the principal burden of the word's Latin root, *fingere*. But it is important to preserve the meaning not merely of making, but also of making up, of inventing things not actually real….[They are] cultural fictions based on systematic, and contestable, exclusions. Moreover, the maker (but why only one?) of ethnographic texts cannot avoid expressive tropes, figures and allegories that select and impose meaning as they translate it. (pp. 6–7)

Various theorists have shifted writing from an apolitical activity to one inherent with masking the complexities of people's lives and creating closures in how the social can be interpreted. Michelle Fine (1994) comments on this in describing how writing academic texts involves "protecting privilege, securing distance, and laminating the contradictions" (p. 72). While these criticisms have an historical presence in prompting social scientists to "grow up in our attitudes toward science" (Fine, 1986 as cited in Lather, 1993), and begin to see the rhetorical and poetic dimensions of scientific texts, the debates among social scientists remain contentious (for a discussion see Richardson, 2000; Nielson, 1995).

While these lines of research have contributed greatly to the denaturalization and politicization of epistemology and writing, the questions that this work opens up for researchers are: What exactly is it about the "conceptual frames," or systems of beliefs and assumptions, that create a situation of hegemony in how we conceptualize and, ultimately, represent the social? What are the core units that congeal as beliefs and assumptions that we employ to create systems of logic? Put differently, what exactly do we, as interpreting and discourse producing beings, bring to the processes of "seeing" (i.e., conceptualizing) and formulating a narrative that imposes, unconsciously, many times, a conceptual order?[3]

The Metaphorical

To engage these questions, I am going to explore the place of the metaphorical in our seeing and writing of the social. I am drawn to the uses of metaphor in these processes after having closely analyzed various writings that discuss somewhat synonymous normalizing elements such as "communicentric bias" (Gordon et al., 1990), "cultural baggage" (Stanfield, 1994), and "civilizational assumptions" (Scheurich & Young, 1997) in the knowing, the seeing, and the writing of race. All of these constructs point to the embeddedness of beliefs and assumptions in our epistemological and ontological systems. Expanding upon this idea, Scheurich and Young (1997) point directly to the assumptions that underpin researchers' conceptual systems to argue that it is these that sustain and create coherent worlds in what we have identified as the modernist project. They state:

> Modernism is an epistemological, ontological, and axiological network or grid that "makes" the world as the dominant western culture knows and sees it. Though this grid has evolved and changed to some degree, it has nonetheless, maintained some kind of coherence and consistency, particularly in terms of some of its primary assumptions (that is, its civilizational level assumptions). (p. 7)

Extrapolating from this idea, the glue that holds the network together is those "primary beliefs and assumptions" about the world and the self.

The question still remains, however, as to what exactly it is about our beliefs and assumptions that permit them to unify and bring coherence to the social. Lakoff and Johnson (1980), among others (e.g., Fiumara, 1995; Richardson, 2000), argue that beliefs and assumptions about the social rely on metaphors that allow an individual to order or conceptualize the world, to describe its characteristics, as well as to denote what it is not. They state:

> Our concepts structure what we perceive, how we get around in the world, and how we relate to other people. Our conceptual system thus plays a central role in defining our everyday realities. If we are right in suggesting that our conceptual system is largely metaphorical, then the way we think, what we experience,

and what we do every day is very much a matter of metaphor. (Lakoff & Johnson, 1980, p. 3)

Metaphors are the "spine" (Richardson, 2000) that permits us as inter-
preters and as writers to conceptualize and link parts into coherent
wholes. Hence, it is this connection between our conceptual systems—or
beliefs and assumptions—and socially constructed and shared metaphors
that form, in part, the entry point into interpreting the realm of the social.

By metaphors, I am referring to those linguistic units that allow us to
understand something else through the linguistic unit itself. Metaphors
are discourses coveted from elsewhere that we use as a stand-in—or as a
description—for explaining and/or interpreting another thing. In other
words, "the essence of metaphor is understanding and experiencing one
kind of thing in terms of another" (Lakoff & Johnson, 1980, p. 5). I place
a great deal of emphasis on metaphors as linguistic or discursive units in
this definition because this characteristic allows us to theorize where
they come from—their history, if you will—and how they circulate
within society and among cultural groups. Hence, metaphors are discourses that are shared socially in interaction and dialogue. They are
passed on through social activity.

Fiumara (1995) describes this interactive process in explaining how
metaphors of the social are deployed in the process of producing meaning. She states: "possible human worlds are collaboratively constructed
and transformed through the unbreakable interaction of listening and
speaking" (p. 5). Similar to Mikhail Bakhtin's (1981) discussion about
the situational and dialogical nature of language use and meaning making, Fiumara also points to the interactional and contextual domains of
how metaphorical structures are shared.

Let us examine some examples of metaphors that social scientists
have employed to construct the social. Educational research communities have circulated among themselves metaphorical conceptual frameworks about "institutional relationships as systems." In addition, when
discussing issues pertaining to race and schools, they have also talked
about schools as being "racially balanced" or "imbalanced." The metaphors of institutions as "systems" and as being in "balance" allow social
scientists to form a spatial, temporal, and categorical relationship of
what these entities are, how they work, or how they should function. The
metaphors allow researchers to see, conceptualize, and envision how
particular social phenomena fit, or are at work, in relationship to our so-

cial setting and context (i.e., the spatial), historical, or chronological sensibilities (i.e., the temporal), and how they relate to other entities or events in our world.

At the same time that metaphors allow individuals to construct coherent conceptual systems, they also function to denote what entities are not. Metaphors have an inscriptive power to discursively bound an identity, to identify its machinations, and to describe the inner workings of an object. It does this all the while that it also negates what an entity is not and how it does not operate. The metaphor that is discursively chained to an object locates the entity's identity within a set of relationships. It provides an interpretation while it also constrains alternative renderings for understanding an entity. This is, indeed, the power of metaphors, they "affirm an identity while also somehow denying it" (Fiumara, 1995, p. 11).

Metaphor, Narrative Structure, and the Prevailing Academic Stories About Race

Considering the current discussions about reconceptualizing how we might see and write social science differently (e.g., Fine, 1994; Ladson-Billings, 2000; Richardson, 1992), the power of metaphor to define and bound may be the key dimension in determining how our conceptual systems function to frame the social when we engage in telling stories about race. The metaphoric is what underlies the assumptions that have contributed to the hegemony of what some have termed "civilizational assumptions" (Scheurich & Young, 1997) or "cultural baggage" (Gordon et al., 1990). When researchers engage in seeing (i.e., conceptualizing) and telling racial stories, the narrative structure, or story line, of these stories is structured metaphorically. Researchers draw upon, albeit unconsciously at times, academic or social narratives that emerge from specific cultural metaphors. These narrative structures inscribe the racial within a specific logic.

For instance, the metaphoric structure of "White man as conqueror" is a pervasive social metaphor that has seeped into and become naturalized as one White, societal metanarrative.[4] Historical renderings—ranging from Andrew Jackson to contemporary interpretations of the first lunar landing—all work from this metaphoric structure. The way of seeing (i.e., interpreting) such phenomena, as well as their representation in text (i.e., writing, film), operates from within this particular framework.

At the same time, the metaphoric structure of the non-White as savage is also circulated, and continues to circulate with some modification, within social science texts. In this structure, a hierarchy is established by metaphorically positioning the non-White subject as animal or uncivilized (see Perea, 1997; Takaki, 1993). The persistent coupling of non-White individuals and groups to this metaphor eventually comes to denote an ontology of the Other. These alleged traits of savagery are inscribed in the White imagination (Baldwin, 1955; Morrison, 1994). To be sure, this ontology was not one established by people of color for the purposes of describing themselves, but was established by White society in its own self-interest (Morrison, 1994). In other words, the metaphorical structure of the "non-White as savage" is the institutionalization of an ontology of a non-White other through projections of discourse whose purpose it is, in all actuality, to define and fortify Whiteness.[5]

Concomitantly, the interpretive and narrative structure of these stories also demarcates a litany of other social relationships that buttress this underlying metaphor. Historically, this has included the production of legal and legislative initiatives (Bell, 1980; Delgado, 1995), literary (Morrison, 1994) and cinematic texts (McCarthy, Rodriguez, Buendía, David, Godina, Wilson-Brown, & Meacham, 1997), and a host of other discursive practices that naturalize the "conqueror" metaphor. For example, many have argued that the legal designation of Blacks as property during the eighteenth and nineteenth centuries functioned, in part, as one site that sustained the metaphor of White men as conquerors (see Morrison, 1994). With the Black population symbolically demarcated as subhuman and as property, the assemblage of biblical (manifest destiny) and/or legal doctrine became the primary vehicles to affirm the conception of White superiority (see Takaki, 1993). The bodies of African Americans became one of the primary sites in which the metaphoric structure of Whiteness as conqueror was exercised.

In contemporary discussions, some scholars have argued that this theme can still be found in multiple, dispersed relations. Popkewitz (1998), for example, has cogently argued that the structure of the individual as conqueror and, specifically, as problem solver underlies contemporary liberalist educational discourse. He asserts that the current appetite for constructivist frameworks of pedagogy is driven by the metaphor of the individual as problem solver, manager, and controller.

The reification, or normalization, of these metaphoric structures about race is also wrapped up in the process of writing. Narrative structures, or the story lines of particular genres of stories, are dialogically interconnected to researchers' conceptual systems (Stanfield, 1994). As a result, particular conceptual systems have come to shape the narrative structure that academic communities are expecting in reporting or representing particular social phenomena. Clifford (1988), for example, has commented on the authority granted to the univocal, or unambiguous, text in the social sciences. As a structure, the univocal text has crystallized into the sign of authority and truth. Instead of emerging as merely a natural manifestation, this genre of writing needs to be seen as an extension of the societal metaphor that places the researcher as the seer of all, and science as *the* definitive word on the real (Denzin, 1997).

Alongside the metanarrative of "White man as conqueror," the dominant metanarrative that prevailed in the social sciences for describing the life worlds of people of color, was one that saw Blacks and other non-White groups as independent in their economic and social development—an outcome of the western narrative of "man" as self-made (Baldwin, 1955). This metanarrative structure emerged in the social sciences in the 1880s and continued through the 1970s and portrayed working-class Blacks and Latinas/os as groups who squandered their resources and lived a culture of deviance. Issues surrounding White racial privilege or White racism were bracketed out of the narrative structure altogether (e.g., Drake & Cayton, 1962; McKenney & Hall, 1972; Park, 1952). The guiding metaphor which conceptualizes the social realm did not permit White social scientists to see themselves as implicated actors in a highly racialized system.

Hence, to recapitulate my central thesis, I am arguing that societal and cultural metaphors structure, in part, researchers' assumptions and worldviews. Prevailing metaphors of the self, the other, and the real have framed how researchers see and know (i.e., their epistemology), as well as underlie the narrative structures that guide their construction of racial stories. These metaphorical structures are not naturally occurring, innately derived constructs, but, rather, they are shared and sustained in dialogic relationships. As many have already cogently articulated, researchers mobilize systems of language to frame, conceptualize, and represent the real (Clifford, 1986; Fine, 1994; Gordon et al., 1990; Scheurich & Young, 1997; Stanfield, 1994).[6] It is at the discursive level that I will turn as a means of developing a way of identifying alternative epistemological frameworks and narrative structures that facilitate the construction of what critical race theorists call "counterstories" (Delgado, 1995).

Articulations of Alternative
Metaphorical Conceptual Systems

To return to my initial discussion pertaining to the article and exhibit about African American photography, there are two questions I want to pursue in this section: (a) How is a framing, such as "self-image as self-defense" an alternative metaphorical conceptual system?; (b) How can researchers align themselves with these conceptual systems in order to think and write differently about the realm of the social?

Organizing an exhibit that tells a story about a group of people asserting a "self-image as self-defense" posture is unique to only a few cultural groups in the United States. Metaphorical frameworks of this type are conceptual systems and narrative structures that are discursively shared among some people of color and some groups of women. To tell such a story requires that the teller, or author, mobilize a different set of propositions about oneself, the other, and the past than what the White, mainstream holds as true. It entails reconceptualizing the way society operates and has operated.

For example, to tell a racial story in which one, or one's community, has had to assert "self-identity as self-defense" involves calling into question the dominant metaphors in which a person or group has been portrayed. It is a conscious negation of narratives that are undergirded by metaphors of African Americans, Asians, or Chicanos as "shifty" or "uncivilized," as well as a proffering of other alternative metaphors of the self (Takaki, 1993). In doing this, they challenge the metaphors that White society has created and sustained through concerted physical, juridical, and discursive practices. Moreover, when an author tells a racial story whose narrative structure takes a seemingly defensive posture, it confronts story lines that depict society as driven toward progress and oriented toward equality (Bell, 1994).

In other words, telling stories about the self and the social provide us with different metaphors than those commonly found in dominant renderings (Collins, 1990; Lorde, 1984). Furthermore, they also allow authors to write about these spheres differently from what was possible within the dominant narrative structures. They accomplish this goal by forcing an author to bring to bear different metaphorical configurations while simultaneoulsy conceptualizing layers of activity differently. In the process, the metaphoric lines between the self, the other, and the social are redrawn and reconcenceptualized.

As the framework organizing the photo exhibit suggests, alternative narrative structures that are underpinned by other metaphors about self, other, and society do circulate within society. These alternatives can be found within the discursive practices (i.e., stories, plays, and music) of some people of color. What these practices offer researchers is an epistemological system and narrative structure that metaphorically envision these relationships differently from what is possible from the systems of the dominant worldview (Gordon, Miller, & Rollock, 1990; Stanfield, 1994). First, they offer metaphors of society and self as multilayered, fluid, and complex. They help an observer see and frame the layers of the self, the collective, and the social as interconnected and whole, rather than define them as discrete and bounded entities. Second, many of these frameworks also work from the premise that power is omnipresent in everyday relations, in the seen and the unseen. That is, many of these alternative epistemological systems narratively privilege the idea that institutional interactions are laden with relations of power, some that appear as surface level manifestations, and others that more commonly appear in underlying and unseen relations. Lastly, and intertwined with the first two characteristics, many alternative epistemological systems narratively begin from the premise that race, and its intersections with gender, greatly matters within institutional contexts. They embark from an understanding that, historically, race and gender are central elements of U.S. social/institutional relations. They commence from the proposition that the story of people of color within U.S. institutions and society is inherently a racial and gendered one.

The most widely recognized examples of alternative metaphorical structures can be found in the work of Patricia Hill Collins (1990), Dolores Delgado Bernal (1998), and Gloria Anzaldúa (1987).[7] These scholars have compellingly identified some of the epistemological frameworks that have guided different communities of color. Although these epistemological frameworks would be well suited for this discussion, I would like to focus on the epistemological and narrative structures that have been articulated around trickster discourses. In particular, I want to highlight how the work of Gerald Vizenor, Luis Valdez, and Shuaib Meacham has collectively offered social scientists alternative metaphorical and narrative structures in which to envision and write about the self, the other, and the social. These scholars have articulated both an epistemological framework and a complementary narrative structure to guide researchers in conceptualizing and constructing research stories about race.

Gerald Vizenor, the Chippewa literary critic, has argued that the narrative structure that Native American Indian tribal communities have relied upon is not the tragic tale of the warrior prevalent in the White social imaginary. Rather, he suggests the narrative structure of native groups is composed of a two-pronged metaphor of the "comedic" and the "tragic." As a conceptual framework, the comedic allows authors to tell stories that recognize the irony of living in a society marked by incoherence and simulation. Meanwhile, the tragic element of this structure allows authors to show how things go awry in turns of contingency and uncertainty. When taken together, this narrative structure demonstrates how factors such as indeterminacy and chance play a role in fostering social relations that are inherently asymmetrical.

To demonstrate how this narrative structure functions, Vizenor (1989) tells the story of costume designer and personal *couturier* Oleg Cassini and his plans to create a line of Indian fashion. The story follows that Cassini realized that he had yet to explore the fashion of American Indians. To pursue this dream, Cassini met with Peter MacDonald, the elected chairman of the Navajo nation. The two forged a joint venture that would produce a "world-class luxury resort" on the Navajo reservation that would "reflect the unique culture and tradition of [Navajo] people" (Vizenor, 1989, p. 8) and would also allow Cassini to create a Native American Indian line of dresses that would accentuate the artistry of the Navajo. The comedic and ironic turn in this narrative unfolds as the various actors comment on the enterprise. For instance, MacDonald states in regard to the authenticity of the resort, "We are creating a Navajo Board of Standards for all new tourist facilities on the Reservation to assure that the Navajo name means quality" (Vizenor, 1989, p. 8).

Meanwhile, Cassini reflects on the design and materials for his new line of Indian-wear and noted, "A good many of my American Indian dresses required intricate beading of a sort that was not available in Italy. I'd been told Hong Kong was the place to find such material" (Vizenor, 1989, pp. 8–9).

The emphasis of the narrative structure that Vizenor describes is on narratively privileging the comedic and the tragic of social interaction. He argues that to tell a story from this epistemological framework entails that the teller attend to how actors are intertwined in serious social encounters. In addition to describing how these encounters are clouded by racial misrepresentations that emerge from a long history of "hyperrealities" about Indians, Vizenor holds that these stories expound upon the resourcefulness of tribal people in the face of injustice and skewed power relations. Hence, for Vizenor, the narrative structure emphasizes the comedic and tragic elements, all the while not losing sight that the stories are about people who have survived, and continue to survive, through hardship.

In similar fashion, Chicanas/os, as well as many other Latinas/os, have operationalized their skepticism of dominant institutions and liberalist rhetoric by interpreting the social through the metaphor of *movidas*.[8] The *movidas* conceptual system is also a trickster discourse that interprets the social at both the surface and underlying levels. In its popular uses, some Chicanas/os speak comically yet tragically about the *movidas* that are in play to name and reinterpret racial practices that White people exercise on a daily basis, yet often go unnamed. It is not uncommon to hear some people say, "*Hay unas movidas que ella jugó*," or, "There are some shady dealings that she engaged in," in situations that defy what is just or expected. The comedic dimension of this strategy has allowed Chicanas/os to cope with the persistent episodes of racism and injustice without losing their sanity, whereas the tragic disposition has permitted them to recognize the severity of these unjust practices.

For example, the Chicana/o "guerrilla theater" of Luis Valdez and *El Teatro Campesino* has put into motion this alternative metaphorical system to proffer alternative interpretations of White/mainstream activities and institutional relationships. Valdez has comically reinterpreted and rewritten these relationships to unmask and reveal those interpretations that have been omitted from "official" renderings. His story lines inter-

ject those understandings that Chicanas/os have circulated amongst
themselves about what "really" is at work in institutional settings. For
instance, in Luis Valdez's (1991) screen play *Zoot Suit,* probably one of
his better known works, the *pachuco* is a trickster figure who interprets
the main character's situation. Smoking marijuana and continually engaged in *basiladas,* or word games and jokes, the *pachuco* makes him-
self visible only to the main character (Henry) in order to make evident
what he is not seeing on the surface. The *pachuco* interjects reminders of
the history of police abuse of Chicano males and of the White racism
that is pervasive in the U.S. judicial system. Valdez does this by placing
the *pachuco* in extratemporal and extraspatial situations in order to illuminate what Henry is not "seeing." It is through these surreal experiences that Henry begins to understand the underlying relations that are
working against him. As such, the *pachuco* comically intervenes in order
to reinterpret the social with more accurate accounts of a highly racialized social and economic system that Chicanas/os have come to know on
a daily basis.

Valdez mobilizes the metaphorical structure of "the social as *movidas"* by narratively identifying other historical relations that are not visible or recognized in metanarratives but that are at play in shaping
surface events. He makes opportunities in the telling of the story to show
narratively how these relations converge to shape social relations between Chicanas/os and White society.[9] Similar to Vizenor, Valdez also
reminds us that these are human stories with serious and comedic intentions.

Lastly, Shuaib Meacham's (1997) theorizing with the metaphoric
structure of the Blues is another alternative or trickster framework for
interpreting the social. He draws from the work of Henry Louis Gates
(1988), Albert Murray (1971), and Robert Ferris Thompson (1983) to
offer an epistemological and narrative structure for envisioning the social field grounded in the aesthetics of working class African Americans.
Meacham suggests that the blues idiom analytically displaces the western conceptual frameworks of hierarchy, division, and categorization, to
conceptualize metaphorically the field of social activity as embodying
the characteristics of jazz.[10]

Meacham operationalizes this framework by analytically and narratively emphasizing how these characteristics can be used to displace
creatively taken-for-granted assumptions about people of color. For ex-

ample, he tells a story of how several young Black males were viewed by the school system as "incorrigible." However, rather than telling a story that depicts the isolated actions of a handful of racist individuals, his analytic style allows him to depict narratively the plurality of discursive fields that work to "name" the actions of Black males in a negative fashion. Similar to a trickster who has one foot within and another outside of the milieu, the blues metaphor allows him to roam diverse fields in order to tell us a story of how the knowledge found in professional educational discourse systematically congeals to affirm the framing of these Black individuals.

In bringing the three elements of break, improvisation, and affirmation to the forefront of his conceptual framework, Meacham re-envisions how to see and write within a more situated and historical African American social space. His framework allows him to reconfigure social relationships, and to narratively foreground dimensions that typically go unexamined to explain the realm of the social.

The (Im)position of Alternative Narrative Structures and Critical Race Theory

The exemplars of alternative epistemological and narrative systems that I have identified all seek to reshape how researchers conceptualize and write research stories about race and society. These systems reflect the understandings about the self, the other, and the social that particular communities of color have generated from interacting within a society that is historically marked by racial distinctions and classifications. Within the last two decades, some scholars have given a great deal of credence and validity to narrative as a means of tapping into these frameworks. The work of critical race theorists, such as Derrick Bell (1994), Richard Delgado (1992), and Patricia Williams (1991), amongst others, have operationalized narrative as a means of "naming one's own reality" (Delgado, 1995, p. 95). Critical race theorists have all placed the telling of stories from a different theoretical and epistemological plane. Their purpose for doing this is twofold:

a) to illuminate how racial codes and practices function in the American judicial and policy arena, and

b) to highlight the narratives, accounts, and anecdotes of people of color that are consciously and unconsciously ignored in the larger social conversation.

Whereas CRT has validated the importance of story as a window into the inner workings of society, the work of scholars such as Anzaldúa, Vizenor, Collins, Valdez, and Meacham have oriented us toward the structure of telling and writing these stories as a means of emphasizing those elements that have been omitted in metanarratives. Collectively, these scholars tell us that, indeed, there is a structure that underlies the telling of stories about race. All the while, they chronicle the historical dimensions that explain how the racial self is subjected to symbolic misrepresentation while consciously interjecting other metaphors of the self, the other, and the social in order to highlight the discursive realm that privileges certain metaphors to circulate over others.

Whereas the parameters these scholars provide researchers do not give us prescriptions for writing, they do provide researchers with metaphors and a narrative structure in which to engage in stories that are parallel in nature to those that critical race theorists have deployed. While the authors I have mentioned have cogently identified the tenets of particular epistemological and narrative frameworks, the articulation of these structures still necessitates that researchers outside of these epistemological communities learn the vernacular of telling the stories from these collectives. The richness in our research "stories" will only come from being able to highlight the idiosyncratic, or unseen, elements people within a community learn to recognize over time. As researchers, these alternative frameworks can only enhance our scholarship. It is not merely, as Ladson-Billings (2000) convincingly argues, a question of "coloring" our scholarship for the sake of inclusion. Rather, these systems will genuinely help researchers see and write from an entirely different vantage point altogether.

Notes

1. This pondering has been a collective enterprise with Dr. Shuaib Meacham. This chapter, then, reflects the understandings and intersections that were made in discussing the potentiality of other epistemological systems in writing the social.

2. My reasoning for placing "seeing" in quotations is to refer to the problematized notion of seeing naturally or in an umediated manner. John Stanfield (1994) and Norman Denzin (1997), amongst others (Lather, 1993; Popkewitz, 1997, 1998), have unmasked the natural stance of seeing to argue that we only see from the conceptual frames that our societal and theoretical orientations allow us to see. They argue that there is no unbiased or unmediated seeing. Rather, researchers are only able to see and name the social as a result of these lenses.

3. The arguments around the discursive nature of representing the real do not negate that there is a reality. Rather, various theorists and philosophers have argued that the only way that we can know the real is through our language, or our linguistic systems of reasoning (Bruner, 1986; Denzin, 1995). Hence, the stakes in the naming of the real have become central in research, particularly around questions of legitimation and validity. What this crisis of representation has left many wondering is, "What is presence, if pure presence is no longer available?" and "What symbolic violence is done through deploying particular representations over others?" (for a discussion see Foucault, 1980; Lather, 1993).

4. I label this as a White societal metanarrative on the premise that this narrative structure is not a universal one that all racial groups employ. Other racial groups have interpreted these social phenomena differently (Gwaltney, 1993).

5. This claim does not undermine Omi and Winant's (1994) central argument about the racial formation process. Rather, it is an attempt to expand on their thesis by being more precise in identifying the units of discourse that are socially interpellated to construct, or frame, race.

6. I qualify this argument as comprising part of the problem on the premise that issues of institutionalization and structuration of these metaphoric systems are also another dimension that need to be kept in mind.

7. For a discussion of these see Denzin (1997) and Ladson-Billings (2000).

8. The English translation for the Spanish word *movidas* literally means "movements."

9. Another writer/director that operationalizes this epistemological framework is John Sayles. His films *Lone Star* and *Men with Guns* narratively excavate the multiple relations (i.e., transnational corporatism) and institutional practices (i.e., racism) that are at work to shape what is seen at the surface level.

10. Meacham posits that within the field of social action we might begin to envision the breaks that are the ritualization of crisis, those initial points in which the norm is disrupted. These are followed by a second phase in which actors engage in improvisational acts that link multiple worlds, traditions, and dialects. Improvisation is an act of creating intersections between disparate forms. Similar to jazz musicians,

Meacham metaphorically envisions actors as creators, where "the soloist calls upon her or his already know, repertoire of skills and knowledge and adapts it to the present challenge" (Meacham, 1997, p. 56). The last phase that Meacham emphasizes is affirmation. In this phase, "the break has been confronted, the improvisation conducted, and a new, yet connected, set of understandings regarding self and circumstance are in place" (Meacham, 1997, p. 57).

References

Anzaldúa, G. (1987). *Borderlands/la frontera: The new mestiza*. San Francisco, CA: Aunt Lute.

Bakhtin, M. M. (1981). *The dialogic imagination* (M. Holquist, Trans.). Austin, TX: University of Texas Press.

Baldwin, J. (1955). *Notes on a native son*. New York: The Dial Press.

Banks, J. A. (1995). The historical reconstruction of knowledge about race: Implications for transformative teaching. *Educational Researcher, 24*(2), 15–25.

Bell, D. A. (1980). *Race, racism and American law* (2nd ed.). Boston: Little, Brown.

Bell, D. A. (1994). *Confronting authority: Reflections of an ardent protester*. Boston: Beacon Press.

Bruner, E. M. (1986). The opening up of an anthropology. In E. M. Bruner (Ed.), *Text, play and story: The construction and reconstruction of self and society* (pp. 1–18). Washington, DC: The American Ethnological Society.

Clifford, J. (1986). Introduction: Partial truths. In J. Clifford & G. E. Marcus (Eds.), *Writing culture* (pp. 1–27). Berkeley: University of California Press.

Clifford, J. (1988). On ethnographic authority. In J. Clifford, *The predicament of culture: Twentieth century ethnography, literature, and art* (pp. 21–54). Cambridge: Harvard University Press.

Collins, P. H. (1990). *Black feminist thought: Knowledge, consciousness, and the politics of empowerment*. New York: Routledge.

Delgado, R. (1992). Rodrigo's chronicle. *Yale Law Journal, 101*, 1357–1393.

Delgado, R. (1995). *Critical race theory: The cutting edge*. Philadelphia: Temple University Press.

Delgado Bernal, D. (1998). Using a Chicana feminist epistemology in educational research. *Harvard Educational Review, 68*, 555–582.

Denzin, N. K. (1995). The poststructural crisis in the social sciences. In R. H. Brown (Ed.), *Writing postmodernism* (pp. 38–59). Urbana: University of Illinois Press.

Denzin, N. K. (1997). *Interpretive ethnography: Ethnographic practices for the 21st century.* Thousand Oaks, CA: Sage Publishers.

Drake, S. C., & Cayton, H. R. (1962). *Black metropolis: A study of Negro life in a northern city.* New York: Harper Torchbooks.

Fine, M. (1994). Working the hyphens: Reinventing self and other in qualitative research. In N. K. Denzin & Y. N. Lincoln (Eds.), *The handbook of qualitative research.* Thousand Oaks, CA: Sage Press.

Fiumara, G. C. (1995). *The metaphoric process: Connections between language and life.* New York: Routledge.

Foucault, M. (1980). Truth and power. In C. Gordon (Ed.), *Power/knowledge: Selected interviews and other writings 1972–1977* (pp. 109–133). New York: Pantheon Books.

Gates, H. L. (1988). *The signifying monkey: A theory of Afro-American literary theory.* New York: Oxford University Press.

Gordon, E. W., Miller, F., & Rollock, D. (1990). Coping with communicentric bias in knowledge production in the social sciences. *Educational Researcher, 19*(3), 14–19.

Goldberg, H. (2000). When asserting a self image as self defense. *New York Times*, April 9. Arts & Leisure, pp. 39, 43.

Gwaltney, J. L. (1993). *Drylongso: A self portrait of Black America.* New York: Random House.

Hurston, Z. N. (1978). *Their eyes were watching God.* New York: Perrenial Press. (Original work published 1937).

Ladson-Billings, G. (2000). Racialized discourses and ethnic epistemologies. In N. K. Denzin & Y. S. Lincoln (Eds.), *Handbook of qualitative research* (2nd ed., pp. 257–278). Thousand Oaks, CA: Sage.

Lakoff, G., & Johnson, M. (1980). *Metaphors we live by.* Chicago: University of Chicago Press.

Lather, P. (1993). Fertile obsession: Validity after poststructuralism. *The Sociological Quarterly, 34*, 673–693.

Lorde, A. (1984). *Sister outsider: Essays and speeches.* New York: Crossing Press.

McCarthy, C., Rodriguez, A., Buendía, E., David, S., Godina, H., Wilson-Brown, C., & Meacham, S. (1997). Race, suburban resentment, and representation of the inner city in contemporary film and television. *Cultural Studies, 1,* 121–140.

McKenney, T. L., & Hall, J. (1972). *The Indian tribes of North America—With biographical sketches and anecdotes of the principals chiefs.* Totowa, NJ: Rowman & Littlefield.

Meacham, S. J. (1997). *Multicultural connections: A study of intertextual linkages.* Unpublished dissertation. University of Illinois, Urbana-Champaign.

Morrison, T. (1994). *Playing in the dark: Whiteness and the literary imagination.* Cambridge, MA: Harvard University Press.

Murray, A. (1971). *South to a very old place.* New York: McGraw-Hill.

Nielson, H. B. (1995). Seductive texts with serious intentions. *Educational Researcher, 24*(1), 4–12.

Omi, M., & Winant, H. (1994). *Racial formation in the United States: 1960–1990* (2nd ed.). New York: Routledge.

Park, R. E. (1952). Magic, mentality and city life. In R. E. Park, *The collected papers of Robert Ezra Park: Vol 2. Human communities: The city and human ecology.* Glencoe, IL: Free Press.

Perea, J. F. (1997). *Immigrants Out! The new nativism and the anti-immigrant impulse in the United States.* New York: New York University Press.

Popkewitz, T. S. (1997). A changing terrain of knowledge and power: A social epistemology of educational research. *Educational Researcher, 26*(9), 18–29.

Popkewitz, T. S. (1998). Dewey, Vygotsky, and the social administration of the individual: Constructivist pedagogy as systems of ideas in historical spaces. *American Educational Research Journal, 35*(4), 535–790.

Richardson, L. (1992). The poetic representation of lives: Writing a postmodernist sociology. *Studies in Symbolic Interaction, 13*, 19–27.

Richardson, L. (2000). Writing: A method of inquiry. In N. K. Denzin & Y. Lincoln (Eds.), *Handbook of qualitative research* (2nd ed., pp. 923–947). Thousand Oaks, CA: Sage.

Richardson, T., & Villenas, S. (2000). "Other encounters": Dancing with whiteness in multicultural education. *Educational Theory, 2*, 425–429.

Rosaldo, R. (1989). *Culture and truth: The remaking of social analysis.* Boston: Beacon Press.

Said, E. (1978). *Orientalism.* New York: Vintage.

Scheurich, J. J., & Young, M. D. (1997). Coloring epistemologies: Are our research epistemologies racially biased? *Educational Researcher, 26*(4), 4–16.

Solorzano, D. (2000, April). *The development of Crtical Race Theory in education.* Paper presented at the annual meeting of the American Educational Research Association, New Orleans, LA.

Stanfield, J. H. (1994). Ethnic modeling in qualitative research. In N. K. Denzin & Y. S. Lincoln (Eds.), *Handbook of qualitative research* (pp. 175–188). Newbury Park, CA: Sage.

Takaki, R. (1993). *A different mirror: A history of multicultural America.* Boston: Little, Brown & Company.

Thompson, R. F. (1983). *Flash of the spirit: African and Afro-American art and philosphy.* Toronto: Vintage Books.

Valdez, L. (1991). *Zoot suit.* Universal City, CA : MCA Universal Home Video.

Vizenor, G. (1989). *Narrative chance: Postmodern discourse on Native American Indian literatures.* Albuquerque: University of New Mexico Press.

Vizenor, G. (1994). *Manifest manners: Postindian warriors of survivance.* Hanover, NH: University Press of New England.

Williams, P. J. (1991). *The alchemy of race and rights.* Cambridge, MA: Harvard University Press.

4

Parent Involvement as Racialized Performance

Gerardo R. López

In many states and cities across the nation, people of color have rapidly grown in number, changing the demographic face of the American spectrum and challenging educational institutions and other social service providers to meet the needs of an increasingly diverse student population (Darder, Torres, & Gutierrez, 1997; Latino Eligibility Task Force, 1993; Perez & de la Rosa Salazar, 1997; Trueba, 1989; Valencia, 1991). If current projections are correct, many of today's so-called "minorities" will be tomorrow's numerical majority (Orfield, 1988; Pallas, Natriello, & McDill, 1989). Policy analysts have already alerted educators of this emerging population and the impact they will undoubtedly have on educational organizations in the future (Bean & Tienda, 1987; Perez & de la Rosa Salazar, 1997; Valencia, 1991). Their collective research suggests that schools will face unique challenges as they increasingly engage with students who are culturally different—many of whom come from immigrant backgrounds and speak languages other than English (Hayes-Bautista, Hurtado, Burciaga Valdez, & Hernández, 1992; Hurtado & García, 1994; Sosa, 1993).

This demographic shift is compounded by data that suggest the economic gap between people of color and non-Hispanic Whites is rapidly growing (Katz, 1989; U.S. Bureau of the Census, 1992; Wilson, 1987). This gap is due, in part, to disproportionate incidents of unemployment, poverty, and other social and economic impediments brought by a changing economic landscape in a de-industrialized society (Carnoy, Daley, & Hinojosa Ojeda, 1990; Orfield & Ashkinaze, 1991; Squires, 1994). The resulting educational impact on marginalized groups is dire: manifested in unequal dropout rates, increased special education placement, and disproportionate representation in lower and unskilled academic tracks (Kirst, Koppich, & Kelley, 1994; Oakes, 1985; Peng & Lee, 1994). In fact, research suggests Chicanos/Latinos, African Americans, and other marginalized groups are more likely to be undereducated than their White middle-class counterparts (Bean, Chapa, Berg, & Sowards, 1991; Buriel & Cardoza, 1988; Chapa, 1989; Romo & Falbo, 1996; Rumberger, 1987, 1991). Policy analysts agree it is in the best interest of everyone to search for better ways to educate these children (Hayes-Bautista, Schink, & Chapa, 1988; Latino Eligibility Task Force, 1993; Valencia, 1991).

In this ever-changing context of educational remedies that aim to fix educational "problems," parental involvement has increasingly received widespread attention as a viable tool for educational reform (Becher, 1986; Eccles & Harold, 1996; Henderson, 1987; Henderson, Marburger, & Ooms, 1986). In fact, the "promise" of parental involvement is touted—by educators, policymakers and practitioners alike—as a key mechanism for educational change and improvement, particularly in schools that enroll a large percentage of children of color (Chavkin, 1993; Clark, 1983; Delgado-Gaitán, 1990, 1994; Moles, 1993; Sipes, 1993). It is the promise of giving the community a voice in school decision-making efforts, as well as the promise of working collaboratively with those that have been historically marginalized from the larger educational conversation (Henderson, Marburger, & Ooms, 1986). It is the promise of working in close conjunction with parents as equal partners and decision-makers in their children's educational lives (Epstein, 1986, 1987, 1990, 1995). It is the promise of fundamentally reforming schools from a top-down managerial structure to a structure that is more caring and respectful of all of its constituents (Henry, 1996). Furthermore, it is the promise of turning schools into true learning organizations, where the spirit of collaboration and partnership is transformed into educational productivity for all children (Henderson, 1987; Moles, 1993). In short, there is widespread agreement in the efficacy of parental involvement as a transformational tool for school reform.

In fact, research consistently finds that children whose parents are involved in their education significantly increase their academic achievement and cognitive development (Becher, 1986; Eccles & Harold, 1996; Henderson, 1987). Moreover, these children demonstrate higher math and reading competency than their peers (Simich-Dudgeon,

1986) and tend to have better attitudes toward homework, standardized tests, and other routine school assignments than those students whose parents are not involved (Peterson, 1989). In addition, research suggests parent involvement often enhances a child's self-esteem, improves parent-child relationships, and helps parents and children develop positive attitudes toward school (Brown, 1989). As a result, children whose parents are involved in their educational lives tend to have better grades, improved test scores, and long-term academic achievement than those whose parents are not involved in their schooling (Peterson, 1989; Simich-Dudgeon, 1986).

Despite the fact that parents from all walks of life have increasingly mobilized in favor of involvement in recent years (Delgado-Gaitán, 1990; Hatch, 1998), and despite the fact that marginalized parents express a deep interest in being involved in their children's educational lives (Williams & Chavkin, 1985), there is a host of evidence that suggests marginalized parents are still not involved at the same rate as White/mainstream parents (Chavkin, 1993; Lareau, 1989; Moles, 1993; Robledo, 1989). This problem of noninvolvement has troubled educators and policy makers in the field who recognize the demographic shift of an increasing ethnic and linguistically diverse student population. They argue that if we are to address the problem of minority student failure effectively, it is imperative that we begin to search for ways to get marginalized parents involved in greater numbers (Chavkin, 1993).

The Problem of Noninvolvement

The problem with the above argument is that it not only subscribes to a particular definition of involvement—a definition that privileges and reifies an a priori set of scripted school-driven involvement practices (Clark, 1983; Lightfoot, 1978)—but it also positions marginalized parents as deficient and/or incapable of positively influencing the educational lives of their children (Auerbach, 1989; Hidalgo, 1998). Moreover, this argument places the onus of school success solely on the involvement practices of the parents, with complete disregard for the social, economic, and organizational factors that also affect student outcomes (Auerbach, 1989).[1] As a result, this argument ultimately blames marginalized parents for their apparent lack of involvement.

Under this perspective, then, schools and other state apparatuses are positioned as being neutral and/or impartial—implying that the so-called problem of minority student failure is neither social nor systemic but that it rests in the individual homes of children. Stated somewhat differently, this argument suggests that minority student failure can easily be re-solved if marginalized parents simply emulate or comply with particular involvement norms. As a result of this deficit thinking, marginalized par-ents have been judged as unconcerned, and perhaps uncaring, when all they have "failed" to do was to be involved in specific or prescriptive ways (Auerbach, 1989; Clark, 1983; Hidalgo, 1998; Lareau, 1989, 1996; Lightfoot, 1978; Sigel & Laosa, 1983).

In this regard, the discourse surrounding parental involvement con-structs a racial division whereby marginalized parents are viewed as lacking the abilities and skills necessary for educational success. Policy solutions, therefore, suggest that parents need to adjust their behavior in order to mimic/emulate mainstream modes of appropriate home-school interactions. These actions include, but are not limited to: bake sales, PTA/PTO, back-to-school nights, volunteering in the classroom, attend-ing school activities, and participating in parent advisory councils and/or school governance councils (see also Epstein, 1984, 1986, 1987, 1988, 1990; Chavkin & Williams, 1989, 1990, 1993; Henry 1996). They also include a host of other activities—e.g., reviewing homework, attending workshops, developing "appropriate" parenting skills, and so forth—that aim to fundamentally change parental practices in order to reinforce the culture of schooling in the home (Sigel & Laosa, 1983). In short, to be involved is to be subjected to these "social regularities" (Foucault, 1972) that engender the rules and roles of appropriate involvement behavior.

Consequently, the problem of (non)involvement is a discursive one: Certain home/school interactions are privileged over others, and schools—as regulatory/disciplinary sites—naturalize these involvement practices while rendering other involvement forms invisible. Certainly, marginalized parents and family members are involved in their children's educational lives. However, much of their involvement forms fall outside traditional/discursive understandings (Hidalgo, 1998; Valdés, 1996). In short, the more pressing problem surrounding noninvolvement rests in a racist educational discourse that fails to explore and validate alternate conceptualizations of involvement.

In order to move away from this racialized economy, we need to begin the process of locating subaltern understandings and manifestations of involvement activity, on the one hand, while recognizing the various ways in which schools minimize and devalue the contributions of parents of color, on the other (Shannon, 1996; Villenas & Deyhle, 1999). By privileging these othered perspectives, we will not only highlight the racial terrain that surrounds parental involvement but also transgress our taken-for-granted assumptions surrounding appropriate home-school interactions and/or parental behaviors. One promising tool toward this end is the use of Critical Race Theory (CRT)—a social, political, and theoretical movement addressing the centrality of race/racism in the larger social order.

Critical Race Theory and Subjugated Knowledge

In recent years, CRT has played an important role in both legal (Crenshaw, Gotanda, Peller, & Thomas, 1995; Delgado, 1995) and educational circles (Ladson-Billings, 1999; Ladson-Billings & Tate, 1995; Parker, Deyhle, & Villenas, 1999). Scholars who write in this area have increasingly moved away from its liberalist roots and have begun an aggressive campaign to analyze the pervasiveness of racism in every aspect of society (Delgado, 1995; Williams, 1995). Rather than subscribe to the belief that racism is an abnormal or unusual concept, critical race theorists begin with the premise that racism is a normal and endemic component of our social fabric (see also Banks, 1993; Bishop, 1998; Collins, 1991; Delgado Bernal, 1998; Gordon, 1990; Ladson-Billings & Tate, 1995; Scheurich & Young, 1997; Tatum, 1997; Tyson, 1998). Racism, in other words, is so ingrained and entrenched in our daily lives that it often assumes normality, and thus, an invisibility that is often taken for granted.

Proponents of CRT suggest that such invisibility works in the interest of a White power structure by minimizing the multiple and subtle ways in which racism is deployed on a daily basis. By "unmasking" the hidden faces of racism, Critical Race Theorists aim to expose and unveil White privilege "in its various permutations" (Ladson-Billings, 1999, p. 12)—revealing a social order that is highly stratified and segmented along racial lines.

As an outgrowth of the Civil Rights and Critical Legal Studies Movements (Crenshaw, Gotanda, Peller, & Thomas, 1995), CRT's premise is to critically interrogate how the law and other juridical apparatuses reproduce, reify, and normalize racism in society. The aim of CRT, however, is not simply to document or describe how racism functions but to serve as a progressive force toward an anti-racist agenda that is the foundation for political struggle and social change (Matsuda, 1996).

One way in which critical race theorists advocate for social change is through the process of counter-storytelling (Delgado, 1995): a process that aims to resurrect the narratives and accounts of people of color; narratives that have been silenced, marginalized, and invalidated in the larger social conversation. These subjugated accounts not only provide a different understanding of reality but also open up possibilities for understanding this reality in new and fundamentally different ways. These are the stories that are not told, stories that are consciously and/or unconsciously ignored or downplayed because they do not fit socially acceptable notions of truth.

For example, if one were to argue that schools actively and willingly support a racist agenda, many educators—conservative and liberal alike—would be greatly offended, finding such statements preposterous and absurd. Whereas some would agree there might be certain curricula and/or instructional practices that are less palatable to nonmainstream students, or perhaps even a handful of truly racist teachers and administrators, most would believe that racism is both uncommon and unusual in educational settings. In short, the belief that schools firmly support a racist economy does not fit our prevailing and espoused beliefs about the nature of schooling.

The role of CRT is to highlight the fact that these beliefs only serve to maintain racism in place; relegating racism to overt/blatant and unmistakable acts of hatred, as opposed to highlighting the ways in which social structures and apparatuses reproduce a system of racial and social inequality. In short, rather than focusing on the more obvious/overt forms of racism, CRT offers a variety of "counterstories" that aim to depict how schools and other organizations play an active role in subordinating marginalized parents and children of color.

Critical race theorists believe there are two differing accounts of reality: the dominant reality that "looks ordinary and natural" (Delgado, 1995, p. xiv) to most individuals, and a "racial reality" (Bell, 1995) that has been filtered-out, suppressed, and/or censored through the normalization process. By revealing these subjugated accounts, CRT hopes to demystify the notion of a racially neutral society and tell another story of a highly racialized social order. In this story, social institutions and practices serve the interest of White individuals.

The purpose of this discussion is to highlight how one specific educational practice—parental involvement—is undeniably laced with racial underpinnings. Rather than accept the "stock story" (Delgado, 1995) of noninvolvement (which suggests marginalized parents are uninvolved in their children's education), this discussion aims to tell a counterstory (Delgado, 1995) of involvement, a story that is not often heard in educational conversations. In this regard, I will utilize a CRT framework to challenge the public stereotype of minority noninvolvement while simultaneously highlighting the various ways in which school practices marginalize, alienate, and blame marginalized parents for school failure (Villenas & Deyhle, 1999). By telling this different account of involvement, I hope to disrupt common assumptions surrounding appropriate parental involvement roles, while calling attention to the racialized terrain in which parental involvement is situated (Hidalgo, 1998).

A Counterstory of Involvement

The following counterstory is taken from a qualitative research study (López, 1999) surrounding the parental involvement beliefs and practices in the homes of academically successful migrant students. The study included a purposeful sample of five migrant families from the Texas Rio Grande Valley and was conducted during a six-month period in 1998–1999. For purposes of this discussion, however, I will elaborate on the involvement beliefs and practices in one particular household.

The research design included a series of observations (N=16) and in-depth individual interviews (N=12) with both immediate and extended family members—in addition to two group interviews, where all members of the immediate and extended family were present. All interviews were audio recorded, transcribed, and analyzed according to traditional qualitative research protocol (Bogden & Bilken, 1992; Denzin & Lincoln, 1994; Lincoln & Guba, 1985; Miles & Huberman, 1994; Patton, 1990).[2] The resulting account contains a fundamentally different understanding and epistemological orientation of what it means to be involved in the academic and educational lives of children.[3]

The Longoria Family

Pablo and Elia Longoria both grew up in small rural *pueblos* not far from the U.S./Mexico border in the Mexican state of San Luis Potosí. Having experienced firsthand the hardships of poverty while growing up and having to sacrifice their own education to work in order to support their families, the Longorias have come to realize the value of an education: firmly believing their own social and economic position as migrant farmworkers is directly related to their limited schooling opportunities while growing up. As a result of their restricted education, the Longorias have made every effort to ensure that their six children have an opportunity to be successful in school—despite the fact that their schooling has been overwhelmingly characterized by constant interruptions.

Although all six Longoria children have managed to negotiate successfully the demands of work, school, and constant mobility, it would appear to many educators that their parents have historically played a small role in helping them achieve these accomplishments. In fact, if one were to view the Longoria household through a traditional academic lens, Pablo and Elia Longoria would appear to be largely uninvolved in their children's educational lives: They never visited any of their children's classrooms during regular school hours, they never served as volunteers at any of their children's schools, and they never served as members of a Parent-Teacher Association (PTA), or any other school decision making body. Moreover, they sparsely attended school activities and functions and never monitored their children's homework or academic progress. Indeed, if viewed through a standard involvement lens, the Longorias have largely played a marginal role in the educational arena.

Perhaps this is because Pablo and Elia Longoria largely understood involvement as something much broader than the enactment of traditional academic roles. For the Longorias, involvement was seen as transmitting to their children the importance of schooling through the lessons of migrant labor. Not only did the Longorias constantly give their children *consejos* [advice] about the importance of continuing their studies, but they also instilled in them a strong belief in education as the primary vehicle to break out of the cycle of poverty that overwhelmingly dominates migrant life.

In this regard, the Longorias largely perceived involvement in a fundamentally different way. For them, involvement was not seen as performing a set of ritualistic predetermined activities, but as teaching their children a more practical lesson surrounding the role of education in the larger social order. In other words, rather than subscribe to normative involvement interpretations, the Longorias chose to be involved in ways that communicated to their children the value of schooling. In order to teach them this lesson, the Longorias exposed their children to the hardships of migratory work at an early age. They believed that if their children saw—and personally experienced—the difficulties of working the field, they would be motivated to put more effort into their studies:

Mr. Longoria: *Para nosotros los Latinos, la única cosa que le podemos dar a nuestros hijos es la herencia del estudio, verdad? Porque no tenemos dinero. No somos ricos. Lo único que le podemos dar es esa oportunidad. No hay nada más. Y uno le pide a Dios que todo le salga bien. No le pedimos al Señor que les de mucho—que dinero, que carros, que sé yo. Solamente que esten bien de salud, que tengan suficiente para vivir—no tanto, nomas suficiente—y que tengan un trabajito menos pesado que el de nosotros. Un trabajo en la sombra, 'pa que no esten en el sol ni el zoquete como uno. Por eso les digo [a mis hijos] que le hechen ganas al estudio. Que agarren una educación para que no sufren tanto en el trabajo. Porque este trabajo es duro. Y ellos sí saben lo duro que es proque lo han hecho toda la vida. Y creo yo que ese es la razon porque se han aplicado tanto en sus estudios. Porque ese trabajo es duro! Y todos ellos lo saben. Saben que si no quieren hacer eso toda la vida van a tener que aplicarse.* [Well for us Latinos, the only thing we can give to our children is the inheritance of an education, right? Because we don't have any money. We're not rich. The only thing we can give them is that opportunity. There is nothing greater than (doing) that. And one prays to God that things go well for them. We don't ask God to give them a lot—like cars, like money, or (things of that nature). Just that they have good health, that they have enough (money) to live—not a lot, but enough—and that they have a job that's less (demanding) than the one we have. A job in the shade, so that they're not in the sun or in the mud like the rest of us. That's why I tell (my children) to apply themselves in their studies. To get an education so that they don't have to suffer as much in their job. Because this job (i.e., migrant labor) is difficult. And they know how difficult it is because they have done it all their lives. And I think that's why they've applied themselves so much in school. Because that work is hard! And they all know that. They know that if they don't want to do that for the rest of their lives, they will have to apply themselves (in school)].

Interestingly, rather than sheltering their children from the harsh realities of migrant work, the Longorias firmly believed their children needed to be exposed to these hardships in order to witness the economic and social conditions that surround the migrant lifestyle. According to the parents, without this firsthand exposure, their children would never fully understand the importance of the education they received:

> Mr. Longoria: *Un año los llevamos para Ohio para que vieran lo duro que es trabajar en la labor.* [One year we took them to Ohio so that they could see how hard it is to work in the fields.]
> Mrs. Longoria: *Y también para poder trabajar un poquito.* [And also to be able to work a little.]
> Mr. Longoria: *O sea, ellos han visto las condiciones que se encuentra uno de pobre como quiera y trabajar para poder tener, y para poder vivir nomás. Ellos han visto lo difícil que es sin tener estudio. Allí vieron lo duro que es y lo que gana uno allá también. Entonces saben que se necesitan enfocar en la escuela si no quieren vivir así también....Entonces ellos ven que tienen que echarle las ganas para salir adelante.* [In other words, they have seen the conditions in which you find yourself if you are poor, and to work to have [money], and just to live. They have seen how difficult it is without an education. There they saw how hard it was and also what you earn there. So they know that they need to pay attention in school if they don't want to live like that....So they were seeing that they have to put effort into it if they want to get ahead (in life)].

This belief in teaching their children the importance of education emerged from the parents' personal history and lived experience as migrant workers. In fact, the Longorias were very strategic in exposing their children to the world of migratory labor: constantly giving them *consejos* about the importance of school and demonstrating to them the limited opportunities available if they chose to circumvent their education. This particular act—informed by social, cultural, and economic conditions—was their way of being involved in their children's educational lives (see also, Delgado-Gaitán, 1994).[4]

The World of Work and School

Rather than seeing school and work as two separate entities, the Longorias firmly believed that educational investments had a direct relationship with the type of job opportunities their children could attain. Not only does this belief demonstrate the economic/market sensibilities of Pablo and Elia Longoria, but it also reveals their values and beliefs surrounding the importance of receiving a solid education. Therefore, for the Longorias, migrant labor was more than a means of subsistence: It was a type of educational experience that engendered specific lessons about life.

To be certain, migrant labor is not only physically strenuous, but the working, living, and earning conditions are less than favorable when compared to the conditions of other manual-labor jobs. The Longorias simply wanted their children to understand that if they dropped out of school, the probability of breaking out of the migrant stream would be difficult:

Mrs. Longoria: *Pues ellos han visto que nosotros hemos sufrido mucho. Yo creo que por eso se han animado a estudiar.* [Well, they have seen that we have suffered a lot. I think that's why they have had the inspiration to study.]

Mr. Longoria: *Así es. Es que ellos han visto como hemos batallado nosotros porque hemos batallado bastante para salir adelante y a base de puro sacrificio y el trabajo. Ellos han visto nuestros sacrificios y como hemos tratado de salir adelante.* [That's right. They have seen how much we've struggled because we have struggled a lot to get ahead on pure sacrifice and work. They have seen our sacrifices and how we've tried to get ahead.]

Mrs. Longoria: *Como se dice: "hay que valorizar el trabajo para saber como vive uno."* [Like they say: "you have to value work to get to know how you live."]

Mr. Longoria: *Por eso es importante enseñarles el valor del trabajo a los muchachos para que vean lo difícil que es. Llevarlos a los trabajos duros—que si estudian no van a andar así: en el sol, en el aire, en el agua. Entiende? Así es.* [That's why it is important to show the kids the value of work so that they see how difficult it is. Take them to the hard jobs—(to make them realize that) if they study they're not going to be (working) like that: in the sun, in the air, in the rain. Understand? That's how it is.]

Mrs. Longoria: *Ellos nos han visto a nosotros trabajar en la labor, y ellos también han trabajado en eso. O sea, ellos saben lo duro que va ser si no terminan la escuela: trabajando como puedan de un lado a otro o como dijo mi esposo en el sol o en l'agua. Porque en eso uno no puede levantarse una madrugada y decir "yo no quiero ir a trabajar porque está muy frío." No. Necesitas trabajar sea como sea—frío, calor, lloviendo, como sea. Por eso los hemos llevado con nosotros: para que vean. Y no nomás el trabajo pero todo: como se vive allí en el mugrero o en lo feo o tener que bañarse uno con agua fría porque no todo el tiempo hay agua caliente. Todo.* [They have seen us work in the fields, and have also worked there. In other words, they know how hard it will be if they do not finish school: having to work from one place to another in rain or shine, like my husband said. Because in that (type of work) one can't wake up in the early morning and say "I don't want to go to work because it's too cold." No. You need to work regardless of how it is—cold, hot, rainy, regardless. That's why we've taken them with us: So that they can see not only the work (we do) but everything: how one lives there in the filth or in ugly (conditions) or having to take a bath with cold water because there's not hot water all the time. Everything.]

Mr. Longoria: *Así ellos se van a aplicar en los estudios para agarrar un trabajo que no sea tan pesado y no van a sufrir tanto.* [That way they'll apply themselves to their studies in order to get a job that's not as difficult and they're not going to suffer as much.]

Interviewer: *O sea, ustedes llevaron sus hijos a la labor por alguna razon?* [Are you saying you took your children to work with you in the fields for a reason?]

Mr. Longoria: *Yo creo que sí. O sea, nunca era para nosotros. Que trabajen para ganar dinero para nosotros. No. Era 'pa que se fueran enseñado. Casi nunca interrumpimos la escuela de ellos. O sea, cuando fuimos para el norte fue en verano. Cuando anduvimos aquí en la labor, fue en verano también que piscamos pepino, tomate, calabazitas, fue en verano—cuando ellos no tenían sus clases. Y los fines de semana también, no cuando ellos tenían sus clases.* [I believe so. In other words, it was never for us. That they go to work earn money for us. No. It was so that they would start learning. We almost never interrupted their schooling. In other words, when we went up north it was in the summer. When we worked here in the fields, it was also in the summer when we picked cucumbers, tomatoes, zucchini, that was in the summer—when they didn't have any classes. As well as on the weekends, when they did not have any classes.]

Mrs. Longoria: *Pues sí se trataba de trabajar toda la semana—pero nosotros éramos los que trabajábamos toda la semana. Ellos no. Ellos, primeramente su educación. Porque lo van a necesitar toda su vida. O sea no queremos que estén como nosotros. No queremos que estén como nosotros de a tiro sin nada de educación.* [Well we did try to work all week long—but we were the ones who worked all week. Not them. Education is their primary thing. Because they're going to need it all their lives. In other words, we don't want them to be like us. We don't want them to be like us (just getting by) without an education.]

In this regard, education was always a priority in the Longoria household; migrant labor was simply a tool to teach their children the value of the education they were receiving. Intrinsically, there seem to be many distinct lessons Mr. and Mrs. Longoria wanted their children to learn through the experience of work:

- To become acquainted with the type of work they do;

- To recognize that migrant labor is difficult/strenuous and certainly not well-paid;
- To realize that without an education, their job prospects would be severely limited.

They believed this type of hands-on learning not only opened their children's eyes to the multiple hardships facing migrant populations, but also helped them develop a consciousness that was geared toward education:

Mrs. Longoria: *Yo creo que mis hijos cuando iban creciendo, ellos iban viendo. Ellos iban viendo y ellos iban aprendiendo y se llevaron con ellos ese mensaje del esfuerzo que hemos hecho nosotros con el trabajo y también con lo que les enseñábamos.* [I think that my children when they were growing up, they would be watching. They would be watching and they would be learning and they learned the message of the effort we have made with work and also everything that we've taught them.]

Interviewer: *Me están diciendo que sus hijos aprendieron esta lección solamente por verlos a ustedes y las condiciones en donde trabajaban?* [So are you saying your children learned this lesson just by observing you and the conditions of work around them?]

Mrs. Longoria: *Es que muchas de las veces no es necesario darles consejos a los hijos. Si los hijos piensan y miran de todo de lo que esta sucediendo con eso basta que vean como se están sacrificando los padres para poder sacarlos adelante o poder darles lo que necesitan.* [It's that many times it's not necessary to give advice to your children. If the children think and observe everything that's happening around them that's enough so that they can see how much the parents are sacrificing themselves to be able to get them ahead or to be able to give them what they need.]

Mr. Longoria: *También los hijos aprecian los sacrificios de sus padres.* [The children also appreciate the sacrifices of their parents.]

Mrs. Longoria: *Pero no creo que es suficiente nomás que vean. Necesitan trabajar y vivir en carne propia esa experiencia. Como se dice: "uno no experimenta en pellejo ajeno." O sea, sí pueden ver lo duro que es trabajar en la labor, pero no se van a dar cuenta de lo pesado que es hasta que ellos mismos lo hagan.* [But I don't think it's enough for them just to watch. They need to work and live that experience in their own flesh. Like we say: "One does not experiment in someone else's flesh." In other words, yes, they can see how hard it is to work in the fields, but they're not going to realize how hard it is until they do it themselves.]

Mr. Longoria: *Ni tampoco se van a dar cuenta si es que quieren trabajar por toda su vida en eso o si quieren seguir estudiando.* [Neither are they going to realize if it is work they want to do for the rest of their lives or if they want to keep studying.]

Taken holistically, the Longorias took their children to work with them so that they could better appreciate the value of the education they were receiving and to make them realize that education played an important role in determining their future job options and opportunities. Toward this end, the Longorias constantly gave their children *consejos*/advice about the importance of school: They could either drop out of school and work in the fields, or they could work on their studies and pursue a different career path. In other words, work was never an option in the Longoria household—the only option given to the children was where they would choose to focus their energies. Not surprisingly, all the Longoria children chose to work hard in their studies.

Children's Educational Successes

Despite the apparent "lack" of formal involvement on the part of the parents, all six Longoria children graduated high school at the top of their respective classes, and all have continued their academic pursuits at the postsecondary level: Josue, the oldest child, graduated sixth in his high school class and holds a B.A. in Biology from the University of Texas at Austin as well as an M.Ed. in Learning and Instruction from the University of Texas Pan-American; Saul, the second oldest, was the salutatorian of his graduating class and holds a B.S. in Chemical Engineering from the University of Texas at Austin; Maricela the third oldest, was student body president of her high school and graduated fifth in her class—she holds a B.A. in psychology from UT Pan-American and is currently attending law school at Saint Mary's College in San Antonio, Texas; Samuel, the fourth oldest, graduated as salutatorian of his high school class and is currently a Computer Engineering major at the University of Texas at Austin; Elvia, the second youngest, graduated third in her class, and is currently an undecided major at Texas A&M University; Moises, the youngest child, graduated as the school valedictorian and recently began his studies at the University of Michigan-Ann Arbor. Their parents are especially proud of their children and pleased with the fact that their children heeded their advice about the importance of working hard at school:

> Mr. Longoria: *Pues yo estoy muy orgulloso. Muy orgulloso. Porque les hemos enseñado el trabajo, como trabajar. Y ellos también han visto lo duro que tra-*

bajamos y se han dado cuenta que eso no es lo que quieren hacer por toda su
vida. Y que bueno que han querido buscarse otra vida, porque ese trabajo que
hago yo es muy duro. Eso sí. Muy duro. [Well I am very proud. Very proud.
Because we have shown them the work, how to work. And they too have seen
how hard we work and they've realized that it's not what they want to do for
the rest of their lives. And that's good that they've wanted to look for another
life because the work I do is very hard. That's right. Very hard.]

Clearly, the Longoria children have been very successful in school
and are doing exceptionally well in their postsecondary careers, despite
the fact their schooling was constantly interrupted by migration, and despite the fact that their parents were never formally involved in their educational lives. It is also clear that Pablo and Elia Longoria understood
involvement in fundamentally different terms. They may not have been
formally involved at the school site, but they were clearly involved in
shaping their children's attitude and consciousness toward education.

Toward a Different Understanding of Involvement

In contrast to the universal, performative, and ritualistic involvement
practices privileged by educators in school settings, the Longorias' understanding of involvement was more personal, pragmatic, and strategic
(see also Delgado-Gaitán, 1994). It is an understanding of involvement
that is inconsistent with traditional interpretations of involvement activity
and, therefore, fundamentally challenges our beliefs about home-school
collaboration and partnerships.

In this rapidly changing social and economic landscape, schools need
to make a greater effort to understand how marginalized parents are negotiating the concept of involvement to become effective partners with
parents on their own terms. Rather than forcing parents to fit into predetermined involvement molds, schools need to begin the process of identifying the unique ways in which marginalized parents are already
involved and search for creative ways to capitalize on these and other
subjugated involvement forms.

In most educational contexts, the concept of taking children to work
would be viewed inappropriate and perhaps immoral. To be sure, this
action would certainly not qualify as a legitimate involvement act. Nevertheless, the Longorias personally recognized these and other socio-

cultural transmissions as legitimate forms of involvement. This was their way of being involved in their children's educational lives:

Interviewer: *Me puede decir un tocante su papel en la educacion de sus hijos?* [Can you tell me a little bit about your role in your children's eduction?]
Mr. Longoria: *No creo que entendi bien su pregunta.* [I don't think I understood your question.]
Interviewer: *Pues quiero saber como esta involucrado en la educacion de shijos?* [Well I want to know how you are involved in your children's education?]
Mr. Longoria: *Bueno, you creo que con lo poco que uno sabe y lo poco que uno tiene, uno trata de ayudarles a los hijos como pueda. O sea, uno quiere enseñarles algo o darles consejos para que ellos salgan adelante.* [Well, I think when one has little (academic) knowledge and little else, one tries to help their children in whatever way they can. In other words, one tries to teach them something or give them advice so that they can come out ahead.]
Interviewer: *De acuerdo. Pero you quiero saber como ha estado involucrado en la educacion de sus hijos. No me puede dar un ejemplo?* [I agree. But I want to know how you've been involved in your children's education. Can you give me an example?]
Mr. Longoria: *Pues como le digo: dándoles consejos ensáñadoles el trabajo, enseñádoles lo duro que es la vida. Porque toda la vida hemos batallado. No somos ricos. Entonces, nos tenemos que mantener a pura base del trabajo. Y ellos saben que pueden lograr mucho mas si tienen estudio. Yo creo que por eso se han animado a estudiar. Porque hemos sufrido mucho y hemos batallado para salir adelante.* [Well like I am telling you: giving them advice, [taking] them to work, showing them how hard life is. Because we have struggled all our lives. We're not rich. So we have to survive by going to work. And they know they can do much more if they have an education. I think that is why they are determined to study. Because we have suffered a lot and have struggled in order to come out ahead.]

Conclusion:
Privileging Subjugated Stories

As a whole, then, there are two competing stories of involvement: a "stock story" (Delgado, 1995) that is widely accepted (and upon which most of our assumptions, policies, and reform strategies are built), and a "counterstory" that challenges this prevailing mindset. The stock story suggests there is a set number of specific or predetermined ways in which parents can be involved in their children's education. The counterstory, such as the one presented in this discussion, aims to broaden these assumptions and challenge fundamental beliefs surrounding appropriate parental roles.   *

The power of the stock story, therefore, rests in its discursive capacity: producing reality (in this case, what is typically understood as involvement and who is considered to be involved) through an economy of disciplinary practices that render other involvement forms invisible (see also Foucault, 1972, 1977, 1980). Unfortunately, this reality not only negates/silences subaltern involvement forms, but positions marginalized parents (and/or other parents who do not perform these traditionally accepted tasks) as uninvolved in their children's educational lives.

In order to move away from this dominant/hegemonic involvement discourse, we must look for practices that stand outside traditional involvement configurations. By identifying these subaltern epistemologies, ways of knowing, and forms of involvement, we can broaden this seemingly racialized discourse and move beyond narrowly defined understandings of how parents and other family members are—and can be—involved in the educational lives of their children.

Notes

1. Although school failure is a factorally complex phenomenon, when children of color fail, it is often attributed to individual and/or personal characteristics such as coming from dysfunctional homes or having certain intellectual or socio-cultural deficits. Conversely, when White/middle class children fail, this failure is often attributed to a host of external/social factors such as media influences, drugs, or peer pressure. These attribution patterns serve only to reinforce racism in the larger social order, while blaming children of color for their academic shortcomings.

2. In contrast to the neutral assumptions that undergird traditional research processes, I believe that research is never ideologically or theoretically pure. In other words, I believe that research is always laced, tainted, and influenced by a number of different factors. What we seemingly choose to research, what constitutes significant findings, whom we write for, and how we write it, are all contingent upon our political commitments, epistemological orientations, academic personnel committees, job prospects, peer acceptance, personal time and energy, and a host of other factors that interact with the written word. Sometimes we may choose to research a particular topic or write in a particular style because we believe it is politically safe. Other times, our social and political commitments place an ethical obligation on us to be more responsible to those whose lives we research (Delgado Bernal, 1998; González, 1999; Hermes, 1999; Lather & Smithies, 1997; Pizarro, 1999; Villenas, 1996).

Whatever the case may be, the final outcome—that is, the written word—is never a
neutral representation of truth.

3. The resulting account provides a powerful counternarrative to the ritualistic prac-
    tices inherent in traditional involvement pursuits. The collective stories and voices
    of the Longoria family were viewed through the lens of Critical Race Theory. The
    stories and testimonies that were shared provide a cogent insight into the strength
    and resiliency of the Latino family unit (Villenas & Deyhle, 1999; Zambrana, 1995),
    the funds of knowledge and belief systems available in Latino households (Moll,
    1992; Vélez-Ibáñez & Greenberg, 1992), and the inability of schools to recognize
    and validate these particular cultural strengths (Villenas & Deyhle, 1999). In this re-
    gard, the use of CRT allowed me to see the data in a fundamentally different way—
    recognizing the strengths of this particular family and the failure of schools to build
    on these strengths and other subjugated involvement forms.

4. To many individuals, the act of taking children to work would typically be seen in a
    negative light. In contrast, a CRT perspective not only highlights the cultural
    strengths of maintaining a close family unit in both the home and work environment
    (see also Zambrana, 1995), but recognizes these acts as engendering particular les-
    sons about a highly racialized and segmented economic order—where so-called "re-
    turns" to educational investments are unequally distributed along racial and class
    lines.

References

Auerbach, E. R. (1989). Toward a social-contextual approach to family literacy. *Harvard
    Educational Review, 59*, 165–181.

Banks, J. A. (1993). The canon debate, knowledge construction, and multicultural educa-
    tion. *Educational Researcher, 22*(5), 4–14.

Bean, F., Chapa, J., Berg, R., & Sowards, K. (1991, June). *Educational and sociodemo-
    graphic incorporation among Hispanic immigrants to the United States.* Paper pre-
    sented at Urban Institute's Immigrants in the 1990s Conference: Washington, DC.

Bean , F., & Tienda, M. (1987). *The Hispanic population in the United States.* New York:
    Russell Sage.

Becher, R. (1986). *Parents and schools.* Urbana, IL: ERIC Clearinghouse on Elementary
    and Early Childhood Education. (ERIC Document Reproduction Service No ED269
    137)

Bell, D. (1995). Racial realism after we're gone: Prudent speculations on America in a post-racial epoch. In R. Delgado (Ed.), *Critical race theory: The cutting edge* (pp. 2–8). Philadelphia: Temple University Press.

Bishop, R. (1998). Freeing ourselves from neo-colonial domination in research: A Maori approach to creating knowledge. *International Journal of Qualitative Studies in Education, 11*(2), 199–219.

Bogden, R., & Bilken, S. K. (1992). *Qualitative research for education: An introduction to theory and methods* (2nd ed.). Boston: Allyn & Bacon.

Brown, P. C. (1989). *Involving parents in the education of their children.* Urbana, IL: ERIC Clearinghouse on Elementary and Early Childhood Education. (ERIC Document Reproduction Service No. ED 308 988)

Buriel, R., & Cardoza, D. (1988). Sociocultural correlates of achievement among three generations of Mexican-American high school seniors. *American Educational Research Journal, 25*, 177–192.

Carnoy, M., Daley, H., & Hinojosa Ojeda, R. (1990). *Latinos in a changing US economy: Comparative perspectives on the US labor market since 1939.* New York: City University of New York.

Chapa, J. (1989). The myth of Hispanic progress: Trends in the educational and economic attainment of Mexican Americans. *Journal of Hispanic Policy, 4*, 3–18.

Chavkin, N. F. (Ed.). (1993). *Families and schools in a pluralistic society.* Albany: State University of New York Press.

Chavkin, N. F., & Williams, D. L. (1989). Low-income parents' attitudes toward parent involvement in education. *Journal of Sociology and Social Welfare, 16*, 17–28.

Chavkin, N. F., & Williams, D. L. (1990). Working parents and schools: Implications for practice. *Education, 111*, 242–248.

Chavkin, N. F., & Williams, D. L. (1993). Minority parents and the elementary school: Attitudes and practices. In N. F. Chavkin (Ed.), *Families and schools in a pluralistic society* (pp. 73–83). Albany, NY: State University of New York Press.

Clark, R. (1983). *Family life and school achievement: Why poor black children succeed or fail.* Chicago, IL: University of Chicago Press.

Collins, P. H. (1991). *Black feminist thought: Knowledge, consciousness and the politics of empowerment.* New York: Routledge.

Crenshaw, K., Gotanda, N., Peller, G., & Thomas, K. (Eds.). (1995). *Critical race theory: The key writings that formed the movement.* New York: New Press.

Darder, A., Torres, R. D., & Gutierrez, H. (Eds.). (1997). *Latinos and education: A critical reader.* New York: Routledge.

Delgado, R. (1995). Legal storytelling: Storytelling for oppositionists and others: A plea for narrative. In R. Delgado (Ed.), *Critical race theory: The cutting edge* (pp. 64–74). Philadelphia: Temple University Press.

Delgado Bernal, D. (1998). Using a Chicana feminist epistemology in educational research. *Harvard Educational Review, 68*(4), 555–582.

Delgado-Gaitán, C. (1990). *Literacy for empowerment: The role of parents in children's education.* New York: Falmer Press.

Delgado-Gaitán, C. (1994). Consejos: The power of cultural narratives. *Anthropology and Education Quarterly, 23,* 298–316.

Denzin, N. K., & Lincoln, Y. L. (Eds.). (1994). *The handbook of qualitative research.* Thousand Oaks, CA: Sage.

Eccles, J. S., & Harold, R. D. (1996). Family involvement in children's and adolescents' schooling. In A. Booth & J. F. Dunn (Eds.), *Family school links: How do they affect educational outcomes?* (pp. 3–34). Mahwah, NJ: Lawrence Erlbaum Associates.

Epstein, J. L. (1984). *Effects on parents of teacher practices in parent involvement.* Baltimore: Center for Social Organization of Schools.

Epstein, J. L. (1986). Parents' reactions to teacher practices of parent involvement. *The Elementary School Journal, 86,* 277–294.

Epstein, J. L. (1987). Parent involvement: What research says to administrators. *Education and Urban Society, 19,* 119–136.

Epstein, J. L. (1988). How do we improve programs for parent involvement? *Educational Horizons, 66,* 58–59.

Epstein, J. L. (1990). School and family connections: Theory, research, and implications for integrating sociologies of education and family. In D. Unger & M. Sussman (Eds.), *Families in community settings: Interdisciplinary perspectives* (pp. 99–126). Binghamton, NY: Hayworth.

Epstein, J. L. (1995). School/family/community partnerships: Caring for the children we share. *Phi Delta Kappan, 76,* 701–712.

Foucault, M. (1972). *The archaeology of knowledge* (A. M. Sheridan Smith, Trans.). New York: Pantheon Books. (Original work published 1969)

Foucault, M. (1977). *Discipline & punish: The birth of the prison* (A. Sheridan, Trans.). New York: Pantheon. (Original work published 1975)

Foucault, M. (1980). *Power/knowledge: Selected interviews and other writings by Michel Foucault, 1972–1977* (C. Gordon, Ed.). New York: Pantheon.

González, F. E. (1999). Formations of Mexicananess: Trenzas de identidad multiples (Growing up Mexicana: Braids of multiple identities). In L. Parker, D. Deyhle, & S. Villenas (Eds.), *Race is...race isn't: Critical race theory and qualitative studies in education* (pp. 125–154). Boulder, CO: Westview Press.

Gordon, E. W. (1990). The necessity of African American epistemology for educational theory and practice. *Journal of Education, 172*(3), 88–106.

Hatch, T. (1998). How community action contributes to achievement. *Educational Leadership, 55*(8), 16–19.

Hayes-Bautista, D., Hurtado, A., Burciaga Valdez, R., & Hernández, A. (1992). *No longer a minority: Latinos and social policy in California.* Los Angeles: UCLA Chicano Studies Research Center.

Hayes-Bautista, D., Schink, W. O., & Chapa, J. (1988). *The burden of support: Young Latinos in an aging society.* Stanford, CA: Stanford University Press.

Henderson, A. (1987). *The evidence continues to grow: Parent involvement improves student achievement.* Columbia, MD: The National Committee for Citizens in Education.

Henderson, A. T., Marburger, C. L., & Ooms, T. (1986). *Beyond the bake sale: An educator's guide to working with parents.* Columbia, MD: The National Committee for Citizens in Education.

Henry, M. (1996). *Parent-school collaboration: Feminist organizational structures and school leadership.* Albany: State University of New York Press.

Hermes, M. (1999). Research methods as a situated response: Towards a first nations' methodology. In L. Parker, D. Deyhle, & S. Villenas (Eds.), *Race is...race isn't: Critical race theory and qualitative studies in education* (pp. 83–100). Boulder, CO: Westview Press.

Hidalgo, N. (1998). Toward a definition of a Latino family research paradigm. *International Journal of Qualitative Studies in Education, 11,* 103–120.

Hurtado, A., & García, E. E. (Eds.). (1994). *The educational achievement of Latinos: Barriers and successes.* Santa Cruz, CA: University of California at Santa Cruz.

Katz, M. B. (1989). *The undeserving poor: From the war on poverty to the war on welfare.* New York: Pantheon Books.

Kirst, M. W., Koppich J. E., & Kelley, K. (1994). School-linked services and Chapter 1: A new approach to improving outcomes for children. In K. K. Wong & M. C. Wang (Eds.), *Re-thinking policy for at risk students* (pp. 197–220). Berkeley, CA: McCutchan Publishing Corporation.

Ladson-Billings, G. (1999). Just what is critical race theory and what's it doing in a nice field like education? In L. Parker, D. Deyhle, & S. Villenas (Eds.), *Race is...race isn't: Critical race theory and qualitative studies in education* (pp. 7–30). Boulder, CO: Westview Press.

Ladson-Billings, G., & Tate, W. F. (1995). Toward a critical race theory of education. *Teachers College Record, 97,* 47–68.

Lareau, A. (1989). *Home advantage.* London: Falmer Press.

Lareau, A. (1996). Assessing parent involvement in schooling: A critical analysis. In A. Booth & J. F. Dunn (Eds.), *Family school links: How do they affect educational outcomes?* (pp. 57–64). Mahwah, NJ: Lawrence Erlbaum Associates.

Lather, P. A., & Smithies, C. (1997). *Troubling the angels: Women living with HIV/AIDS.* Boulder, CO: Westview Press.

Latino Eligibility Task Force. (1993). *Latino student eligibility and participation in the University of California: Report number one of the Latino Eligibility Task Force.* Santa Cruz, CA: University of California at Santa Cruz.

Lightfoot, S. L. (1978). *Worlds apart: Relationships between families and schools.* New York: Basic Books.

Lincoln, Y. L., & Guba, E. G. (1985). *Naturalistic inquiry.* Beverly Hills, CA: Sage.

López, G. R. (1999). *Teaching the value of hard work: A study of parental involvement in migrant households.* Unpublished doctoral dissertation, University of Texas Austin.

Matsuda, M. J. (1996). *Where is your body? And other essays on race, gender and the law.* Boston: Beacon Press.

Miles, M. B., & Huberman, A. M. (1994). *Qualitative data analysis: An expanded sourcebook.* Thousand Oaks, CA; Sage.

Moles, O. C. (1993). Collaboration between schools and disadvantaged parents: Obstacles and openings. In N. F. Chavkin (Ed.), *Families and schools in a pluralistic society* (pp. 21–49). Albany: State University of New York Press.

Moll, L. C. (1992). Bilingual classroom studies and community analysis: Some recent trends. *Educational Researcher, 20*(2), 20–24.

Oakes, J. (1985). *Keeping track: How schools structure inequality.* New Haven: Yale University Press.

Orfield, G. (July, 1988). *The growth and concentration of Hispanic enrollment and the future of American education.* Paper presented at the annual conference of the National Council of La Raza, Albuquerque, NM.

Orfield, G., & Ashkinaze, C. (1991). *The closing door: Conservative policy and Black opportunity.* Chicago: University of Chicago Press.

Pallas, A. M., Natriello, G., & McDill, E. L. (1989). The changing nature of the disadvantaged population: Current dimensions and future trends. *Educational Researcher, 18,* 16–22.

Parker, L., Deyhle, D., & Villenas, S. (Eds.). (1999). *Race is...race isn't: Critical race theory and qualitative studies in education.* Boulder, CO: Westview Press.

Patton, M. Q. (1990). *Qualitative evaluation and research methods* (2nd ed.). Newbury Park, CA: Sage.

Peng, S. S., & Lee, R. M. (1994). Educational experiences and needs of middle school students in poverty. In K. K. Wong & M. C. Wang (Eds.), *Re-thinking policy for at risk students* (pp. 49–64). Berkeley, CA: McCutchan Publishing Corporation.

Perez, S., & de la Rosa Salazar, D. (1997). Economic, labor force, and social implications of Latino educational and population trends. In A. Darder, R. D. Torres, & H. Gutierrez (Eds.), *Latinos and education: A critical reader* (pp. 45–79). New York: Routledge.

Peterson, D. (1989). *Parent involvement in the educational process.* Eugene, OR: ERIC Clearinghouse on Educational Management. (ERIC Document Reproduction Service No. ED 312 776)

Pizarro, M. (1999). Adelante: Toward social justice and empowerment in Chicana/o communities and Chicana/o studies. In L. Parker, D. Deyhle, & S. Villenas (Eds.), *Race is...race isn't: Critical race theory and qualitative studies in education* (pp. 53–81). Boulder, CO: Westview Press.

Robledo, M. (1989). *The answer: Valuing youth in schools and families.* San Antonio, TX: Intercultural Development Research Association.

Romo, H., & Falbo, T. (1996). *Latino high school graduation: Defying the odds.* Austin, TX: University of Texas Press.

Rumberger, R. W. (1987). High school drop outs: A review of issues and evidence. *Review of Educational Research, 57,* 101–121.

Rumberger, R. W. (1991). Chicano dropouts: A review of research and policy issues. In R. R. Valencia (Ed.), *Chicano school failure and success: Research and policy agendas for the 1990's* (pp. 64–89). New York: Falmer Press.

Scheurich, J. J., & Young, M. (1997). Coloring epistemologies: Are our research epistemologies racially biased? *Educational Researcher, 26*(4), 4–16.

Shannon, S. M. (1996). Minority parental involvement: A Mexican mother's experience and a teacher's interpretation. *Education and Urban Society, 29*(1), 71–84.

Sigel, I. E., & Laosa, L. M. (Eds.). (1983). *Changing families.* New York: Plenum Press.

Simich-Dudgeon, C. (1986). *Parent involvement and the education of limited-English-proficient students.* Washington, DC: ERIC Clearinghouse on Languages and Linguistics. (ERIC Document Reproduction Service No. ED 279 205)

Sipes, D. S. B. (1993). Cultural values and American-Indian families. In N. F. Chavkin (Ed.), *Families and schools in a pluralistic society* (pp. 157–174). Albany: State University of New York Press.

Sosa, A. (1993). *Thorough and fair: Creating routes to success for Mexican-American students.* Charleston, WV: ERIC Clearinghouse on Rural Education and Small Schools.

Squires, G. D. (1994). *Capital and communities in Black and White: The intersections of race, class, and uneven development.* Albany: State University of New York Press.

Tatum, B. D. (1997). *Why are all the black kids sitting together in the cafeteria? And other conversations about race.* New York: Basic Books.

Trueba, H. T. (1989). *Raising silent voices: Educating the linguistic minorities for the 21st century.* New York: Harper & Row.

Tyson, C. (1998). Coloring epistemologies: A response. *Educational Researcher, 27*(9), 21–22.

U.S. Bureau of the Census. (1992). *Statistical Abstract of the United States 1992*. Washington, DC: U.S. Government Printing Office.

Valdés, G. (1996). *Con respeto: Bridging the distances between culturally diverse families and schools: An ethnographic portrait*. New York: Teachers College Press.

Valencia, R. R. (1991). *Chicano school failure and success: Research and policy agendas for the 1990's*. London: Falmer Press.

Vélez-Ibáñez, C., & Greenberg, J. B. (1992). Formation and transformation of funds of knowledge among US-Mexican households. *Anthropology and Education Quarterly, 23*, 313–335.

Villenas, S. (1996). The colonizer/colonized Chicana ethnographer: Identity, marginalization, and co-optation in the field. *Harvard Educational Review, 66*(4), 711–731.

Villenas, S., & Deyhle, D. (1999). Critical race theory and ethnographies challenging the stereotypes: Latino families, schooling, resilience and resistance. *Curriculum Inquiry, 29*(4), 413–445.

Williams, D. L., Jr., & Chavkin, N. F. (1985). *Final report of the parent involvement in education project* (Report NO. NIE–400–83–0007). Washington, DC: U.S. Department of Education.

Williams, P. J. (1995). *The alchemy of race and rights: Diary of a law professor*. Cambridge, MA: Harvard University Press.

Wilson, W. J. (1987). *The truly disadvantaged: The inner city, the underclass and public policy*. Chicago: University of Chicago Press.

Zambrana, R. (Ed.). (1995). *Understanding Latino families*. Thousand Oaks, CA: Sage.

5

Multicultural Education in Teacher Training Programs and Its Implications on Preparedness for Effective Work in Urban Settings

Jennifer Ng

As a self-proclaimed, established pioneer in race coverage, *Newsweek* published an article titled "The New Face of Race" (Meacham, 2000b) which declared the onset of a "quiet, daily revolution" (p. 40). Bringing information from the "real lives lived on the front lines," the article warned that the Age of Color—a new chapter in American history where "the nuances of brown and yellow and red mean more, and less, than ever"—is "not a futuristic vision; it's here" (p. 40).

What is the new face of race in America? According to the article, California's White population shares its new "minority" status with Hawaii, New Mexico, and Washington, DC. Florida and Texas will also have a White minority population before the end of the decade. Projections show that by 2010 Latinos will surpass African Americans as the largest minority group, and by 2020 the Asian American population will double in size from 10 million to 20 million people. Along with the domestic changes reflecting life span and fertility rates, the Bureau of Labor Statistics has also noted that the number of foreign-born workers in the U.S. is at its highest level in seven decades (Meacham, 2000b).

The language of battle in a discussion of race suggests political tensions, and the idea of a winner and loser is inherent in the comparison. It hints at the institutional and societal privilege of whiteness without explicitly testifying to the related history of oppression and invisibility of people of color. The allusion to struggle does, however, directly address the fight for—and for some groups, the maintenance of—power, resources, and privilege.

Statistics document the racist plight and powerlessness people of color disproportionately face. In 1990, six of the nation's eight largest cities had more than half of their populations made up of racial minorities, mostly African American or Latino (Ginzberg, 1993). Identifying racial minority populations in urban centers is important because over 80% of concentrated poverty areas in the United States are found in the country's 100 largest cities (Kasarda, 1993). Although the current poverty rates for all racial minority groups have fallen below or equaled the lowest rate ever recorded for each group, the March 2000 supplement to the Current Population Survey shows that the poverty rate for African Americans is still about three times the poverty rate for Whites (U.S. Census Bureau, 2000). Inner-city residents are isolated by deliberate city planning (Noguera, 1996) and have little state or national electoral power relative to their more affluent suburban counterparts (Anyon, 1997). With the shift from an industrial to a service based economy, most of the new jobs in urban areas are either highly specialized or do not pay a living wage (Wilson, 1996; Zinn & Eitzen, 1999).

The interlocking oppressions people of color face in urban communities also affect children's education at public neighborhood schools. Approximately 76% of the students enrolled in urban schools are African American or Latino/a, and over 40% of these schools are deemed high-poverty schools by the Department of Education (Anyon, 1997). Over one-fifth of the country's poor and 35% of the total student population with limited English proficiency also attend urban schools. It is projected that in less than 25 years more than half of these students will be living in poverty (Orfield, 1993). Despite these statistics, urban schools are consistently funded at a lower rate than suburban schools (Council of Great City Schools, Educational Testing Service, National Commission on Teaching and America's Future, and U.S. General Accounting Office as cited by Anyon, 1997).

Discussions of urban education are, for the most part, discussions of issues that affect students of color most significantly. Educational research has consistently contributed examples of how public education fails students of color (Anyon, 1997; Fordham, 1997; Hamovitch, 1996; Kozol, 1991). It has also described some innovative, successful, and liberatory case studies as exceptions to institutional patterns of failure (Ladson-Billings, 1994; O'Connor, 1997; Rose, 1989, 1995). Understanding the findings and/or critiques from educational research to more broadly achieve effective teaching for students of color in urban settings is essential; examining the current use of multicultural education theories and methods in teacher training programs is one avenue for such an analysis.

In this chapter, I argue that four particular shortcomings of multicultural education in teacher training programs can considerably limit the effectiveness of teacher preparation to work in urban schools. First, multicultural education—when separated from its foundation in historical and political movements of social change—results in a limited understanding of the concept as a whole. The end result is student training in the use of alternative types of educational materials, activities, and social skills rather than a fundamental awareness of a lived theory in practice. Second, multicultural education in teacher training programs functions as more than just its explicit organization and curriculum. A lack of attention to the implicit, suggested messages fueling the program can be of great detriment to a program's overall effectiveness. Third, instruction regarding multicultural approaches in teacher training programs too often lacks insight into the social and psychological situations of participants as they encounter various stages of racial identity development. Finally, the absence of a sincere critique of White privilege in multicultural education allows for the continuation of ignorance regarding institutional and societal forms of oppression, and assures the current status of multicultural education as anything but revolutionary.

In concluding the chapter, I discuss areas in need of continued research as well as argue for the incorporation of more qualitative analysis documenting the experiences of preservice teachers of color, critical studies on youth culture, and longitudinal surveys of teacher attitudes and practices.

What Is Multicultural Education?

Gloria Ladson-Billings and William Tate (1995) explain, "Multicultural education has been conceptualized as a *reform* movement designed to *effect change* in the school and other educational institutions so that students from diverse racial, ethnic, and other social-class groups will experience educational *equality*" (emphasis added, p. 61). Through assimilationist goals in the 1950s and searches for authentic racial/ethnic identities of a more pluralistic nature after the civil rights struggle in the 1960s, many of the current manifestations of multicultural education are "trivial examples and artifacts of culture" (p. 61). Multiculturalism, the philosophy behind multicultural education, is now often understood as not only the basis for learning about many cultures but the inclusion of all differences (i.e., racial, ethnic, cultural, linguistic, ability, gender, sexual orientation). It is used by some educators synonymously with the term "diversity" (Ladson-Billings & Tate, 1995).

Multicultural education that views all differences to be equal and similar can be problematic for several reasons. For example, discussion of racial minorities and homosexuals under the shared umbrella of "multicultural education" ignores much of the conflict that may exist between individuals within the groups. Ladson-Billings and Tate (1995) state, "The tensions between and among these differences is rarely interrogated, presuming a 'unity of difference'" (p. 62). Another problem with such a broad definition of multicultural education is that it tends to confuse definitions of "race" and "culture." It obscures the socially constructed nature of race and racial identity, mistaking it with the definition of culture—a shared system of behaviors and beliefs that characterize particular groups (Cameron & Wycoff, 1998).

A false understanding and categorization of various groups and differences leads to what Akintunde (1999) terms "modernist multiculturalism." Such an approach casts discrimination in abstract, hypothetical terms so that oppression continues to be understood only on an individual basis. If the individual understands discrimination and its consequences as a function merely reflecting personal choice, then a critical examination of institutional, societal, and epistemological oppression is hindered, and anyone can be an oppressor or oppressed. Akintunde compares the situation to that of murder: "The concept exists but someone has to commit it in order for it to happen" (p. 2). In this view, racist acts occur only on individual levels in intentional ways. Furthermore, Akintunde states:

> Through [modernist multiculturalist] efforts to increase an "understanding" of "others" it actually reinforces and cements "otherization" and reinforces and perpetuates White supremacy. In addition, such efforts, though not explicitly stated, are in fact designed to help "Whites" learn to see "others" as their equal. Of course, implied in such thinking is that "others" are assumed inferior and need to be raised to the status of "Whites." (pp. 5–7)

In similar fashion, multicultural education also needs to be reconnected to its desire for reform and educational equality. When "others" are believed to be inferior and the continued education of Whites can lead them to an "understanding" of the other, neither social change nor social justice will result. Crenshaw (1988) argues, "Antidiscrimination discourse is fundamentally ambiguous and can accommodate conservative as well as liberal views of race and equality." As a result:

> The current multicultural paradigm is mired in liberal ideology that offers no radical change in the current order....[W]e unabashedly reject a paradigm that attempts to be everything to everyone and consequently becomes nothing for anyone, allowing the status quo to prevail. (Ladson-Billings & Tate, 1995, p. 62)

A crucial point in such a critique of multicultural education is that the concept should not be abandoned but that it could be improved. Educational researchers have put forth helpful characteristics, theories, and typologies of effective multicultural education. Banks and Banks (1995) describe five necessary components of multicultural education:

1) *content integration*, the use of diverse content and experiences in instruction;
2) the *knowledge construction process*, an analysis and understanding of cultural assumptions, frames of reference, and biases that affect how knowledge is constructed;
3) *prejudice reduction*, focused on developing more positive attitudes regarding race, ethnicity, and gender;
4) *equity pedagogy*, techniques to support the academic achievement of students from diverse racial, ethnic, and social backgrounds;
5) an *empowering school culture and social structure*, allowing for all students to experience equality and cultural empowerment.

In addition, Ladson-Billings (1994) characterizes aspects of culturally relevant teaching such as recruiting teachers with an expressed interest in the education of racial minority children, helping teachers develop reflective thinking to critique the system in productive ways, providing cultural immersion opportunities, modeling of culturally relevant teachers, and so forth.

Akintunde (1999) recommends a shift from modernist to *postmodernist multiculturalism* that exposes White supremacy and privilege, eradicates the notion of race and its accompanying syndromes, and deconstructs the dominant, "neutral" Western canon. Giroux (1994) advocates the serious use of cultural studies to inform educational pedagogy and the application of Peter Euban's distinction between *political education*—which refers to the cultivation of "the capacity for judgment essential for the exercise of power and responsibility by a democratic citizenry" (p. 302)—and *politicizing education*, defined as "pedagogical terrorism in which the issue of what is taught, by whom, and under what conditions is determined by a doctrinaire political agenda that refuses to examine its own values, beliefs, and ideological construction" (p. 302). Similarly, McLaren's (1995) version of *liberal multiculturalism* that teaches students about racial and ethnic minorities and attempts to project a more positive image of these groups is less ideal than a *critical and resistance multiculturalism* that assumes the representation of difference and is understood through larger social struggles that necessitate social, cultural, and institutional transformation. Carter's (2000) typologies of the assumptions fueling multicultural education are also useful, in that they allow educators to compare the ideology of various approaches to multicultural education, recognize their advantages and disadvantages, and help them uncover their implicit assumptions.

Multicultural Education: An Interrogation of the Texts and Subtexts in Teacher Education Programs

As discussed above, students in public schools are more racially, ethnically, and linguistically diverse than ever before. This diversity, however, is not the case in the preservice teacher population. African Americans, Latinos, Asian Americans, and Native Americans make up less than 10% of those entering the teaching profession, and this percentage is steadily declining (American Association of Colleges for Teacher Education, 1987). More specifically, 6.8% of prospective teachers are African American, 2.7% are Latino, and the number of Asian American and Native American teachers is negligible. The percentage of school administrators of color has also dropped from 12% in the 1970s to 6% in the 1990s (Gay, 1997). Furthermore, the racial makeup of the teacher educator population is quite homogeneous. Eighty-eight percent of full-time faculty in education are White; eighty-one percent of this faculty are between the ages of 45 and 60, or older (American Association of Colleges for Teacher Education, 1994).

According to research cited by Cochran-Smith (1995), teachers are most able to "understand, set appropriate expectations, and provide strategic support for students who are like themselves in culture, race, and ethnicity" (p. 542). This is not to suggest that White teachers are unable to teach racial minority children successfully. Rather, the way that teachers learn to think about multicultural education from their university faculty, peers, and program supervisors/cooperating teachers is of utmost importance. As Grant & Zozakiewicz (1995) discuss, preservice teachers are most likely to engage issues of multicultural education thoughtfully after specific initiation, encouragement, or requirement by a mentor knowledgeable and concerned about multicultural education. One way to assess a teacher education program's underlying philosophy, its explicit goals, and its efficacy in preparing teachers in multicultural education is to consider its texts and subtexts (Cochran-Smith, 2000). The *text* of a program includes its course sequence, fieldwork experiences, reading and writing assignments, and certification procedures. Within the text itself is a *subtext*—what messages the materials, discussions, and activities convey directly as well as subtly, how people's reading and interpretations of particular books are affected by their subjectivity and experience, and what happens in response to the text of the program that is not planned or necessarily made public.

A catalog of courses offered by teacher training programs suggests a quantifiable commitment to multicultural education. However, as Young and Laible (2000) emphasize, "The incorporation of a few competency entries that include the words race, gender, culture, and diversity do not reflect a serious attempt at addressing these critical problems [of racism and the equitable education of children of color]" (p. 387). The text of a teacher training program also includes the way by which preservice teachers are advised to organize and register for course requirements. As a reactive approach to the need for multicultural education, too many teacher training programs "created appendages in the form of workshops, institutes, and courses to deal with the 'problem' of culturally different students" (Ladson-Billings, 1999, p. 218). This marginal status of multicultural education left the "core of American education with its attendant White, middle class values and perspectives intact. Multiethnic or multicultural education was synonymous with 'minority' education [and] teachers, despite cultural 'training,' continued to function within a Eurocentric framework" (Goodwin, 1997, p. 9). As quoted by Ladson-Billings (1999), Zeichner asserts, "Despite a clear preference for the integrated approach [where issues of diversity occur throughout course work and field experiences], the segregated [add-on] approach is clearly dominant in U.S. teacher education programs" (p. 223).

The ways that preservice teachers respond to the text of teacher training programs through a range of expressed and observable behaviors provide insight into the subtext of particular programs. One response to the add-on approach of multicultural education is that the course work is seen as a "necessary evil." Ladson-Billings states, "Even at schools, colleges, and departments of education with well-regarded teacher preparation programs, students talk of "getting through the diversity requirement" (p. 240). The internalized effects of such beliefs lead preservice teachers to see multicultural education as benefiting the education of students of color only, and some express their exasperation with multicultural education because they want to learn how to teach *all* children (Cochran-Smith, 1995, 2000). Preservice teachers come to see that "diversity, like cultural deprivation and the state of being at risk, is that 'thing' that is other than White and middle class" (Ladson-Billings, 1999, p. 219). Well-meaning individuals may at best then conceive of multicultural education as a human relations effort—as a way to "treat everyone the same," "learn to get along with all types of people," and "accept diversity" (Grant & Zozakiewicz, 1995, p. 267). Alternatively, smart and successful preservice teachers figure out how to superficially talk the talk and play the game of political correctness without developing a political stance on teaching (Cochran-Smith, 1995; Sleeter, 1995a, 1995b).

Interestingly, preservice teachers of color often voice a different opinion of the program's multicultural education component than their White counterparts. Cochran-Smith (2000) recounts her concerted efforts to design a teacher training program with a progressive, explicit examination of race and race issues and her shock at hearing the criticism of preservice teachers of color. She explains,

> [O]ne student teacher, a Puerto Rican woman, raised her hand and said with passion and an anger that bordered on rage, "Nothing! This program does *noth-*

ing to address issues of race!" After a few seconds of silence that felt to me like hours, two other students—one African American and one Black South African—agreed with her, adding their frustration and criticism to the first comment and indicating that we read nothing and said nothing that addressed these questions. I was stunned. (p. 160)

Students critiqued the program's lack of racial minority representation in the faculty, stating that they felt little validation on the issues they wanted to discuss as women and prospective teachers of color. They also stressed the need for "inclusion" to be even more inclusive, recognizing the absence of Asian American and Native American experiences from the too common dichotomy of Black and White. These students' criticisms were not necessarily shared by their White counterparts, some of whom privately expressed that the degree of focus on race issues was "just right" or "too heavy." The fact that such disparate student responses resulted from the same text compiled by the teacher training program highlights the importance of being cognizant of the program's subtext.

Racial Identity Development: The Social and Psychological Effects on Preservice Teacher Preparation for Transformatory Multicultural Education

Many preservice teachers enter their training programs with unchallenged beliefs regarding American meritocracy (Sleeter, 1995b) and very little interaction with people unlike themselves. This lack of experience preservice teachers have with interrogating their own assumptions and reflecting on their involvement with different people can hinder their thorough understanding of multicultural education and its potential for social change and justice (Banks & Banks, 1997; Carter, 2000; Cochran-Smith, 1995, 2000; Cooney & Akintunde, 1999; Grant & Zozakiewicz, 1995; Hamovitch, 1996; McIntyre, 1997; Nevarez, Sanford, & Parker, 1997; Richardson & Villenas, 2000; Young & Laible, 2000). While discussing race issues with other students in teacher training programs, preservice teachers may work through and between different stages of racial identity development (Carter, 2000; Lawrence & Tatum, 1997).

Racial identity refers to a person's psychological response to her/his own race. Carter (2000) explains, "It reflects the extent to which one identifies with a particular racial group and how that identification influences perceptions, emotions, and behaviors toward people from other groups" (p. 875). This insight is of great significance, for it helps teacher educators understand the social, psychological, and academic needs of preservice teachers in their programs. Furthermore, such insight helps students "see" their beliefs and actions in a theoretical framework of racial identity development, and guides preservice teachers in establishing some degree of autonomy to investigate their motives and their intentions as educators. Carter also contends, "The paradigms one espouses matter because they form the basis from which one attempts to influence and intervene in the lives of others" (p. 873). The racial identity development models Carter proposes are worth reviewing.

Separate models of development exist because of the differing experiences of Whites and racial minorities in a hegemonic society. For Blacks and people of color, Carter suggests there are four distinct stages of identity development:

1) the *conformity/pre-encounter* phase, characterized by the racial minority's external self-definition to reflect a preference for the dominant race and a negative attitude towards one's own race;
2) the *dissonance/encounter* phase, where the individual begins to experience feelings and attitudes that reflect confusion and conflict regarding her/his own group and the dominant racial group;
3) the *immersion-emersion* phase, represented by the individual rejecting both the dominant culture and race and turning instead into an exploration of her/his own race and developing an internal definition of self; and
4) the *internalization/integrative awareness* phase, distinguished by the individual's commitment and pride in her/his own race and culture which allows her/him to function more capably within the dominant society as well as show an active support of nonracist perspectives through social and political activism.

Conversely, Carter suggests there are six stages that constitute the White racial identity model:

1) the *contact* phase, where an individual expresses satisfaction with the racial status quo and is unaware of racism and her/his own participation in such a system of oppression
2) the *disintegration* stage, which is characterized by the individual's tension in having to choose between commitment to her/his own racial group or challenge the social order of injustice as well as the recognition that people are not really color-blind;
3) the *reintegration* phase, which refers to an idealization of the individual's own racial group allowing her/him to believe in society's message of her/his entitlement;
4) the *pseudo-independence* stage, which marks the individual's attempt at self-definition and acceptance of racial and cultural differences, even though it may lead to marginal status within her/his own group;
5) the *immersion-emersion* stage, which reflects the individual's search for a nonracist, positive White identity and fellowship with other Whites as a source of knowledge about race and racism; and
6) the *autonomy* stage, which is symbolic of the individual's reconciliation of self with an understanding of racism and commitment to dismantle oppression in all forms.

Both racial identity models suggest constant and nonlinear processes, and particular experiences or events often serve as catalysts for movement within the models (Carter, 2000; Tatum, 1992). Use of the models in teacher training programs serves several purposes. It emphasizes the various social and psychological statuses of people even within the same racial group. In other words, shared skin color and physical characteristics are insufficient predictors to locating a person's degree of cultural identification (Carter, 2000). The models also reveal that oppressive consequences can result from well-intentioned individuals. This is observable in many school interactions and programs specifically meant to address issues of race and inequality (Fine, 1991; Fordham, 1997; Hamovitch, 1996; Meacham, 2000b). Working with the models, preservice teachers can understand that their attitudes, actions, and reactions embody externally perpetuated definitions of self and function on a developmental continuum. Therefore, personal stances about race are not so simple as being a racist or to not being a racist. Preservice teachers can delve into detailed, situated discussions about the complexities and nuances of various developmental stages in personal as well as societal life. The models also go beyond the usual tendency to center discussion of the consequences of racism on the victims (McIntyre, 1997) to include the role of those who are complicit and benefit from oppression. Finally, in coming to understand the developmental stages of racial identity, preservice teachers using the models can understand that their active participation in abolishing racism and other oppressions is essential and illustrates the only means by which a just society can be established.

The benefits of understanding racial identity development also extend to those who educate preservice teachers. They can recognize and make some sense of White students' resistance to certain ideas as well as empower racial minority students to transcend the limited, painful compromises frequently associated with academic participation and success (Cochran-Smith, 1995, 2000; Fordham, 1997; Gordon, 2000; Meacham, 2000a; Richardson & Villenas, 2000). Understanding the social and psychological origins of these issues helps teacher educators better connect common themes from students' responses and improve the existing curriculum to satisfy students' educative processes (Cooney & Akintunde, 1999). Because of the stress on development, the models accentuate the need for integrated multicultural education in teacher training programs. The arrangement of academic years and class schedules frustrate the continuity of racial identity development within teacher training programs, especially if the discussions are limited to token classes on race (McIntyre, 1997). Furthermore, racial identity theories also apply to the lived experiences and positions of teacher educators themselves. They should be used to challenge teacher educators' own stances and inform assessment as to the program's effectiveness. Cochran-Smith (1995) describes the tension that arises from inviting students to formulate new insights by using the authority of a professor's role to impose the "correct" perspectives. She writes:

> We must acknowledge the fact that if we influence students' views about race and teaching, it is not because we open their eyes to *the truth*, but to a great extent because we use professional status and personal charisma to persuade them of the perspectives we believe will support their efforts for social justice. (p. 562)

As is the case in all teacher and student interactions, the dynamics of the relationship formed depend on the individuals involved. Viewing these associations with an understanding of racial identity development and their combined effects provide a more accurate picture of how the models function in actual educational relationships. Carter (2000) distinguishes four relationship types: parallel, regressive, crossed, and progressive. A *parallel* relationship is often stagnant because both teacher and student are at the same level of racial identity development (i.e., an affluent White teacher working with affluent White children). A *regressive* relationship reflects the student's more developed racial identity development and includes that student's experience of feeling unheard, devalued, and ignored by a teacher with less mature racial identity development. A *crossed* relationship occurs when the teacher and student are situated at opposite racial identity stages, and such a relationship can be the source of great tension and conflict. Most ideal for both teacher training programs and school classrooms is a *progressive* relationship where teachers can utilize their more developed racial identity to facilitate each student's learning and growth. An understanding of the social and psychological aspects of racial identity development in individuals as well as the dynamic results from human interaction allow teacher educators to work toward the goal of preparing preservice teachers for progressive reform.

The Challenge of Locating White Privilege in Multicultural Education

Multicultural education will not lead to social change as long as it remains the study of other people's differences from the White or middle-class norm. Nor will social change arise from multicultural education that insists all people share a common, human condition. The theorizing of whiteness—not as a deconstruction of each racial group separately, but rather, the problematic ways in which the normalized status of whiteness organizes the perception of other groups' deviance—needs to be a sincere component of multicultural education (Thompson, 1999). McIntyre (1997) insists, "The call to view multicultural education as a social movement [includes] a challenge to White educators to explore their racial locations in hopes of eradicating racism and racial oppression in educational institutions (and in ourselves)" (p. 654). Through the challenging process of locating and questioning whiteness and White

privilege, preservice teachers can understand the covert aspects of racism which may contradict their own assumption that "unless one uses a
racial epithet one cannot prove any racist behavior" (Kailin, 1999, p.
736). Also, a historical examination of the ways that racism has de-
pended and functioned on the normalization of whiteness (Takaki, 1993)
might instill in preservice teachers a sense of urgency concerning the
need to restructure school institutions (McIntyre, 1997).

The problematic absence of whiteness theorizing in multicultural
education counteracts many school activities and reforms meant to improve the lives of students of color. In my experience working with a
program for "at-risk" middle school girls in Houston, Texas, I observed
several occasions illustrating this lack of insight to White privilege and
the normalized status of whiteness. The group, Shaping Her Attitudes
and Developing Essentials for Success (SHADES), was comprised of
girls identified by subjective teacher recommendations. With few exceptions, the girls were racial minorities, came from poor families, and were
chosen for the program because of their observed behavior in classrooms
and school hallways. The adult sponsors were all female, predominantly
White, affluent, and many lived over an hour's drive away from the
school site. Recitation of the SHADES pledge, written by the group's
faculty founders, was required of the girls at the beginning of each meeting. Some of the promises in the pledge included "always [conducting]
myself as a young lady whether in public or private," and "[adjusting]
my mind and heart to effectively deal with circumstances beyond my
control." The group's vision statement read, "Our program is designed to
help at-risk young ladies develop positive self-esteem, develop proper
values, and empower themselves to make good choices." Planned activities featured a guest speaker from a local cosmetology institute to talk
about hygiene and appropriate dress, the school nurse to address absti-
nence and the consequences of sexual promiscuity, and a presentation of
formal dinner etiquette done by the counselors of the school. One first-
year, White teacher from the Midwest prepared a new seminar to be
added to the group's yearly programming. She wanted to share her personal experiences battling anorexia and bulimia. The reactions of the
girls during the session were of compassion—because the teacher explained that she had been in the hospital for treatment—but also confusion. The White teacher, as well as many sponsors in the group, were not
sensitive to the realities of the girls' lives. They did not recognize that

many of these girls were all too familiar with hunger because of poverty and that the struggle to achieve the "standard of beauty" is drastically different for females of color.

Although well-intentioned, the SHADES philosophy assumed the girls' deficiency because of their families and home life, socioeconomic status, race, and lack of measured academic success. The teachers involved neither recognized their own privilege, nor the need for the girls' ownership and voice in the program. Its connection to a *culture of poverty* thesis and promotion of meritocracy maintained the teachers' authority to "help" these girls and did not lead to change. The program sought to *culturally* assimilate students by teaching behavior patterns of the dominant group as a means to satisfy the goal of *structural* assimilation, the full inclusion of students into the organizations and institutions of the dominant group (Gordon, 1961). This result is similar to Hamovitch's (1996) observations of a school group seeking to socialize "at-risk" students founded on a conservative *ideology of hope*. Hamovitch argues that this ideology publicly ignores the institutional and societal oppression these students face, justifies blaming the students and their families for choosing not to adopt the values and behaviors of success, and reflects the teachers' fears of straying from a positive, uplifting, but un-critical understanding of American society (see also hooks, 1994). Charles Wilson, as quoted by Kailin (1999), explains:

> [B]ehind the words exists an entire reality which protects the professional educators' self-esteem at the expense of the children; protects the educators' status at the expense of the community's interests; protects whites at the expense of the Blacks; protects the middle class from competition with those who they feel aren't ready, or don't deserve the good things of this glutted society. (p. 743)

The perpetuation of ignorance surrounding the dynamics of racism are unacceptable, especially for preservice teachers who will inherit the power to affect children's lives. Through effective multicultural education in teacher training programs, preservice teachers can learn to interrogate their whiteness and understand that color-blindness not only shields their own esteem from damage but also dismisses the real experiences of their students' lives (McIntyre, 1997). Preservice teachers must become conscientious of and continue to fight the tendency to exploit or glamorize their students' situations so that they can act as saviors or

"White knights" (p. 664) and instead conceptualize their mission as allies in the work of empowerment and self-sustenance (see also Cochran-Smith, 1995; McIntyre, 1997).

A further caution exists in making analogies between oppressions as a means of understanding different experiences. As Thompson (1999) points out, "Part of the elusiveness of whiteness stems from the fact that it is never *just* whiteness" (p. 148). With a majority of preservice teachers and teacher educators' status as women, comparisons between sexism and racism in multicultural education are of qualified benefit to concerted efforts to address race. Grillo and Wildman (1997) caution that "analogies [provide] both the key to greater comprehension and the danger of false understanding" (p. 45).

One effect of analogizing sexism and racism is that it "makes the analogizer forget the difference and allows her to stay focused on her own situation without grappling with the other person's reality" (p. 44). This would suggest not only that the focus of race in conversation is lost, but that many people can speak expertly on an experience they do not sincerely understand. Grillo and Wildman consider this a move to steal the center. They argue, "Part of being a member of a privileged group is being the center and the subject of all inquiry in which people of color and other nonprivileged groups are the objects" (p. 46). Although White women's attempts to understand racism through their lived experiences in a sexist society are natural and well-meaning, opportunities must be created for people of color to be heard and share their insights.

Another consequence of making comparisons between sexism and racism is that it fosters essentialism of sex and race (Collins, 2000; Fordham, 1997; Grillo & Wildman, 1997; hooks, 1984). A working definition of these terms as separate categories assumes that they can be neatly distinguished, and such an assumption further obscures the presence of females of color whose experiences lie at the intersection of the two categories. bell hooks (1984) states that both Black men and White women have led movements for liberation that favor their own interests at the continued expense of others' oppression. She emphasizes, "Women in lower class and poor groups, particularly those who are non-White, would not have defined women's liberation as women gaining social equality with men since they are continually reminded in their everyday lives that all women do not share a common social status" (p. 18). Women of color do not possess the same experiences or privileges of other groups oppressed by racism or sexism; their survival in and between these oppressions is more complicated than essentialist notions would suggest.

Research Implications: Reinforming Teacher Training

Effective multicultural education is essential in preparing preservice teachers who will have an impact on—and responsibility for—the lives of forthcoming generations of Americans. It is not the answer to issues that only concern racial minorities, nor is it the answer to some preservice teachers' desires for a prescriptive, methodological approach to education. It must be conceived of as a participatory movement of reform dependent on the continued investigation of issues raised in this chapter and guided by informed research into additional avenues of relevance. As proposed by Grant (1999), these avenues might be loosely organized into the following categories:

- systems of reasoning
- power
- ideology
- building alliances
- methods and procedures

Specifically, one such area is the impact of preservice teachers' perceptions regarding urban or "minority" schools. Groulx's (2001) research on preservice teachers' perceptions of minority schools suggests that indeed, many preservice teachers have difficulty envisioning themselves as teachers of urban, minority children. Using a survey to assess the significance of *similarity* (shared racial/ethnic, socioeconomic, and linguistic backgrounds between teacher and students), *ideal students* (referring to behavioral and motivation issues as well as parental involvement), *diversity* (range of racial, class, language, and ability differences), and *security* (including building safety and sufficient resource allocation concerns), Groulx's measures regarding preservice teachers' preferences for particular work environments also gets at underlying assumptions and perceptions of urban schools. Quantitative analysis showed issues of school safety, security, and parental support as the most important characteristics overall. These preferences were negatively and significantly correlated with expressed interest and comfort for working in schools with predominantly African American student populations. Preservice teachers exhibiting these preferences were more interested in working at suburban and/or private schools. Groulx's qualitative data demonstrated preservice teachers' assumptions that urban schools would be unsafe, students would lack motivation and discipline, parental involvement would be low, the environment would be uncomfortable because of language and cultural differences, and the challenge of the situation would be more than they believed they were ready to handle professionally. These findings correspond with other research outcomes revealing many teachers' implicit negative connotations of urban schools serving primarily students of color versus the more positive connotations of suburban, White schools (Fordham, 1997; Ladson-Billings, 1999; Tran, Young, & DiLella, 1994).

The power of popular images in perpetuating these assumptions is great, and very few real experiences inform or challenge preservice teachers' ideas. Groulx (2001) reports:

> [M]any participants said they found it difficult to even envision a predominantly African American or Hispanic school such as those described in the survey; such schools were remote from their educational experience, and few had even visited a predominantly minority school for any length of time. They said it was *only natural* that the overwhelming majority of them would prefer suburban and/or private schools. (emphasis added, p. 83)

With unchallenged stereotypes and erroneously constructed understandings of urban minority schools, many preservice teachers see their preferences—and ultimately, their actions—as "only natural." There is a lack of connection between the work of teaching and the process of social justice (Sheets, 2000).

Even so, research suggests that this lack of connection does not exist for all preservice teachers and that some preservice teachers in fact choose teaching careers because they see the process of education linked to the work of social justice (Ball, 2000; Hood & Parker, 1994; King, 1999; Ladson-Billings, 1994). Frequently, these preservice teachers are people of color who want to return to their communities and teach, "in an effort to incorporate possibilities for self-love" (Meacham, 2000a, p. 577). As Hood and Parker (1994) urge, preservice teachers of color "can provide insights for future changes in the teacher education program to benefit all students and faculty" (p. 169).

For example, although researchers have explored the shortage of Asian Americans in the teaching force (Gordon, 2000; Rong & Preissle, 1997), more qualitative research focused on the experiences of existing Asian American preservice teachers could offer insights necessary for modifying teacher preparation courses. One popular strategy employed by the faculty in my certification program to develop self-reflection involved writing and sharing autobiographical narratives of literacy development. We would, as a class, discuss the similarities of our experiences and then consider how our future students would probably be different racially, linguistically, and economically.

Having lived all my life in a small, midwestern university town, I was used to my life story being different from my peers. I had grown up being the only Asian American in a White community; in fact, I was usually the only person of color. I learned how to be comfortable by not drawing attention to my differences and remaining silent because of this circumstance. As a second generation, American-born person of Chinese descent who spoke English as a primary language and had been socialized in very "American" ways, I recalled too many situations where the complexities of my identity had been used to interrogate the authenticity of my citizenship. The liberal stance of my teacher preparation program did help me begin to express ideas surrounding issues such as race, but for the most part, race remained in my mind something that my future diverse students would have.

In my first teaching job at a predominantly African American and Latino/a urban school, I felt confident and excited about being able to discuss race and racism openly with people for whom it really mattered. I was, however, shocked and completely unprepared to face students' questions about *my* racial identity. Learning to respond to my students' inquiries with the same openness I expected from them was an intimidating process and one that I had generally been shielded from as I "passed" quietly for White in my certification program. How might a teacher education program be informed by my individual experiences? Perhaps it would recognize its reliance upon overly simplistic dichotomies of "us" versus "them" and "Black" versus "White."

Related to this awareness would be an effort to convey the ethnic, regional, linguistic, historical, and generational diversity of groups categorized by umbrella terms such as "Asian" and "Hispanic." It might also find ways to require its students to engage in self-critique and take comparable risks into realms of purposeful discomfort. As Ropers-Huilman and Graue state, "our standards for our own and others' knowing are strongly influenced by positioned statuses we bring to that knowing. Our knowing processes exist in synergy with our cultural identities—each enhancing and disrupting the other (1999, p. 238).

Further research to build upon current case studies of model teacher education programs and activities (Ladson-Billings, 1999; Tran, Young, & DiLella, 1994; Zeichner et al., 1998), strategies of modeling and mentoring from university-based teacher preparation through actual field experience (Gay, 1995), and the valuable incorporation of critical studies on youth and popular culture into teacher preparation (Mahiri, 1998; McLaren, 2000) should also be pursued. Lastly, the evolving characteristics, attitudes, and practices of teachers in urban schools over time (Groulx, 2001) need to be investigated and used to reinform methods of teacher education.

Researchers who pursue any of these topics can also benefit, I believe, from incorporating tenets of Critical Race Theory—such as the significance of storytelling and critiques of White liberalism (Ladson-Billings, 1998; Ladson-Billings & Tate, 1995)—with those of feminist theory (e.g., Collins, 2000; Gilligan, 1982; hooks, 1984; Pipher, 1994) and cultural studies (e.g., Giroux, 1993; Giroux & McLaren, 1994) in order to get at the complexities too often hidden in discussions of multiculturalism and education. Because these theories emphasize the need for giving traditionally marginalized voices attention, preservice teachers can perhaps come to understand the embeddedness of racism and learn to expose it in its various forms. The intentional use of emotions or distanced, third-person perspectives in storytelling can help preservice teachers "analyze the myths, presuppostions, and received wisdoms that make up the common culture about race and that invariably render blacks and other minorities one-down" (Delgado, 1995, p. xiv). Once these assumptions are revealed, preservice teachers can learn to interrogate them through a critical understanding of White liberalism—to ask the questions of *who benefits?* And, *are significant changes being made?* Only then can preservice teachers posing such questions begin to envision their roles in a larger movement for social justice.

Conclusion

As demographic trends project, sometime during the course of this century, over half of all Americans will trace their ancestry back to non-White, non-European countries. Even now, the debate and process of redefining what it means to be American occurs not just in society at large, but also in teacher training programs and other educational circles committed to serving the country's population. Issues of multicultural education are central to this interaction between a search for national identity and the content of educational curriculum and practice. The context of urban schooling offers a site from which we can measure both the urgency and effectiveness of multicultural education.

References

Akintunde, O. (1999). White racism, white supremacy, white privilege, and the social construction of race. *Multicultural Education, 7*(2), 2–8.

American Association of Colleges for Teacher Education (AACTE). (1994). *Briefing books*. Washington, DC: Author.

American Association of Colleges for Teacher Education (AACTE). (1987). *Teaching teachers: Facts and figures*. Washington, DC: Author.

Anyon, J. (1997). *Ghetto schooling: A political economy of urban educational reform*. New York: Teachers College Press.

Ball, A. F. (2000). Empowering pedagogies that enhance the learning of multicultural students. *Teachers College Record, 102*(6), 1006–1034.

Banks, C. A., & Banks, J. A. (1995). Equity pedagogy: An essential component of multicultural education. *Theory Into Practice, 34*(3), 152–158.

Banks, C. A., & Banks, J. A. (1997). Reforming schools in a democratic pluralistic society. *Educational Policy, 11*(2), 183–193.

Cameron, S., & Wycoff, S. (1998). The destructive nature of the term race: Growing beyond a false paradigm. *Journal of Counseling and Development, 76*(3), 277–285.

Carter, R. (2000). Reimagining race in education: A new paradigm from psychology. *Teachers College Record, 102*(5), 864–897.

Cochran-Smith, M. (1995). Uncertain allies: Understanding the boundaries of race and teaching. *Harvard Educational Review, 65*(4), 541–570.

Cochran-Smith, M. (2000). Blind vision: Unlearning racism in teacher education. *Harvard Educational Review, 70*(2), 157–190.

Collins, P. H. (2000). What's going on? Black feminist thought and the politics of post-modernism. In E. A. St. Pierre and W. S. Pillow (Eds.), *Working the ruins: Feminist poststructural theory and methods in education* (pp. 41–73). New York: Routledge.

Cooney, M. H., & Akintunde, O. (1999). Confronting white privilege and the "color blind" paradigm in a teacher education program. *Multicultural Education, 7*(2), 9–14.

Crenshaw, K. W. (1988). Race reform and retrenchment: Transformation and legitimation in antidiscrimination law. *Harvard Law Review, 101*, 1331–1387.

Delgado, R. (Ed.). (1995). *Critical race theory: The cutting edge.* Philadelphia: Temple University Press.

Fine, M. (1991). *Framing dropouts: Notes on the politics of an urban public high school.* Albany: State University of New York Press.

Fordham, S. (1997). "Those loud black girls": (Black) women, silence, and gender "passing" in the academy. In M. Seller and L. Weis (Eds.), *Beyond black and white: New faces and voices in U.S. schools* (pp. 81–111). Albany: State University of New York Press.

Gay, G. (1995). Modeling and mentoring in urban teacher preparation. *Education and Urban Society, 28*(1), 103–118.

Gay, G. (1997). Multicultural infusion in teacher education: Foundations and applications. *Peabody Journal of Education, 72*(1), 150–177.

Gilligan, C. (1982). *In a different voice: Psychological theory and women's development.* Cambridge, MA: Harvard University Press.

Ginzberg, E. (1993). The changing urban scene: 1900–1960 and beyond. In H. G. Cisneros (Ed.), *Interwoven destinies: Cities and the nation* (pp. 33–47). New York: W. W. Norton.

Giroux, H. A. (1993). *Border crossings: Cultural workers and the politics of education.* New York: Routledge.

Giroux, H. A. (1994). Doing cultural studies: Youth and the challenge of pedagogy. *Harvard Educational Review, 64*(3), 278–308.

Giroux, H. A., & McLaren, P. (Eds.). (1994). *Between borders: Pedagogy and the politics of cultural studies.* New York: Routledge.

Goodwin, A. L. (1997). Historical and contemporary perspectives on multicultural teacher education. In J. King, E. Hollins, and W. Hayman (Eds.), *Preparing teachers for cultural diversity* (pp. 5–22). New York: Teachers College Press.

Gordon, J. A. (2000). Asian American resistance to selecting teaching as a career: The power of community and tradition. *Teachers College Record, 102*(1), 173–196.

Gordon, M. M. (1961). Assimilation in America: Theory and reality. *Daedalus, 90,* 263–285.

Grant, C. A. (1999). Introduction: The idea, the invitation, and chapter themes. In C. A. Grant (Ed.), *Multicultural research: A reflective engagement with race, class, gender, and sexual orientation* (pp. 1–8). London: Falmer Press.

Grant, C. A., & Zozakiewicz, C. A. (1995). Student teachers, cooperating teachers, and supervisors: Interrupting the multicultural silences of student teaching. In J. M. Larkin & C. E. Sleeter (Eds.), *Developing multicultural teacher education curricula* (pp. 259–278). Albany: State University of New York Press.

Grillo, T., & Wildman, S. (1997). Obscuring the importance of race: The implication of making comparisons between racism and sexism (or other isms). In A. K. Wing (Ed.), *Critical race feminism* (pp. 44–50). New York: New York University Press.

Groulx, J. (2001). Changing preservice teacher perceptions of minority schools. *Urban Education, 36*(1), 60–92.

Hamovitch, B. (1996). Socialization without voice: An ideology of hope for at-risk students. *Teachers College Record, 98*(2), 286–306.

Hood, S., & Parker, L. (1994). Minority students informing the faculty: Implications for racial diversity and the future of teacher education. *Journal of Teacher Education, 45*(3), 164–171.

hooks, b. (1984). *Feminist theory from margin to center.* Boston, MA: South End Press.

hooks, b. (1994). *Teaching to transgress: Education as the practice of freedom.* New York: Routledge.

Kailin, J. (1999). How white teachers perceive the problem of racism in their schools: A case study in "liberal" lakeview. *Teachers College Record, 100*(4), 724–750.

Kasarda, J. D. (1993). Cities as places people live and work: Urban change and neighborhood distress. In H. G. Cisneros (Ed.), *Interwoven destinies: Cities and the nation* (pp. 81–124). New York: W. W. Norton.

King, J. E. (1999). In search of a method for liberating education and research: The half (that) has not been told. In C. A. Grant (Ed.), *Multicultural research: A reflective engagement with race, class, gender, and sexual orientation* (pp. 101–119). London: Falmer Press.

Kozol, J. (1991). *Savage inequalities: Children in America's schools.* New York: Harper Perennial.

Ladson-Billings, G. (1994). *Dreamkeepers.* San Francisco, CA: Jossey-Bass Inc.

Ladson-Billings, G. (1998). Just what is critical race theory and what's it doing in a *nice* field like education? *International Journal of Qualitative Studies in Education, 11*(1), 7–24.

Ladson-Billings, G. (1999). Preparing teachers for diverse student populations: A critical race theory perspective. *Review of Research in Education, 24* , 211–247.

Ladson-Billings, G., & Tate, W. F. (1995). Toward a critical race theory of education. *Teachers College Record, 97*(1), 47–68.

Lawrence, S. M., & Tatum, B. D. (1997). Teachers in transition: The impact of antiracist professional development on classroom practice. *Teachers College Record, 99*(1), 162–178.

Mahiri, J. (1998). *Shooting for excellence: African American and youth culture in new century schools.* New York: National Council for Teachers of English and Teachers College Press.

McIntyre, A. (1997). Constructing an image of a white teacher. *Teachers College Record, 98*(4), 653–681.

McLaren, P. (1995). White terror and oppositional agency. In P. McLaren & S. Sleeter (Eds.), *Multicultural education, critical pedagogy, and the politics of difference* (pp. 33–70). Albany: State University of New York Press.

McLaren, P. (2000). Gangsta pedagogy and ghettocentricity: The hip-hop nation as coun-
terpublic sphere. In K. A. McClafferty, C. A. Torres, & T. R. Mitchell (Eds.), *Challenges of urban education: Sociological perspectives for the next century* (pp. 227–
269). Albany: State University of New York Press.

Meacham, J. (2000a). Black self-love, language, and the teacher education dilemma: The
cultural denial and cultural limbo of African American preservice teachers. *Urban
Education, 34*(5), 571–596.

Meacham, J. (2000b, September 18). The new face of race. *Newsweek*, pp. 38–60.

Nevarez, A., Sanford, J. S., & Parker, L. (1997). Do the right thing: Transformative multicultural education in teacher preparation. *Journal for a Just and Caring Education, 3*(2), 160–179.

Noguera, P. (1996). Confronting the urban in urban school reform. *The Urban Review,
28*(1), 1–19.

O'Connor, C. (1997). Dispositions toward (collective) struggle and educational resilience
in the inner city: A case analysis of six African-American high school students.
American Educational Research Journal, 34(4), 593–629.

Orfield, G. (1993). *The growth of segregation in American schools: Changing patterns
of segregation and poverty since 1968.* A report of the Harvard project on school
desegregation to the National School Boards Association. Washington, DC: National School Boards Association.

Pipher, M. (1994). *Reviving Ophelia: Saving the selves of adolescent girls.* New York:
Ballantine Books.

Richardson, T., & Villenas, S. (2000). "Other" encounters: Dances with whiteness in
multicultural education. *Educational Theory, 50*(2), 255–273.

Rong, X. L., & Preissle, J. (1997). The decline in Asian American teachers. *American
Educational Research Journal, 34*(2), 267–293.

Ropers-Huilman, B., & Graue, B. (1999). Stumbling toward knowledge: Enacting and
embodying qualitative research. In C. A. Grant (Ed.), *Multicultural research: A reflective engagement with race, class, gender, and sexual orientation* (pp. 228–239).
London: Falmer Press.

Rose, M. (1989). *Lives on the boundary.* New York: Penguin Group.

Rose, M. (1995). *Possible lives.* New York: Penguin.

Sheets, R. H. (2000). Advancing the field or taking center stage: The white movement in multicultural education. *Educational Researcher, 29*(9), 15–21.

Sleeter, C. E. (1995a). Teaching whites about racism. In R. J. Martin (Ed.), *Practicing what we teach: Confronting diversity in teacher education* (pp. 117–130). Albany: State University of New York Press.

Sleeter, C. E. (1995b). White preservice students and multicultural education course-work. In J. M. Larkin & C. E. Sleeter (Eds.), *Developing multicultural teacher education curricula* (pp. 17–29). Albany: State University of New York Press.

Takaki, R. (1993). *A different mirror: A history of multicultural America.* Boston: Back Bay Books.

Tatum, B. D. (1992). Talking about race, learning about racism: The application of racial identity development theory in the classroom. *Harvard Educational Review, 62*(1), 1–24.

Thompson, A. (1999). Colortalk: Whiteness and "Off White." *Educational Studies, 30*(2), 141–160.

Tran, M. T., Young, R. L., & DiLella, J. D. (1994). Multicultural education courses and the student teacher: Eliminating stereotypical attitudes in our ethnically diverse classroom. *Journal of Teacher Education, 45*(3), 183–189.

U.S. Census Bureau. (2000). *Poverty: 1999 highlights.* [Available on-line: http://www.census.gov/hhes/poverty/poverty99/pov99hi.html]

Wilson, W. J. (1996). *When work disappears: The world of the new urban poor.* New York: Alfred A. Knopf, Inc.

Young, M. D., & Laible, J. (2000). White racism, antiracism, and school leadership preparation. *Journal of School Leadership, 10,* 374–415.

Zeichner, K. M., Grant, C., Gay, G., Gilette, M., Valli, L., & Villegas, A. M. (1998). A research informed vision of good practice in multicultural teacher education: Design principles. *Theory Into Practice, 37*(2), 163–171.

Zinn, M. B., & Eitzen, D. S. (1999). *Diversity in families.* New York: Addison-Wesley Educational Publishers, Inc.

6

On Whose Terms?
The (In)visibility of the
Latina/o Community at
the University of Illinois at
Urbana-Champaign

Arisve Esquivel

I am American/I was born here/and I've lived my whole life here/But your "we" doesn't speak for me./I refuse to be a part of/your blind patri-otic/acceptance of/a history of oppression.
—Eduardo Alexander Rabel, 1997

The struggle to forge a space for people of color in U.S. society can be traced to the colonial era. While history is always telling, the history of people of color remains to be fully told. In fact, the Latino student in the poem above speaks of the marginality, silencing, and invisibility he experiences within U.S. society on a daily basis—a history that is often left out of traditional historical accounts. Due to the imbedded racism within U.S. society, the histories that are documented usually represent people of color in a negative light and/or marginalize, depoliticize, and reify a sanitized and politically neutral historical account. Such marginalization impacts the ability to address contemporary problems faced by people of color in a more holistic and contextualized fashion. Because the urgency and history of such problems are not made apparent in these renderings, their histories—and by extension, the histories of people of color—often seem to lack legitimacy.

An example of such omission can be seen in the virtual absence of historical literature, personal testimonies, and other documentation that unveil the struggles and issues faced by students of color in predominantly White institutions of higher education. This absence is problematic because it not only minimizes the hostile racial climate that students of color historically have faced in traditionally White institutions but also renders invisible the university's consistent failure to take positive steps to address these particular concerns.

To be sure, issues regarding access, retention, curriculum, and campus climate all contribute to minority students' relative success at a university setting. A university's unwillingness, or inability, to examine its own exclusionary practices not only demonstrates its indifference toward students of color, but also suggests a general reluctance to address minority students' needs as an overall university goal. In many cases, such a refusal occurs despite repeated opposition and protest by students and faculty of color. Indeed, it is often the case that such opposition usually falls on deaf ears.

It is thus critically important to contextualize and historicize minority students' struggles in traditionally White institutions in order to understand that the issues they raise are not new. With this in mind, this discussion examines the history of Latina/o students at a predominantly White institution of higher education as well as the university's dismal attempt to address their needs in a holistic and sincere fashion.

Background and Significance of Study

In the late spring of 1968, the University of Illinois at Urbana-Champaign (UIUC) implemented an initiative to bring at least 500 minority freshmen to campus for the fall semester. Of the approximately 580 minority freshmen admitted in the fall of 1968, the majority were African Americans with only a handful of Latinas/os. Since minority students were greatly outnumbered by a predominantly White majority, Latina/o students sought to create a space for themselves at the university. They believed that a cultural center would provide a physical space to support and expand their community within the university. Although they were small in number, Latina/o students actively fought for a cultural center. They mobilized by writing letters, meeting with administrators, and holding protests on campus to draw attention to their demands. They believed their success as students was directly tied to the preservation of their cultures, especially because the university was a foreign environment to many of them. Latina/o students also demanded change within the university's structure, including a re-examination of curricular offerings and an improvement in the overall campus climate. UIUC administrators proved, at times, to be allies—at other times they were obstacles—in the students' struggle to forge a community within the university setting.

This study attempts to document this struggle by outlining the invisibility and organizational silencing of Latina/o students' voices, needs, and concerns by UIUC officials. University administrators' actions and inactions are analyzed to highlight:

- how historical narratives were documented
- how the "color-blind" perspective of administrators was constructed, and
- the experiences of Latinas/os at a predominantly White institution.

The struggle of Latina/o students is examined in light of how students fought for liberation of their minds and acceptance of their cultures on the university campus. In the end, this chapter examines the impact of the Latina/o students' struggle, the larger implications for the educational attainment of Latinas/os at the national level, and Latinas/os full incorporation within institutions of higher education.

As such, this study contributes to the literature on higher education and its focus on Latinas/os. It historicizes the development and implementation of Latina/o Studies and the cultural center at UIUC which have not been previously documented. Lastly, by employing a theoretical framework that combines Critical Race Theory (CRT) and Latina/o Critical Race Theory (LatCrit), this study also contributes to the expansion of both frameworks, and their utility for conducting historical research on the experiences of racial minorities in traditional White institutions of higher education.

Theoretical Framework

CRT situates race at the center of historical analysis and provides a space in which to address the problems people of color experience within a White power structure (Crenshaw et al., 1995; Solorzano, 1998). It exposes society and its systems as normalizing Whiteness and privileging

Whites. For instance, institutions of higher education appear, on the surface, to be neutral and colorblind. However, their existing structure and
daily practices—from admission policies to curricular offerings and the
overall lack of organizational and administrative support—marginalizes
students of color. CRT exposes this by documenting and valuing people
of color's narratives and counterstories (Delgado, 1989; Tate, 1997).

LatCrit specifically places Latinas/os at the center of analysis and
speaks to the omission of Latinas/os within CRT (LatCrit III Symposium, 1999). CRT's Black/White paradigm does not expose spaces for
Latinas/os to be heard, thus a LatCrit lens widens the scope of CRT
without challenging its fundamental tenets (Solorzano, 1997, 1998; Valdes, 1996). Since LatCrit emerged from CRT, I find it useful to employ
both theoretical lenses within this discussion.

In this instance, I utilize Latina/o students' counterstories to deconstruct the "official" stories circulated by university personnel about particular campus events. By reconstructing historical narratives and
employing a CRT/LatCrit framework, one begins to see who belongs,
who is valued, and the falsity of inclusion at the UIUC campus.

Moreover, CRT/LatCrit opens up the discussion of who is a "citizen"
at UIUC and consequently, who wields the power to be heard and the
issues that will be addressed. In this regard, the discourse of both
groups—Latina/o students and university administrators—is examined
using a dual methodological approach.

Methodology

The data used for this analysis are contained within the University of
Illinois Library Archives and include letters, internal memos, flyers,
notes, and other miscellaneous print items. When possible, I have noted
the author(s) of each document and the exact location as outlined by the
archives' system of classification.[1]

When I first began my research, I was informed by a library archivist
that no holdings regarding Latina/o students existed. Upon further questioning, the archivist believed the only way to access any information
would be to look at La Casa Cultural Latina's archival records (La Casa
Cultural Latina is the Latina/o cultural center on campus). This is reflective of the Black and White binary that Foley (1997) discusses: "[T]he

rigid boundaries of Black-White race relations fail to account for groups, like Mexicans, located somewhere in the ethnoracial borderlands between whiteness and blackness" (p. xiv). By racializing archival categories it becomes increasingly difficult for scholars to conduct historical research of this nature because the histories of certain groups have been relegated to a marginal status within the institutional setting. Furthermore, these actions represent vehicles by people of color and their histories systematically silenced and marginalized in colleges and universities of higher learning (see also Donato & Lazerson, 2000).

In this discussion, I utilize archival records to reconstruct the experiences and stories of Latinas/os on the UIUC campus. I will attempt to demonstrate how these stories directly contradict the "official" stories of the UIUC administration—a story that suggests Latinas/os were always welcomed and supported on campus. This juxtaposition between "official" accounts and "counternarratives" highlights the tensions between stories (Delgado, 1989) and the students' struggle to survive in a racially inhospitable climate.

Findings

Latinas/os, predominantly Mexicanas/os, have been residing in the state of Illinois in substantial numbers since 1916. In 1968, however, the Special Educational Opportunity Program admitted over 500 new minority students, the majority of whom were African American. Prior to this initiative, the admission rates of Latinas/os at UIUC were so low as to be essentially nonexistent.

Nevertheless, the accessed data indicate that Hispanic[2] undergraduate and graduate students had a significant increase in numbers beginning in 1967. In this year, records indicate there were 25 undergraduate Hispanics students and 20 Hispanic graduate students—while the combined student body was 30,407. By the time La Casa Cultural Latina was established in 1974, there were 149 Latina/o undergraduates and 68 Latina/o graduate students within a total student body of 35,045.

As Table 1 suggests, these numbers have improved, but they have not drastically shifted since 1974. In fact, by 1998, Hispanic undergraduates numbered 1,453 while Hispanic graduate students totaled 261 (Admissions and Records Office, 1998).[3] The fact that university minority student totals have remained somewhat constant throughout this period is due in significant part to efforts by undergraduate and graduate students themselves to recruit and enlist prospective students of color.

Table 1: Latina/o Undergraduate and Graduate Student Enrollment

Year	Hispanic Under-graduate Students	Hispanic Graduate Students	Combined Hispanic: Under-graduate and Gradu-ate Students	Combined Minority Under-graduate and Gradu-ate Students	UIUC Total Com-bined Student Population
1967	25	20	45	675	30,407
1974	149	68	217	1,801	35,045
1998	1,453	261	1,714	8,178	36,330

Nevertheless, the small Latina/o student population is a powerful reminder of the changes that need to be made in the university system and provides a context for understanding why Latina/o students began to push for changes in the university structure.

Negotiations of Space and Priorities:
Initial Proposals for La Casa Cultural Latina

Given the campus climate of the late 1960s (less than 2% of UIUC students were students of color) and the need to support one another, Latina/o students believed that a cultural center could provide a base for support. La Colectiva Latina, formerly known as the Urban Hispanic Organization, was the main student organization that pushed for the development of La Casa. By 1975, La Colectiva Latina promoted a tripartite mission:

- To promote activities which emphasize the life-style and the cultural heritage of the typical Latino student, which includes Chicano's, Puerto Rican's, Cuban's, Central American's, [sic] etc., all whose homes are the United States;

- To develop programs which can satisfy the intellectual, cultural, social, and recreational needs of the Latino student;

- To serve as a lobbying group which is designed to further the
  causes of Latino students; to represent the Latino students to
  the administration and officials of the University in matters of
  immediate and future concern of the Latino students. (La
  Colectiva Latina Proposal, March 6, 1974)

While Latina/o students were the catalysts for the cultural center, other
units within the university publicly supported their initiative; including
the office of Campus Programs and Services, and the Program of Bilin-
gual/Bicultural Education. Consequently, each independently submitted
formal proposals for the establishment of La Casa to the office of Vice-
Chancellor for Campus Affairs at UIUC.

La Colectiva Latina's Proposal

In a letter addressed to the Vice-Chancellor for Campus Affairs, La
Colectiva Latina submitted a proposal indicating that they would meet
with him at a later date to discuss their recommendations (La Colectiva
to Vice-Chancellor for Campus Affairs, April 23, 1974). Their request
briefly outlined four main components of the proposed cultural center:

- Background
- Objective
- Purpose of the Center
- Overview

In the "Background" section, students explained how they actively
increased their own admission rates at UIUC and how the university
needed to provide adequate support services and programs for retention.
Furthermore, they explained, "Our emphasis is no longer on compensa-
tory measures, but on establishing creative and concrete programs aimed
at Latinos. The programs will be based on the idea of self-determination
for the Latino" (La Colectiva to Vice-Chancellor for Campus Affairs,
April 23, 1974).

The "Objective" section described the goals of the Latino Cultural House. The students envisioned a cultural house as providing "a viable role in the university life [both] academic, and social" (La Colectiva to Vice-Chancellor for Campus Affairs, April 23, 1974). Thus, through the cultural house, Latina/o students could become active, contributing members on the UIUC campus. In the students' eyes, the purpose of the cultural house would not only benefit Latina/o students but the entire UIUC community. Hence, as students pondered ways in which a cultural center would serve their needs, they also considered the role it could play in expanding the cultural, intellectual, and social horizons of the larger campus. As they explain in the "Overview" section:

> The overall effect of the Cultural House, through its activities and programs, will contribute to the acknowledgement of our pluralistic society. The mainstream of educational thought is slowly progressing from one of domination by monolingual, monocultural ideas to one where value is placed on the multilingual, multicultural makeup of our society. Through [sic] the establishment of a Latino Cultural House is no giant step, nevertheless, it is a step in the right direction. (La Colectiva to Vice-Chancellor for Campus Affairs, April 23, 1974)

As a whole, Latina/o students envisioned a cultural center that foreshadowed a contemporary emphasis on diversity and inclusivity. Although students were able to demonstrate the need for a cultural center, the complexity of running it would prove to be a further obstacle.

Director of Bilingual/Bicultural Program's Proposal

In a letter addressed to the Dean of Campus Programs and Services, the Director of the Program of Bilingual/Bicultural Education also expressed his support for the cultural center. He explained that, "This house will provide the students with an invaluable opportunity to engage in joint cultural programs, academic activities, and many other constructive endeavors" (Director of Bilingual/Bicultural Education Program to Dean of the Office of Campus Programs and Services, April 3, 1974). The Director of the Bilingual/Bicultural Education Program believed the cultural house could serve as the basis for its activities. Furthermore, it could house the resources and materials collection generated by the Bilingual/Bicultural Education Program so that more people could have access to the information. Moreover, he saw three main objectives for the Latino Cultural House:

1. To stimulate and enhance the intellectual growth of Latino students by providing them with the proper orientation; proper atmosphere and facilities to meet, share each other's knowledge, plans and concerns; place of relaxation.

2. To stimulate the collection, development and creation of educational materials on Latino cultures, such as, folklore, literature, dancing, music, and art.

3. To integrate educational concerns with the need for a closer relationship, in the spirit of friendship, of all Latinos from different countries and from our own. (Director of Bilingual/Bicultural Education Program, n.d.)

The Director of the Bilingual/Bicultural Education Program also posed and answered several questions:

1. *Why is it important to have a house, which would have the functions, mentioned above? Can all this be done elsewhere?* It is hard enough to be a foreigner or a minority student or a minority student in an institution as large and complicated as ours. Latino students need a place they can call "home," where their language is spoken, their art is displayed, their activities and concerns are important, where friends gather informally and reinforce each other's commitment to education. Guidance and help is not sought for in the elegant room of an instructor's office. Help, advice and encouragement are more readily asked for and given in a culturally familiar environment.

2. *Would not this house become a center for political "radicals"?* In my opinion, a cultural house for Latino students would be the least likely place to organize a revolution. Latino students are serious and hardworking young people, thoroughly committed to their academic work. They are aware of the social problems of minorities in this country and that is the reason why they are preparing themselves at the U of I. If they have some suggestions to make to the administration, they will make them following the dictates of reason and in the proper manner.

3. *How would this house be managed and taken care of?* I would suggest that the BBP be in charge of the management and become a clearinghouse for the activities related to the Latino Cultural House. The presence of the BBP would give the house an atmosphere of serious academic concern, intellectual growth, of constructive and organized effort at improving educa-

tion for the Latinos in this state and in the entire country. (Director of Bi-
lingual/Bicultural Education Program, n.d.)

In items two and three this person conceptualizes a center constructed
around the interests and the needs of the institution as opposed to needs
and interests defined by students. If this would truly be a place that students could call "home," he left unanswered the role they would play in
making their own "home." Another troubling aspect with this letter is
how "radical" students are constructed. He draws a distinction between
"serious" students caring about education (who, presumably, are not
radical) versus "radical" students who cannot be committed students.
This interpretation, however, does not allow a "radical" student to have
the attributes and characteristics of a committed student. In this regard,
his response reinforced the policy values of other university officials.

In short, despite his intentions, the Director of the Bilin-
gual/Bicultural Education Program reifies the good student/bad student
dichotomy. As such, Latinas/os' citizenship within the university structure is immediately called into question. This position serves only to reinforce the university's implicit desire to privilege students who did not
question the status quo. In essence, campus officials sought diversity, but
on their own terms (Taylor et al., 1997).

The Office of the Vice-Chancellor for Campus Affairs
and the Office of Campus Programs and Services

During this period, administrators at both University of Illinois campuses (Urbana-Champaign and Chicago Circle) struggled to address
and/or understand their Latina/o constituencies. Less than two weeks
after a hearing on the Chicago campus regarding the lack of support
given to the Latina/o community, UIUC's Vice-Chancellor for Campus
Affairs, in a letter addressed to UIUC's Office of the Chancellor, stressed
the importance of avoiding the difficulties of the Chicago Circle Campus: "Don't let that sort of thing happen here" (Vice-Chancellor for
Campus Affairs to Chancellor, April 29, 1974). The Vice-Chancellor for
Campus Affairs goes on to say:

So far, with the help of ... [UIUC Administrators] and the nebulous but moder-
ate leadership of our Latino students, we have kept turmoil and controversy out

of the campus, at least insofar as our Latino relations are concerned. Now we
are at a point where we can make real steps forward, not just to avert difficulty,
but to add some penicillin, not a band-aid. (Vice-Chancellor for Campus Affairs to Chancellor, April 29, 1974)

The Vice-Chancellor for Campus Affairs then discusses a possible site
for the cultural center and where funding would come from. He believed
that the establishment of such a center was "the answer to some of the
critics that we are not far-sighted and concerned about the welfare and
needs of minority students" (Vice-Chancellor for Campus Affairs to
Chancellor, April 29, 1974). He ends the letter by saying, "As I said earlier, this is a very real possibility for us to make some real progress with
the very small but ever growing Latino community here on campus"
(Vice-Chancellor for Campus Affairs to Chancellor, April 29, 1974).

While university administrators publicly maintained the appearance
of supporting Latina/o students and La Casa, there was an entirely different "internal" conversation that was taking place among the UIUC administration. In a "confidential" memo addressed to the Vice-Chancellor
for Campus Affairs, the Dean of the Office of Campus Programs and
Services discussed the funding and overseeing of the Latino Center. In
this letter he expressed his preference to keep his position confidential
since "this could be a politically explosive proposition" (Dean of the Office of Campus Programs and Services to Vice-Chancellor for Campus
Affairs, April 23, 1974). This letter details the Dean's belief that the Latino Cultural Center be placed under the aegis of the Campus Programs
and Services Office because the Afro-American Cultural Center was already housed there. According to the Dean of the Office of Campus Programs and Services, the funding for La Casa ($13,500 at the time) should
come from the Student Relations Program. The "politically explosive
proposition," however, was due to the fact that funding was readily
available from a different source:

> A final comment must be made which is a factor we must face. We do have
> some $100,000 plus for intellectual and cultural programs. Yet we have a zero
> amount for our Latino students. I cannot see how we can justify this for too
> long a period of time. (Dean of the Office of Campus Programs and Services to
> Vice-Chancellor for Campus Affairs, April 23, 1974)

In other words, while the Dean of the Office of Campus Programs and
Services was aware of the need to provide for Latina/o students, he knew

that none of the intellectual and cultural program funds were utilized for the Latina/o population.

Even more problematic was another statement made by the Dean of the Office of Campus Programs and Services in that same letter: "It is an erroneous assumption to believe that the Latino student, whether here on this campus or any other, will integrate truly with the normal flow of campus activities" (Dean of the Office of Campus Programs and Services to Vice-Chancellor for Campus Affairs, April 23, 1974). This particular dean, who publicly supported Latina/o students, now reveals a position that questions Latinas/os' citizenship by implying an unwillingness or inability on their part to integrate into the normal flow of campus activities. Even though he publicly claims to be a strong supporter of La Casa, he candidly doubts that Latina/o students would ever integrate fully into the university's community. Furthermore, his use of the term normal indicates that he considers Latinas/os to be unlike mainstream/White university students. Delivering a further blow, he privately confesses a personal belief that Latina/o students are linguistically and expressively lacking: "There are significant numbers of Latino students who are deficient in speaking English and Spanish. Thus, a center with the proper facilities can prove most beneficial for our Latino students" (Dean of the Office of Campus Programs and Services to Vice-Chancellor for Campus Affairs, April 23, 1974). Rather than negotiating with Latinas/os to shape the mission and programs of the proposed cultural center, he was inclined to improve programs based on his perception of Latina/o cultural traits.

A general administrative resistance accompanied these sentiments to the establishment of a cultural center, as indicated in the follow-up letter from the Vice-Chancellor for Campus Affairs to the Dean of the Office of Campus Programs and Services:

> As I told you the other day, the Chancellor is not very enthusiastic about us accepting another major responsibility for an ethnic centered program. However, based upon the problems of the times and our very sincere efforts to bring about some resolution regarding the Latino feeling lost on campus, I am sure that he will move on it as rapidly as possible. (Vice-Chancellor for Campus Affairs to Dean of the Office of Campus Programs and Services, May 3, 1974)

The university's unwillingness to develop the cultural center suggests a general lack of organizational support for Latina/o issues and concerns.

Consequently, problems encountered by Latina/o students take on a different light as students continue to encounter "hidden" obstacles and/or resistance.

While the "public" discourse maintained by the university suggests a strong support for the development of a cultural center, the "private" discourse reveals the institutionalized perception of Latinas/os as deficient and problematic. Even though the university ultimately approved the establishment of La Casa, it did not provide the adequate funds to support it and ensure its success.

By deploying graduate students as directors of La Casa and hiring undergraduates to serve as office workers, the university placed an insurmountable burden on students to keep La Casa afloat. Despite the fact that the university benefited from the events, programs, and recruitment efforts generated by La Colectiva Latina, students were never given any public credit for their efforts.

The Legacy of Struggle Continues

The struggle to sustain and expand a space within UIUC continued long after the development of La Casa. Students continued to encounter obstacles at different levels. However, they were determined to maintain, improve, and expand opportunities for Latina/o students such as enrollment growth, academic presence, and program offerings which would benefit the campus as a whole. While it is impossible to cover all the events that transpired since La Casa was founded, there are some key events that need to be highlighted. By examining these points of struggle, I will attempt to demonstrate that contemporary problems faced by Latina/o students are historically grounded. While there have been some advancements and accomplishments, the university has systematically failed to fully accommodate the needs of students from different backgrounds.

This struggle for respect and acceptance is exemplified in the two student sit-ins of 1992: April 29 at the UIUC Office of Minority Student Affairs and Cinco de Mayo (May 5) at the UIUC Henry Administration Building. The issues that prompted the protests—Latina/o recruitment and retention, increased representation of Latinos in faculty and administrative ranks, the elimination of Chief Illiniwek as the university mascot,

and the development of a Latina/o Studies Program—can be traced back
to the same issues that Latino students faced in the late sixties and seven-
ties.[4] Indeed, not much had changed to provide a welcoming environment and climate for Latina/o students. Despite the fact that negotiations
between the students and the administration came to a halt during the
subsequent academic year, students resumed negotiations in 1994. This
time, the focus of student concerns was on the development and implementation of a Latina/Latino Studies Program.

This struggle for legitimacy, space, and validation is the same struggle that has plagued Latina/o students at UIUC for decades. By understanding La Casa's origins and its legacy, we can see the evolution of the
Latina/Latino Studies Program. Only when we contextualize this struggle
are we able to understand the parallels and connections that students
have historically faced at the UIUC campus.

Contemporary Struggles

In the spring of 2001, Latina/o students continued to push the university to address their needs. This time, the focus of contention was the
UIUC history department. During a ten-year span, from 1990 to 2000,
the history department only hired one Latino scholar. When the Latino
professor left the campus, students felt that his resignation was greatly
influenced by a general lack of departmental support. When the history
department began interviewing possible candidates to fill the position,
students urged the history department to do a "cluster hire" of two
equally strong Latina/o candidates. To show their support, students wrote
a letter to the department and attached a petition with 117 UIUC student
signatures.

What transpired, however, was another disappointing moment in the
long history of mistreatment, miscommunication, and mistrust between
Latina/o students and UIUC administrators. Not only did the history department challenge some of the student signatures as being false, but also
their hiring selection was the single candidate the students had *not* chosen.[5] Despite the fact that the history department and other university
officials have cooperated with students to discuss their concerns about
these faculty hires, they continue to insist that no problems exist within
the history department. This attitude clearly demonstrates how little the

administration and faculty are informed about the needs of the Latina/o community on campus.

At this point in time it remains to be seen if a meeting with the provost will result in concrete changes or the usual symbolic university gesture. While university officials maintain they are concerned with issues affecting the Latina/o community, they continue the traditional "official" double-speak. The university uses meetings with high-ranking officials—such as the provost—as "proof" that they are addressing the concerns of Latinas/os. However, action is missing within the policies they enact. There must come a time when universities have to deal with the rhetoric they espouse and directly deal with the issues at hand (Larson, 1997). It will remain to be seen if the university will continue with its symbolic rhetoric and action or take concrete steps to address the legitimate issues and concerns raised by Latina/o students.

Discussion

This study has demonstrated how UIUC administrators in the late sixties and UIUC administrators today have implemented inclusion on their own terms. It suggests that while administrators seem to espouse inclusion, their actions clearly indicate an entirely different objective. This contradiction demonstrates the importance of documenting historical research on race in higher education and the importance of narratives and counternarratives to reveal this contradiction.

This analysis has traced the early efforts by Latina/o students to improve conditions on the UIUC campus. Analysis of the data suggests that Latina/o students forged and located a community within La Casa. Over time, the Latina/o community on campus has increased, but the basic needs of recruitment, retention, respect, inclusion, and acceptance remain the same. The struggles of Latina/o students from the late sixties to 2001 are inextricably linked. Therefore, it is critically important to view these struggles as continuous rather than as isolated/explosive incidents.

By employing CRT/LatCrit to analyze the events that historically transpired at UIUC, it opens up a space to bring issues of race to the center of this discourse. Through the use of counterstories, one begins to see how Latina/o students have historically been marginalized, and how this marginalization continues to the present day. CRT/LatCrit highlights the racism that is embedded within the UIUC campus and defines what Latina/o students are fighting against. In this regard, CRT/LatCrit provides an analytical basis from which Latina/o students can continue to demonstrate their needs. Lastly, CRT/LatCrit demonstrates the connection between the past and the present as well as holding the university accountable for past and present wrongdoings.

Latina/o students have historically demonstrated that it is not enough to get admitted to the university; they understood that in order to succeed within the institution they had to set up a support system. The support system they fashioned was the development and implementation of La Casa. Students believed they had a right to be at UIUC and that they had a right to have their needs/concerns addressed.

The negotiations that occurred placed a heavy burden on the students because they had the dual responsibility of being both students and activists. However, many of these students had no other choice. Students were willing to sacrifice their time and effort to improve campus conditions, but they were not willing to assimilate into a structure that that did not respect their cultures, their histories, and their individuality/subjectivity. Latina/o students firmly believed that change had to occur, not only for their benefit but also for the benefit of future generations to come.

Conclusion

Taken holistically, we can see how the events that led to the development of the La Casa left a lasting impact on future generations of Latina/o students. This link can be seen in the actual painting of the mural in 1975 to the struggle to preserve it in the mid-nineties. Latina/o students continued to push the UIUC administration to address their needs/concerns, which ultimately resulted in the two sit-ins in 1992. As a result, the sit-ins provided the catalyst for the development and implementation of the Latina/Latino Studies Program. Moreover, the continued push by students to improve the hiring and retention of Latina/o faculty and Latina/o scholars was demonstrated in the discussions with the history department in the spring of 2001.

UIUC Latina/o students have continually proven that they will not accept inclusion as it stands and will continue to demand inclusion on their terms. If this history of struggle and contestation is not recognized, then, as the opening epigraph suggests, a whole segment of the U.S. population is rendered invisible. By contextualizing the campus climate at UIUC, a clearer picture emerges of the past and present relationship between Latina/o students and university administrators. This context, in turn, provides an opportunity for future university administrators—both local and national—to better serve their Latina/o constituency. Perhaps most importantly, this context provides a space for Latina/o students to reclaim their history at UIUC and use it to improve conditions for all UIUC students.

Notes

1. Please note that references are made to offices and programs to underscore the fact that correspondence, proposals and negotiations represented official or organizational rather than personal responsibility. Also, there existed some confusion regarding the classification used within the archives. For example, some documents were in folders with dates that conflicted with the date on the specific document. In order to be as precise as possible I noted all the information given—even though it appears, at times, that I have the wrong date.

2. The term Hispanic is used here because this is how Latinas/os are categorized in the data. Please note that I object to using this term, since it is not reflective of the diversity, which exists within Latinas/os. Furthermore, the term Hispanic does not allow for gender distinctions. I will use the terms Latina/o and/or Latinas/os in this dicussion, unless I am reporting findings that use the former term. I also use the plural terms cultures and histories because—while people of color have commonalities and share a collective history and culture—I do not want to suggest that there exists only one true culture or one true history (Oboler, 1995). In this study, the racial/ethnic categories, upon which the data are based, depend on voluntary self-reporting submitted to the university.

3. Admissions and Records Office Statistics (Nov. 3, 1998). Undergraduate, Graduate and Professional Enrollment by Racial/Ethnic Category University of Illinois at Urbana-Champaign, fall 1967 to fall 1998. Note: "Enrollment as of the 10th day of instruction. The distinction of enrollment by racial/ethnic categories is based on voluntary self-reported data. Foreign students are not included in these racial/ethnic counts. Source: OAR. OAA: 11/3/98 MAW." Note: The term *Hispanic* is very broad and it is unclear how U.S. Permanent Residents fit into the data.

4. CRT/LatCrit, as stated previously, recognizes the importance of narratives and practice. I was one of the students involved in attempting to effect positive change after the 1992 Latina/o student actions. Although, CRT/LatCrit provide me with a legiti-

mate space in which to discuss my involvement, I have decided not to do so. My
reasons for this are difficult to explain, but I will briefly attempt to do so in this
footnote:

I find it difficult to explain my involvement for various reasons. First, because
I'm still in the middle of it, it is hard to reflect on what has transpired. Too often I
find myself questioning the decisions and actions we have taken. Was there a better
way? Instead of making things better did we mess up things even more? How can
we be smarter, stronger? Did we get our message across? It is difficult to live with
the contradictions that being involved on campus entails. The contradictions exist
within the reality of being a doctoral student who believes in the power of education
but being proven through university officials' words and actions that we do not belong here. How do I reconcile this? Will I ever come to conclusions that I can live
with? The spaces and borders that we have had to (re)cross in order to get the university to address our needs come with repercussions. Some repercussions are very
obvious while others are subtler almost like shadows. Thus, I feel that I need more
time to sort out what I'm thinking and what I have experienced before I can write
about it. While I have numerous questions the following perspectives are clear in my
mind because they have emerged from discussions with fellow Latina/o students
who are involved on this campus.

Striving to get the needs and concerns we face as minority students, specifically
Latina/o students, addressed at a predominantly White university has been difficult
and discouraging at numerous levels. As students we have had to learn how to navi-
gate the institution as we have gone along. We have been fortunate, however, that
previous students passed down their expertise and knowledge. Nonetheless the fact
remains that we are undergraduate and graduate students; we work part- or full-time
jobs; we have responsibilities to our families back home; and some of us have children of our own. These factors have made our activism come at a much higher price.
Although we recognize the responsibility that comes with what we have undertaken,
at times it is an overwhelming burden.

Throughout this process, we often feel that we are doing the jobs of administrators, but without the benefits of time, money, or recognition. Many of the things we
have asked for and demanded over the years should already exist on this campus.
We have learned that the only way to improve things on this campus is to undertake
the work ourselves. This role reversal has come at a price. On the one hand, we have
learned much, especially how institutions work. On the other, we are frequently de-
moralized. To understand my point, ask yourself these questions. If you are trying to
change an institution because its existing structure does not provide a space in which
people like you can succeed, why would you want to continue to be part of that institution? If administrators by both their words and (in)actions insult and demean
you, why should you be motivated in your classes? If the administration does not diversify its faculty, administrative staff, and student body, how does that encourage
you to pursue a master's degree or doctoral work?

There have been so many difficult questions with no easy answers. However
one thing has been a constant even when we look back to when Latinas/os first
started coming here. The only way this institution has really changed is when stu-

dents have made them change. Thus, the counterstories that exist on and about this campus have to be documented, especially because the administration has demonstrated not to value, recognize, and prioritize Latina/o students' needs and strengths. The counterstories of these students have to be documented so that future generations of students become aware that the problems they experience have roots in the past. Having this knowledge raises the stakes to a new level. Will the UIUC administration truly value and recognize its Latina/o constituency as it does with its White constituency? I would argue that if the university espouses the importance of having a diverse campus and a commitment to diversity, then it must address the concerns of Latina/o students in an aggressive/proactive manner instead of its typical resistance to change until, and only until, the university is portrayed in a negative public light. As one undergraduate Latina student stated at a meeting last semester regarding the lack of Latina/o faculty in the history department: "We have had to sacrifice our time, our classes, in other words our education to be here to fight for more education, a better education." How much longer will students have to do the work of paid administrators?

5.   The reason for this was that students wanted them to hire all three candidates but were told that it would never happen and to only select two. Thus, the chances of hiring two would be better than three. Students were not opposed to the candidate hired by the history department. However, students wanted a cluster hire and not just one person. Students wanted a cluster hire to build up the Latina/Latino Studies Program and the History department. Despite the History department's assertions that not all three candidates were qualified, students believed all of them were competent candidates.

References

Archival Sources

[All archival sources were obtained from the University of Illinois, UIUC Library University Archives, La Casa Cultural Latina Records (RS 41/64/40).]

La Colectiva Latina Proposal. (1974, April 6). La Casa Cultural Latina Records, University of Illinois, UIUC Library University Archives, Box #2, Folder Correspondence, 1974–1976.

La Colectiva Latina to Vice-Chancellor for Campus Affairs. (1974, April 23). La Casa Cultural Latina Records, University of Illinois, UIUC Library University Archives, Box #3, Folder Cultural Center Proposal, 1974–1975.

Dean of the Office of Campus Programs and Services to Vice-Chancellor for Campus Affairs. (1974, April 23). La Casa Cultural Latina Records, University of Illinois, UIUC Library University Archives, Box #2, Folder Correspondence, 1974–1976.

Dean of the Office of Campus Programs and Services to Vice-Chancellor for Campus
    Affairs (April 23, 1974), La Casa Cultural Latina Records, University of Illinois,
    UIUC Library University Archives, Box #3, Folder Cultural Center Proposal, 1974–
    75.

Vice-Chancellor for Campus Affairs to Chancellor. (1974, April 29). La Casa Cultural
    Latina Records, University of Illinois, UIUC Library University Archives, Box #2,
    Folder Correspondence, 1974–1976.

Vice-Chancellor for Campus Affairs to Dean of the Office of Campus Programs and
    Services. (1974, May 3). La Casa Cultural Latina Records, University of Illinois,
    UIUC Library University Archives, Box #2, Folder Correspondence, 1974–1976.

Director of Bilingual/Bicultural Education Program to Dean of the Office of Campus
    Programs and Services. (1974, April 3). La Casa Cultural Latina Records University
    of Illinois UIUC Library University Archives, Box #2, Folder Correspondence,
    1974–1975.

Director of Bilingual/Bicultural Education Program. (n.d.). "The Latino Cultural House,"
    La Casa Cultural Latina Records University of Illinois UIUC Library University Ar-
    chives, Box #2, Folder, Correspondence, 1974–1976.

Books and Articles

Admissions and Records Office Statistics. (1998, Nov. 3). Undergraduate, Graduate and
    Professional Enrollment by Racial/Ethnic Category University of Illinois at Urbana-
    Champaign, Fall 1967 to Fall 1998.

Crenshaw, K., Gotanda, N., Peller, G., & Thomas, K. (1995). *Critical race theory: The
    key writings that formed the movement*. New York: The New Press.

Delgado, R. (1989). Storytelling for oppositionists and others: A plea for narrative.
    Michigan Law Review, 87, 2411–2441.

Donato, R., & Lazerson, M. (2000). New directions in American educational history:
    Problems and prospects. *Educational Researcher, 29*(8), 4–15.

Foley, N. (1997). *The White Scourge: Mexicans, Blacks, and Poor Whites in Texas
    Cotton Culture*. Berkeley, CA: University of California Press.

Larson, C. (1997). Is the land of Oz an alien nation? A sociopolitical study of school-
    community conflict. *Educational Administration Quarterly, 33*(3), 312–350.

LatCrit III Symposium. (1999). *University of Miami Law Review, 53*(4).

Oboler, S. (1995). *Ethnic lables, Latino lives: Identity and the politics of (re)presentation in the United States.* Minneapolis: University of Minnesota Press.

Rabel, E. A. (1997). Untitled. In F. M. Padilla (Ed.), *The struggle of Latino/Latina university students: In search of a liberating education* (pp. 128–129). New York: Routledge.

Solorzano, D. G. (1997). Images and words that wound: Critical race theory, racial stereotyping, and teacher education. *Teacher Education Quarterly, 24,* 5–19.

Solorzano, D. G. (1998). Critical race theory, race and gender microaggressions, and the experience of Chicana and Chicano scholars. *International Journal of Qualitative Studies in Education, 11,* 121–136.

Tate, W. (1997). Critical race theory and education: History, theory, and implications. *Review of Research in Education, 22,* 195–247.

Taylor, S., Rizvi, F., Lingard, B., & Henry, M. (Eds.). (1997). *Educational policy and the politics of change.* New York: Routledge.

Valdes, F. (1996). Latina/o ethnicities, critical race theory, and post-identity politics in postmodern legal culture: From practices to possibilities. *La Raza Law Journal, 9*(1), Spring.

7

Critical Race Theory and Its Implications for Methodology and Policy Analysis in Higher Education Desegregation

Laurence Parker

The historical mission and cultural focus of a college or university has an impact on the policy focus of the institution. The policy process in public institutions of higher education is developed and shaped by many important players including state boards, politicians, influential alumni, business leaders, faculty, administrators, as well as the political composition within these groups. The important issue for Critical Race Theory and educational policy analysis surrounds the *cultural climate* of public colleges and universities in the postdesegregation era: Who shapes it, how, and for what reasons? Public historically Black colleges and universities (HBCU) represent roughly 3% of colleges and universities nationally, and they enroll 18% of African American undergraduates. Historically, the majority of these institutions have been under-funded by state legislatures (Brady, Eatman, & Parker, 2000). However, these institutions have managed to produce 42% of African Americans who acquire the B.A. degree (Brown, 1999). The unique historical and cultural mission of these institutions has played a critical role by providing support for a special population of students who have been underserved by public schools. The public HBCUs fulfill their service mission by providing equal educational opportunities and equity outcomes for African American students in a racially and culturally supportive environment. Higher education desegregation since the U.S. Supreme Court's *U.S. v. Fordice* (1992) and *Ayers v. Fordice* (1995) has focused on remedies that address institutional race neutrality through the eradication of state policies which serve to funnel Black students to the HBCUs, and White students to historically or traditionally White institutions (TWIs). Because there is a legal component in the establishment of the educational and cultural mission of higher education institutions, the question arises as to whether this type of remedy focus not only serves to legally define the goals and purpose of the institution and student opportunities, but also whether such a component protects a college's or university's existence and power from more fundamental legal challenges. David Kairys (1990), a leading critical legal scholar, noted the important legitimating function that the law serves to rationalize the wealthy and powerful in U.S. society. The climate and culture of the institution, faculty, and administrative control over educational decisions, and concern over student choice as higher education consumers, serve as convenient and effective legal shields that the federal courts and some systems of higher education have erected for TWIs to protect themselves from public HBCU challenges to resources, access and power, as well as African American student challenges to recent bans on affirmative action.

In this chapter, I will examine the *Fordice* decision and the other higher education desegregation litigation through Critical Race Theory tied to educational policy analysis. The most important issue raised from this combined perspective is how the law exerts a form of hegemonic control over people of color, and how it ignores critical counternarratives about the role of race in U.S. law and society (Gotanda, 1991). The critical race theorists also see the value in stories and history as forms of narrative that can be used to present legal evidence of discrimination (Matsuda, 1987; Bell, 1988; Delgado, 1989; Johnson, 1994). Diversity as a compelling state interest is important, and the Fourteenth Amendment should be seen as requiring remediation when violations are found. The evidence of past discrimination linked to present-day effects should be specific and particularized to inform policy for effective and creative remedies. A university or state higher education system's simple admission of guilt is not enough to escape their duty to actively pursue equity and social justice for minority students. Critical Race Theory in higher education desegregation argues that the past does make a difference. The university and federal judges in these cases may point with pride to past accomplishments of cultural institution building to create race-neutral campuses. However, it should follow that these same universities may not deny the reality and lingering impact of past racial exclusion and discrimination. Because the past does make a difference, one cannot ignore the history of racism, which hinders us from making affirmative steps to remedy the violation.

The U.S. Supreme Court and the federal district courts have used a "color-blind" frame to reach their decisions in *Fordice*. To be sure, the Court's ruling against the Mississippi freedom of choice plan and the continuance of a dual system of higher education was a partial victory for advocates of civil rights and for African Americans. However, the Court did not recognize the importance of public HBCUs in their decision. In addition, the *Fordice* ruling may be sending and reinforcing the message that public TWIs are superior to public HBCUs; consequently, HBCUs are seen as expendable within the larger social order (Bell, 1979; Johnson, 1993). This in turn will solidify the caste system of higher education through the continued concentration of academic power and resources in the TWIs rather than solidifying and strengthening HBCUs (Hood, 1984).

The first part of this chapter will provide readers with an overview of Critical Race Theory and its criticisms of traditional legal perspectives (e.g., pragmatism, instrumentalism, progressivism). This part will also connect Critical Race Theory to discussions of methodology focused on race. The purpose here is to provide illustrative frameworks that link and trace the historical origins and racialized effects of policy decisions. The second part of this chapter will review the salient facts, issues, and holdings of the *Fordice* and *Knight* cases. Part three will critique these higher education desegregation cases from a Critical Race Theory perspective linked to educational policy. One of the main points I will attempt to show is how the U.S. Supreme Court and the federal district court in *Fordice* ignored the historical relationship of white control and domination that had a deleterious impact on HBCUs specifically and African Americans in general. I will also argue that qualitative research and policy analysis connected to Critical Race Theory serve to document the counternarratives of discrimination that should be heard and recognized by the courts. Public HBCUs have historically played a very important role in expanding college access to people of color—and some of the counternarratives in this chapter will highlight this fact. Second, the legal irony of higher education racial desegregation has presented the dilemma of the color-blind constitutional view of the law mandating open access for all and the removal of the vestiges of past discrimination. However, the forced accommodation of African American students in TWIs was coupled with a denial of the unique mission of the historically Black institutions in the post-*Fordice* era. Therefore, the central position this chapter develops is how the federal courts can order policies requiring equal protection for all students, yet fail to acknowledge that such a solution can have an unintended deleterious impact. In this case, HBCUs have struggled to balance their specific educational mission in the face of increased calls for more White students on these campuses in order to receive court-ordered resources, while African American students have to deal with a hostile racial climate by attending public traditionally White institutions.

An Overview of Critical Race Theory
and Its Link to Educational Policy Analysis

CRT, as a critique of racism in the law and society, emerged as an outgrowth of the critical legal studies movement that took place at the Harvard Law School in the early 1980s (Crenshaw et al., 1995). The law professors and students in this group began to question the objective rationalist nature of the law and the process of adjudication in the U.S. legal system. They criticized the way in which the real effects of the law served to privilege the wealthy and powerful in U.S. society while having a deleterious impact on the rights of the poor to use the courts as a means of redress. Out of this growing critique of the role of law in society, a strand of critical scholarship emerged through the writings of Derrick Bell, Mari Matsuda, Richard Delgado, Angela Harris, and Kimberlé Crenshaw (Tate, 1997). These scholars argued that the critical legal studies movement did not go far enough in challenging the specific racialized nature of the law and its impact on persons of color. Bell, Delgado, Crenshaw, and other early critical race theorists made several distinct claims that gave shape and emphasis to their arguments:

- Racism is a normal daily fact of life in society, and the ideology and assumptions of racism are ingrained in the political and legal structures as to be almost unrecognizable. Legal racial designations have complex, historical and socially constructed meanings that insure the location of political superiority of racially marginalized groups.

- As a form of oppositional scholarship, CRT challenges the experience of White European Americans as the normative standard. Instead, CRT grounds its conceptual framework in the distinctive contextual experiences of people of color, and their lived racial oppression, through the use of literary narrative knowledge and storytelling. The ultimate goal of this effort is to challenge the existing social construction of race.

- CRT attacks liberalism and the inherent belief in the law to create an equitable and just society.

CRT advocates pointed out the legal racial irony and liberal contradiction of the frustrating legal pace of meaningful reform that has eliminated blatant hateful expressions of racism, yet, kept intact exclusionary relations of power. Critical Race Theorists argued that the law—particularly civil rights laws of the 1960s—was targeted to combat classical racism (Katz, Glass, & Cohen, 1973). This type of racism was characterized by *overt* acts such as grossly offensive behavior toward others, legal segregation and discrimination, or acts of racial violence. The moral authority of the civil rights movement served to weaken this form of racism in the U.S., and most White European Americans saw the law as a vital tool in helping to eliminate classical racism. However, one of the main tenets of CRT has been that while classical racism has subsided, everyday racism has risen.

This type of racism can be characterized as those mundane practices and events that usually go unnoticed in every life (Essed, 1991). The actions associated with everyday racism are subtle, automatic, nonverbal exchanges and societal practices that maintain racism firmly in place. Furthermore, everyday racism is incessant and cumulative and is seen in everyday actions by individuals and groups, as well as in institutional policies and administrative practices. Critical Race Theory sought to expose the flaws of the color-blind view of everyday social relations and boldly suggested that the hope of ending discrimination and racism through legal means was, in large part, a falsity. Racism persisted not because of some philosophical contradiction between equality and justice but simply because the larger social order was willing to tolerate and accept racial inequality and inequity.

Critical Race Theory's roots can also be partially traced to previous social science race-based critiques related to the epistemological and ontological construction of race and racialism within modernity. The legal theories related to race share commonalities with other critical theoretical positions related to race and history, philosophy, and the social sciences. For example, Goldberg (1993) argued that in order to understand modernity and its evolution, one had to understand the ontology of race, racialism, and how each played a fundamental role in shaping major philosophical, political, and scientific thought. Smedley (1999) examined the development of the ideology of race as a worldview in the North American continent. She traced the origins of racial ideology in the U.S. to British conflicts with other national groups such as the Irish, in order to fully examine how these groups opposed to British colonialist expansion became racialized by the British for justification purposes connected to domination and exploitation.

Stanfield (1999) also asserted that in race-centered nation states (e.g., the U.S., United Kingdom, South Africa, Brazil), the sociological myth of racial categories is a powerful primary socialization tool that has a tremendous impact on social perceptions, social status, and social identity of all societal members. Racial categorization is a part of cognitive psychological thinking, in that it refers to the ways people think about humans defined in terms of races. It links social and cultural attributes to physical attributes. Therefore, reasoning is based on racial categories and it is more or less commonly accepted in these countries—despite the fact that the rhetoric of color-blindness is commonly used as a pretext to continue to justify hierarchical racial divisions. Feagin (1992, 2000) also discussed the role that microaggressions played on traditionally White college campuses by creating a hostile environment for African Americans that resulted in what he termed "cumulative racism," or a convergence of all the of the subtle—yet still prejudicial—putdowns and actions that marginalized groups' experiences on college campuses because of their race. All of these examples are illustrative of how other critical research on race connects to CRT, resulting in an interdisciplinary and encompassing framework of racial theory from a critical interdisciplinary perspective.

Given the critical race-based positions that were developed in other fields, its coupling with CRT has given the theory expanding explanatory power to address the myriad elements of race, its role in shaping law and the nation state, personal and group identity, distribution of goods and services, and institutional practices and policies. Since its inception, CRT has not locked itself into a singular line of criticism against the law and society regarding race (Hayman, 1995). Rather, CRT has evolved from its early focus on African Americans—and the impact of the law on Black/White European American relations—to examining how issues related to the law and immigration, national origin, language, globalization, and colonization are related to race.

The LatCrit and critical Asian American legal studies movements emerged from this line of critique, calling for a type of "Critical Race Theory" specific to these groups of color (Chang, 1993; Haney-López, 1997; "Special Issue," 1996). For example, LatCrit has drawn similarities with CRT regarding the racism within U.S. law. However, the LatCrit movement sees itself grounded more in documenting, through narrative storytelling, how aspects of race, ethnicity, language, and national origin converge to "otherize" Latinos and Latinas within the U.S. racial context. Asian American Critical Race Theory borrows from poststructuralism for a critical reading and tracing of the use of language and the law to create Asian Americans as "honorary Whites" whose fears can be played against other groups of color regarding affirmative action and admissions to elite public universities. However, these groups can also have the law used against them as it was in the case of Japanese "internment camps" during WWII.

Critical race feminism has also emerged as an area of study with respect to women of color and their connection to the law and public policy's impact on their lives as women, both in the U.S. and in other parts of the world (Wing, 1997). Queer theory, Marxism, and postcolonial theory have also seen connections and conflict with CRT in terms of identity and multiple groups that racialized individuals belong to (see, for example, Carbado, 2000; Iglesias & Valdes, 1999; Tanaka & Cruz, 1998, on specific works related to LatCrit, CRT, and its intersections and conflicts with gay/lesbian/transgendered identity). Indeed, CRT has expanded the direction of critical positions taken in relationship to theories of race and the law. These new avenues, coupled with the experiential and situated knowledge of people of color, makes CRT an appropriate research lens in education for analyzing racial inequality in the law and society.

The connection between CRT and education serves the dual purpose of providing a race-based interdisciplinary theoretical framework of analysis to the study of education laws, policies, and administrative procedures that have a deleterious impact on racial minorities in K-12 and higher education settings (Roithmayr, 1999). CRT—and its LatCrit and Asian American critical race counterparts—can also benefit from the qualitative and quantitative research process by adding methodological enhancement of the data used as evidence in racial discrimination cases (Parker & Lynn, in press). This statement is not to say that other critical perspectives on race and education should be ignored—because they too provide more detailed analysis and theoretical perspectives on issues related to representation, identity, discrimination, and positive racial struggle for social justice by minority students and communities (see for example, McCarthy & Crichlow, 1993; Natriello, 1999). However, the issues for CRT are more specific: How have key policy decisions influenced the conditions and outcomes of students of color? Why, how, and for what purposes do schools and postsecondary institutions reinforce racial, class, and gender inequality for students of color? How do students of color and their parents/communities respond to race, class, and gender inequality?

In addressing these research issues, CRT's connection to qualitative studies in education can be defined as a framework—or a set of basic perspectives, methods, and pedagogy—that seeks to identify, analyze, and transform those structural, cultural, and interpersonal aspects of education that maintain the subordination of students of color. CRT and educational policy analysis also seeks to foster an engagement with critical race praxis and positive change toward racial justice in the schools and higher education institutions (Solorzano, 1998; Solorzano & Yosso, in press).

Much of the literature in education related to CRT addresses its origins and links to specific educational issues and policies. Ladson-Billings and Tate (1995) pushed for using CRT in education to deconstruct fundamental assumptions behind seemingly race-neutral policies and ideology about the education of African American children and other students of color. Tate (1997) traced the origins of CRT and elaborated on the positions of key thinkers that were integral to the formation of the CRT movement. He also suggested ways in which CRT could be linked to educational research by calling for specificity in using CRT as a tool to unmask the effects of racism in educational institutions. Solorzano (1997, 1998) looked at using CRT in higher education settings, first as a

theoretical framework to examine the teacher education discourse surrounding the abilities of children of color, and then as a vehicle to look at
the impact of microaggressions in graduate school settings and its cumulative impact on Chicano-Chicana students. In other words, Solorzano
also used CRT to analyze the seemingly race-neutral language of policy
that focused on providing equal educational opportunity and quality education for meritorious minority graduate students. However, the student
counternarratives in his research illustrated how they endured the everyday racism of graduate school, as White European American professors
and students made these Chicano-Chicana students feel as if they did not
deserve to be at elite institutions of graduate study.

Building on this theme, Villalpando (2000) used CRT, LatCrit, and
case study research methods to identify institutional climates related to
race in higher education settings, and found that some of the campus environments were inhospitable to Chicano-Chicana students. However, he
also used CRT, LatCrit, and critical race praxis to analyze how these students forged racial-ethnic support networks to combat the racism on
campus and to take advantage of educational opportunities and serve the
local Chicano community. Villenas, Deyhle, and Parker (1999) used
CRT to trace how civil rights laws were used to combat "classical racism" in the form of major constitutional and statutory violations that
were perpetuated against the Navajo nation in San Juan County, Utah
(*Meyers v. Board. of Ed. of San Juan Sch. Dist.*, 1995). In this case, the
federal district court found that the school district engaged in various
discriminatory actions—from failure to provide bilingual education, to
tolerating and encouraging de facto racial segregation—and provided
inequitable funding to Navajo schools. Brady, Eatman, and Parker (2000)
utilized CRT as a methodological framework in a slightly different way:
through an examination of higher education funding disparities. Rather
than relying on narrative and storytelling as data, they used the descrip-
tive statistical data to tell the story about higher education disparities between public HBCUs and TWIs.

Other researchers in education have linked CRT to critical epistemological standpoints to create a more holistic and intersecting framework
that incorporates narratives and storytelling of personal/collective memory and experiences. Furthermore, those involved in the studies were
active participants in the research process. For example, researchers have
discussed how CRT could be linked to Chicana feminist epistemology

(Delgado Bernal, 1998), personal understandings of "Mexicananess" (Gonzalez, 1998), the racial and gendered experiences of young Mexicanas in California high schools (Pizarro, 1998), and the formation of a Latino/a family research paradigm that focuses on families as opposed to individuals (Hildago, 1998). In addition, Banning (1999) has looked at using CRT to address whiteness, White privilege, and contradictions in feminist pedagogy through her participatory research study that examined classroom discourse at a predominantly White college class taught by a White female feminist instructor. Ladson-Billings (1998) also discussed CRT's use in analyzing the impact of racism in school policy actions related to curriculum, instruction, and school funding. Lynn (1999) added to this perspective by researching African American teachers who teach within a critical race pedagogical framework as they inform African American students as to the importance of their race/culture as a bridge to learning and success.

To be sure, Ladson-Billings (1998) issued a caveat about jumping on CRT as the next theoretical bandwagon of leftist education scholarship. However, she also started her article by asking what CRT was and what was it doing in a "nice" field such as education. Part of the answer has come from debates surrounding the utility of CRT and other nontraditional forms of research inquiry in education. Another part of the answer can be found by looking at the use of CRT to examine the origins, development, implementation, and evaluation of educational policy and how critical race methodology can be a useful framework to help guide this inquiry. The reception of CRT in the field, however, has been anything but nice, as some critics have voiced serious concern over the proliferation of these critically challenging paradigms—labeling them as mere identity politics masked as scholarship and charging them with diluting the overall quality of educational research (López, 2001). In short, CRT has not crossed over into the field to any significant extent and is virtually absent in the area of educational policy.

Indeed, standard approaches to educational policy are still the norm: focusing on the articulation of decisions to systematically address a specific problem. The policy process has been typically defined as a series of decisions regarding actions taken in terms of what to do (policy development), decisions on how to do it, and decisions on how to assess outcomes through assessment and evaluation (Lee, 1998). Although these areas are seemingly distinct, the policy process is interconnected, and decisions made in one vector process will have an effect on the other domains. Specific special interest groups at the international, federal, and state levels all play various competing roles in the policy influence process in education. Furthermore, the impact of policies on the local context—as well as theoretical and new empirical/methodological debates in the policy field—will have an impact on shaping the future direction of educational policy (Cizek, 1999).

The history of educational policies, particularly at the federal level, also offers potential insights as to how historical analysis can be used to inform key present-day policy decisions for agencies (Vinovskis, 1999). However, these comprehensive approaches to policy analysis in education ignore the more critical interpretations of the policy process. For example, Ball (1990) focused on critical educational policy analysis to document the complex realities of policy making in education, which would include showing how influence, pressure, dogma, expediency, conflict, compromise, error, and pragmatism all play a role in the policy process. Furthermore, Ball criticized the "neat and superficial" way that the policy process has been presented; surely, the policy process in education is "messy" (p. 9).

Scheurich (1994) has also provided a similar critique, calling for the use of Foucault and poststructuralism to critically examine the language of policy in education to unearth its hidden meanings and symbolic power. He used the term *policy archeology* as a useful metaphor for researchers to engage in this type of critical policy analysis that also takes into account who is left out of the policy process (namely, racial minority groups). Pillow (1997) added to this important critical work in educational policy analysis by calling attention to how policy language is often used to declare a "crisis" in education. This "crisis talk" alerts the nation about actions that should be taken to solve a specific educational problem. However, a careful tracing of the policy language and its intent reveals a different story.

Pillow found this to be the case in her qualitative research study on the development and implementation of teenage pregnancy prevention policy that was, on its face, intended for all young girls, but was specifically targeting African American females (despite the fact that young White women had more personal and social problems related to teenage pregnancy than their African American peers). Young (1999) also discussed the limitations of traditional policy analysis models in education that have typically relied on a rationalist theoretical framework driven by empirical research methods. Young instead argued for multiple theoretical frameworks used in educational policy analysis in order to capture the dynamics of the policy context. Drawing from her research on parental involvement policy, Young used critical analyses to examine power relations at an elementary school and how the discourse and language of policy in this area supposedly supported inclusion of parents, but actually served to exclude Mexican American parents from participation.

Drawing from these efforts, I pose the following question: How does race, racialism, and racism play a role in determining policy design, implementation, and outcomes? I believe CRT is important here because it situates race (and its intersections with other areas of identity) at the center of the policy analysis. Given that CRT views racism as a central part of how society is organized and governed, it helps explain and illustrate how and why racism is accepted and taken for granted by White society.

In this regard, CRT adopts a healthy skepticism of the liberal promise of racial reform, as well as a general distrust of conservative notion of color-blind or blanket applications of laws and policies. CRT can also be used to help trace "public relations" policy—or PR-olicy (Lugg, 1996)—to help determine whether policy proposals are driven more by public relations rhetoric or by values that are truly rooted in social justice and equity. In addition, CRT can inform race and educational policy by asking a more fundamental research policy question: Will White European Americans support policies that are harmful to minorities that would otherwise not be tolerated if those same policies were applied to the majority (White) population?

House (1999) asked this question in a corollary to William Julius Wilson's thesis that Americans generally support policies that seemingly benefit all Americans, but draw the line at policies—like welfare and affirmative action—that are seen as benefiting minorities:

> While William Julius Wilson suggests that Americans will not support policies seen to benefit minorities primarily, Americans do seem to support policies which are detrimental to minorities. They would not support massive retention if it were applied to the majority populations. The Chicago suburbs fail less than one percent of their students. If one looked at the explicit rationales for Chicago's neighborhood schools and Chicago's later retention program if students do not obtain a set cutoff score on a standardized test, one would be puzzled by apparent contradictions. Yet both sets of policies are fully consistent

with the underlying beliefs about [the racial inferiority of] minorities and with the educational policies applied to minorities. (House, 1999, p. 9)

House traced the impact of various educational policies and concluded that these practices can be explained and justified without reference to race. Local school finance issues, standardized testing, grade retention, and differential curricula stem more from American beliefs in individuality, autonomy, and freedom. However, when one examines the impact of these policies over the long term, their combined effect is to provide minorities with an inferior education that the majority of Americans would neither tolerate nor accept for their own children.

We can see an illustration of this in "reverse discrimination" cases brought forth by White European Americans in higher education. For example, anti-affirmative action bans were passed by statewide referenda in California and Washington that barred any state or local agency from using race as a basis for granting preferential treatment to any individual or group in state programs of admissions or job hiring (Ayers, 1995; Taylor, 2000). Despite efforts by Mexican American politicians and political activist groups to pressure the University of California Board of Regents to reverse the anti-affirmative action ban in its nine institutions, the effects of it have still been felt across the state. Specifically, there has been a significant drop in Latino/a, Chicano/a, and African American student enrollment at both the undergraduate and graduate/professional levels, particularly at flagship institutions such as the University of California at Berkeley. In fact, UC Berkeley saw its African American undergraduate enrollment drop from 252 in 1997 (the last year in which affirmative action was still in effect), to a mere 143 students in the year 2000, whereas the undergraduate Chicano/a student population went from 385 in 1997 to 228 in 2000. UCLA was also severely impacted: There were no African American students admitted to its law school in the fall 2000 term under the Proposition 209/affirmative action ban (Schmidt, 2001).

Critical Race Theory seeks to expose these types of color-blind policy initiatives as clear manifestations of racial discrimination. The critical race legal position challenges the dominant racial ideology through law and seeks to use the power of the courts to "further the goal of eradicating the effects of racial oppression" (Crenshaw, 1988, p. 134). Such a position argues that White European Americans have enjoyed a tremendous legal advantage over people of color. Such power has been effectively wielded in U.S. society because it has been legitimized through law to such an extent that White people have come to *expect* certain legal rights and priviliges (Harris, 1993). In higher education, White property rights through merit-based admissions have been legitimized through the use of anti-affirmative action measures such as Proposition 209 in California and other federal lawsuits claiming reverse discrimination. Under this reasoning, White European Americans are innocent victims under affirmative action—their higher education property rights are sacrificed to lesser "qualified" minority student applicants. A critical race policy analysis of this assumption reveals an expectation of a right through an admissions policy based on racially blind merit. In this same vein, Critical Race Theory—connected to educational policy analysis—can also be used to examine how *Fordice* was a decision that protected White institutions as property but placed limitations on public HBCUs and the property interest of African Americans. The significance of critical race policy analysis, therefore, indicates a tolerance, if not acceptance, of higher education inequity for public HBCUs that would never be considered for traditionally White institutions.

CRT Methodology for the Study of Race and Higher Education

Solorzano and Yosso (in press) developed critical race methodology in terms of its utility as an analytical framework to ask research questions, review literature, analyze data, and form conclusions and recommendations. They discussed five tenets of a CRT methodology:

1) placing race and its intersectionality with other forms of subordination at the center of research
2) using race in research to challenge the dominant scientific norms of objectivity and neutrality
3) having the research connected with social justice concerns
4) making experiential knowledge central to the study and linking this knowledge to other critical research and interpretive perspectives on race and racism
5) the importance of transdisciplinary perspectives that are based in other fields (e.g., women's studies, African American studies, Chi

cano/a-Latino/a studies, history, sociology) to enhance understanding
of the effects of racism and other forms of discrimination

Solorzano and Yosso posit that CRT methodology represents a challenge
to the existing modes of scholarship by analyzing the ideology of racism,
its impact, and the counternarratives used by persons of color to research
that has typically not placed race at the center of social science study or
has rendered it as an identity politics issue, not one deserving of serious
attention through research.

In this study, CRT methodology and critical race policy analysis
were utilized to examine higher education desegregation litigation. This
research has been part of a larger project that examines the historical and
current role of ideological power in higher education especially as they
relate to African Americans (Parker, Hood, & Anderson, in press). The
research for this project began in 1992, and the methods utilized have
focused on news accounts, court records, interviews from key expert
witnesses, and higher education data. Secondary sources through law
review articles, books, and journal articles were also used for the purpose
of collecting information and providing supporting documentation.

CRT methodology and critical race policy analysis in education were
important to not only frame the research issues, but also to interpret the
evidence and provide a lens of focus for higher education implications.
Some of the critical questions central to the study (and that comprised
part of the interview protocol) were:

1) What would be the most important educational and legal reasons for
   upgrading the status of public HBCUs to a level comparable to that
   of TWIs—particularly flagship state institutions?
2) How will the historical missions of both HBCUs and TWIs change
   as a result of the *Fordice* mandate?
3) What is the evidence regarding discrimination of African American
   students at public TWIs and the unique aspects of educational opportunity at the public HBCUs?

Using parts of critical race methodology for content analysis, we
have been looking at the recurring policy patterns and central legal and
education themes that emerged in respective desegregation cases. In the
next section of this chapter, I will summarize the historical and present-

day legal position of color-blindness and meritocracy, which has historically been viewed as a window of meritorious access to higher education
for African Americans.

A Discussion of Selected Cases in Higher Education Desegregation

The legal history of public HBCUs has been one of continual discrimination and battles surrounding control over resources, the stated
vision and/or mission of the college, and autonomy over future policy
directions. The early case law related to desegregation and the educational and cultural importance of HBCUs has been discussed by others
(Preer, 1982; Kujovich, 1987; Johnson, 1993; Stefkovich & Leas, 1994;
Freeman, 1998). Even though African Americans had their own institutions, they were woefully inferior to the vast resources of the TWIs'
graduate schools and what they could offer in terms of faculty prestige
and professional opportunities. Therefore the Court reinforced the importance of the salutary effects of desegregated educational opportunity under the U.S. Constitution for African Americans. Key issues emerged
from the higher education desegregation case law and federal civil rights
enforcement in this era and one of them was the formidable resistance of
southern states to desegregation in the aftermath of the *Brown v. Board
of Education* (1954) U.S. Supreme Court ruling. There was also continued failure to provide equitable resources to the public HBCUs. Finally,
there was the slow erosion of federal civil rights enforcement of racial
equality laws due to weak compliance remedies and a benign federal effort to make state systems of higher education conform to tighter desegregation standards (Halpern, 1995; Williams, 1997).

In Alabama, the African American plaintiffs charged that the dual
system of higher education restricted the mission of the public HBCUs to
prevent them from developing a comprehensive offering of graduate and
undergraduate programs (*Knight v. State of Alabama* 1991, 1994, 1995).
The plaintiffs in this case also charged that the TWIs used the seemingly
neutral criteria of standardized entrance exams to limit the access of African American students to their institutions. Even the few African
American students who met the test score criteria and were admitted to
TWIs faced hostile resistance and/or indifference to their successful ma-
triculation as students. This discrimination continued through the gradu-

ate school experience as they faced even more rigid admissions criteria and subjectivity by departmental admissions committees—issues that were further compounded by the lack of African American faculty to serve as mentors and advisors. The state, as a defendant, refuted these assertions by claiming that no student had been excluded from the TWIs based on race—in a blatant attempt to distinguish themselves from their HBCU counterparts—and that all potential students could exercise their freedom to enroll in any institution of their choice.

In response, the plaintiffs were able to present historical evidence of the state's strong resistance to the integration of African American integration at TWIs. For example, George Wallace campaigned for governor under the platform of resistance to segregation, and he vowed to stand in the way of African American students if the courts forced integration into the University of Alabama at Tuscaloosa.

In June of 1963, Wallace made good on his campaign promise and physically blocked the entrance to the university's Foster Auditorium as the first African American students entered to register for classes under federal court order. According to one of the expert witnesses at the *Knight* hearings, "Wallace...never wanted it to seem that the government of Alabama was voluntarily integrating" (Thornton 1991, p. 165). The message was clear. Segregation may have been defeated, but the vigorous resistance would be continued at all costs, and at the detriment of African American students and HBCUs.

For example, the plaintiffs also cited the personal testimonies of current and former African American students, who emphasized the historical patterns and acts of discrimination they experienced on TWI campuses, as well as recent racial incidents that fostered an unwelcoming climate for learning. For example, University of South Alabama officials repeatedly failed to acknowledge acts of racist "free speech" directed toward African Americans, such as a 1989 incident at one of the TWIs where an African American student was confronted with writing on her dormitory room door which stated "Nigger go back to Africa." When she reported the transgression to the associate director of housing, the student was told, "Don't worry about it. It's probably just a couple of boys who have had too much to drink and they're probably just kidding, probably just having some fun" (Post-trial Proposed Findings, 1990, pp. 392–393). This lack of sensitivity to the gravity of such a situation is reflective of the administrative use of discretion to sanction racist speech, and the use of policy to resist certain claims made by interest groups (Taylor, Rizvi, Lingard, & Henry, 1997).

African American graduate students also encountered a hostile environment at the TWIs in Alabama. The evidence submitted by the *Knight* plaintiffs indicated that during the 1983–1990 period, Auburn University awarded 567 doctoral degrees, but only 13 or 2.3% of them went to African Americans (Post-trial Proposed Findings, 1990, p. 335). The paucity of African American Ph.D.s was largely attributed to TWI's opposition to the expansion of the doctoral programs at HBCUs and the TWI's failure to admit or graduate African American students. Many departments have never conferred a doctoral degree to an African American. A similar pattern was also reflected in the low number of faculty at the TWIs, because no TWI in the state had more than 5% of African Americans as professors (Post-trial Proposed Findings, 1990, p. 281).

The federal district court ruling questioned the good faith efforts of the TWIs to implement a freedom of choice plan, given the historical and current evidence of discrimination. As one example, the court found that the sole reliance on standardized test scores for admission was a discriminating and determining factor that suppressed the number of African American students attending Auburn University. Furthermore, the court noted historical inequities in the allocation of financial resources to HBCUs and integration into the TWIs. Federal district court judge Murphy considered this history to be important when he fashioned a remedy requiring the state to provide over $95 million to the HBCUs for the upgrading of the infrastructure at their campuses and the expansion of their course offerings. The court also placed itself in charge of monitoring these remedies.

When this ruling was challenged by the state, the U.S. Court of Appeals for the 11th Circuit upheld the previous district court decision by finding that the state's system of distributing resources and programs to the state's HBCUs and TWIs was the direct result of the past de jure segregated system (*Knight v. State of Alabama*, 1994). Another important aspect of the federal appeals court ruling addressed the issue of historically tracing the marginalization of African American history, thought, and culture at the TWIs. On the appeal, the African American students charged that the design of the curriculum and core course content at Alabama's TWIs was not widely integrated into campus academic experiences. The federal appeals court did indeed acknowledge the First

Amendment right of the faculty to define the college curriculum. However, the court also saw importance of clarifying whether or not the marginalization of African American history, thought, and culture was
rooted in the past regime of segregation. As a result, this issue was remanded to the lower court for review (*Knight v. State of Alabama*, 14 F.
3d 1534, 1533). On this issue, Judge Murphy ruled there was no pur-
posive intent at TWI campuses to suppress African American studies
throughout the curriculum (*Knight v. State of Alabama*, 1995, p. 348).
Believing the issue was one of access as opposed to content, Judge Murphy made an unanticipated recommendation and ordered the use of "diversity scholarships" for *White* students to attend the historically Black
Alabama State University and Alabama A & M. In 1999, however, a
Black graduate student challenged this mandate on the grounds that explicit cross-race student recruitment programs should not be used for desegregation purposes. The Center for Individual Rights supported the
student by arguing that the state had already fulfilled its mandate to desegregate its higher education system and that current student choice
should not be grounded in correcting the past through reverse discrimination of any kind based on race (Hebel, 2001b; for more on this view see
Schiff, 1985).

In the *Fordice* case and previous Mississippi decisions (i.e., *Ayers v.
Allain*, 1987, 1990), the lower federal courts upheld the state of Mississippi's assertion that freedom of choice was equally available to everyone in the state, despite the admitted history of discrimination against
HBCUs and the failure of achieving true integration at TWIs. These
lower court decisions in *Fordice* demonstrated how a history of racism
and discriminatory treatment against HBCUs and African Americans was
completely ignored (Brown, 1992). If the courts were more aware of how
the history of racial discrimination influenced student choice, then it
would have been more evident that "freedom of choice" has been used
by states as a historical pretext to uphold institutional segregation in its
higher education system (Blake, 1991; Halpern, 1992).

U.S. v. Fordice (1992) originated in 1975 when African Americans
of Mississippi filed suit against the state and its traditionally White institutions of higher education. The African Americans charged that the defendants created and maintained a dual and unequal system of higher
education that was based on race which consequently violated the 13th
and 14th Amendments to the United States Constitution as well as Title

VI of the Civil Rights Act of 1964. This case was one of several which originated in southern states between 1969 and 1977 in an effort to not only correct these constitutional and statutory violations, but also to seek a more direct remedy for the discrimination that the *Adams v. Califano* case had failed to address. In response, the defendants in Mississippi asserted that the state department of education as well as the TWIs had good-faith nondiscriminatory and nonracial admissions and operational policies, and that the racial makeup of colleges and universities in Mississippi could not be traced to any action by the state. Furthermore, the state maintained that freedom of choice in higher education gave all students, regardless of race, the opportunity to be admitted into any state institution if they met the established requirements for admissions.

The African American plaintiffs in *Fordice* challenged the state's assertions of the existence of a nonracialized educational system and nondiscriminatory nature of higher education in Mississippi. The *Fordice* plaintiffs charged that the discrimination was most reflective in the policies of the state department of education including use of ACT scores in student admission decisions, the location of off-campus centers, the designation of institutional missions, disparities in funding and programs, as well as the racial composition of the faculties.

The federal district court held in favor of the state in *Ayers v. Allain*. The lower federal courts held that neither the educational policy of differential ACT scores for admissions, nor the funding disparities constituted discrimination. To be sure, the district court engaged in extensive findings of fact, and the conclusions of law followed that a state had an affirmative duty to dismantle the previously segregated system of higher education. However, the legal standard of analysis set by the federal district court called for greater emphasis to be placed on current higher education policies to ensure that they were racially neutral. When the federal district court applied this standard of legal analysis to the facts brought out in the trial, the court found no violation of federal law; the states as defendants were fulfilling their duty to remove the previously segregated system. The African American plaintiffs appealed, and the federal court of appeals for the 5th Circuit affirmed the decision of the district court. Not surprisingly, the most notable part of this decision addressed the issue of students' "free choice" in selecting an institution of higher education.

The court of appeals also held that higher education did not call for particular remedies to correct past discrimination because individuals were free to choose the college or university they wished to attend. Furthermore, the state had no affirmative duty to assure that African Americans enter a profession with or without the support of historically Black colleges and universities. The court of appeals distinguished higher education from the public school setting where attendance was mandatory. In the public school arena, the United States Supreme Court held in *Green v. New Kent County School Board* (391 U.S. 430) that the state had an affirmative duty to dismantle its unitary segregated school system. However, the differences between higher education and the K-12 school system were too pronounced for the legal standard in *Green* to be applied to this case. Therefore, the court of appeals acknowledged that the plaintiffs had raised important racial concerns about admissions, faculty, resources, and programs. However, the federal constitutional and statutory claims did not call for the systematic dismantling of public higher education in Mississippi.

In the *Fordice* case, the African American plaintiffs made similar claims to their counterparts in Alabama by asserting the existence of discriminatory effects in the dual system of higher education. In this case, the state admitted this past historical discrimination, but then countered by asserting that the past no longer applies to the current situation because all students in the state had the "freedom" to apply and attend any institution of their choice. The plaintiffs also maintained that the use of standardized tests had a deleterious impact on African American students admissions to the TWIs and also depressed the numbers attending the HBCUs. The state maintained that the use of the examinations was merely another attempt by the TWIs to upgrade the overall system of higher education. Alvin O. Chambliss, the attorney for the plaintiffs, articulated the counterargument in his opening statement:

> The historical discrimination hurt black people in five different ways. Equal access, they were shut out. It segregated them, and then when they got in they got lesser programs, funding facilities, reputation. And it denied black people leadership opportunities and employment opportunities in the five white schools which were the schools of choice so to speak. Black people are still experiencing those norms, and the system, rooted in the days of apartheid in Mississippi still exists. Nothing has changed. You have the misuse of the ACT. The university center dominated by junior college; in addition to the three white schools, still stands in the shadow of Jackson State University. You have black people still feeling hostility at the University of Mississippi, and basically the system

is substantially intact from 1962 until now, 99 percent of the white students go
to white schools. (Chambliss, 1991, p. 5)

In the lower federal court rulings, the state's freedom of choice plan
was upheld due to a previous decision on race, freedom of choice and 4-
H clubs in *Bazemore v. Friday* (478 U.S. 385). This was a critical point
of contention for the U.S. Supreme Court as they questioned the state's
comparison between racial choice and 4-H clubs, to the complexities of
higher education with regard to possible discrimination. The state's reliance on the freedom of choice argument proved to be its undoing because, in an eight-to-one decision, the U.S. Supreme Court overturned
the previous rulings and held that the vestiges of state sanctioned discrimination still remained.

At issue for the Court was whether the state of Mississippi had made
a genuine effort to eliminate the Jim Crow policies of separation and discrimination in higher education. The Court noted the historical resistance
to integration that was exemplified by the controversy surrounding James
Meredith's entrance to Ole Miss in 1962, and the reality that the racial
patterns of student enrollment in same-race institutions remained virtually unchanged from the late 1960s to the initial filing of the suit against
the state. The Court ruled that this history strongly contributed to the present-day discrimination in the state's higher education system that was
reflected by the use of standardized college admissions tests and the historical missions of colleges and universities. The U.S. Supreme Court
remanded the case to the lower federal courts with three inquiries:

1. whether it would be practicable and consistent with sound educa-
    tional policies and practices to eliminate effects of the "race neutral"
    policies
2. whether the state's operation of higher education was constitution-
    ally sound
3. to inquire about the feasibility of a complete re-examination of
    higher education in the state to eventually dismantle the former de
    jure system.

In 1995, the ruling by Federal District Court Judge Neal Biggers ordered no closures of public HBCUs and TWIs and directed approximately $35 million in improvements toward the HBCUs (Jaschik, 1995).
The judge called on the state to consider the creation of more profes-

sional programs at Jackson State University as well. However, the ruling was criticized because it called for overall higher standardized test scores and grade point averages in academic high school courses in order to gain entrance into the public colleges and increasing the White European American presence at the HBCUs by providing race-based scholarships for them, which in reality would not change racial enrollment patterns but would limit African American student access to higher education because of poor high school preparation. By the spring of 2001, state and federal officials reached a tentative settlement of the long *Fordice* litigation. The settlement called for $503 million to be spent over seventeen years to enhance programs at the public HBCUs, and increase White enrollment to 10% of the student body to be eligible for this funding. Some African American leaders at the HBCUs were critical of the decision because it put an unfair burden on their institutions to simultaneously recruit White students while having to build struggling programs without addressing the more specific needs of these institutions (Hebel, 2001a). However, Federal District Judge Neal Biggers soon invalidated the settlement (*Ayers & U.S. v. Musgrove & State of Mississippi*, 2001). Judge Biggers ruled that the proposed plan was too costly, that there was no public debate about the plan with concerned citizens in the state, and moreover, that the plan did not address the central issue of the eradication of "any policies which prevent black students from attending historically white universities or which may channel black students to historically black universities and white students to historically white universities" (*Ayers & U.S. v. Musgrove & State of Mississippi*, 2001, p. 5). Although a hearing for public debate happened in the fall of 2001, a larger issue still remained: The equal protection burden under *Fordice* placed the desegregation of institutions (through cross-race student enrollment programs) at the center of the policy actions as opposed to academic institutional enhancement at the public HBCUs to attempt to achieve the same goal.

Fordice Aftermath and Continuing Policy Controversies

At least four critical issues have evolved as policy dilemmas after the United States Supreme Court's decision in *Fordice*. First, the legal standard for proving racial discrimination in higher education required the federal courts to determine whether the state's polices are traceable to the prior legally segregated system, and if these policies still have a deleterious effect on segregation. Second, the federal courts should determine if such policies have sound educational justification despite being rooted in the prior de jure system. A third issue emerging from the *Fordice* standard was how the lower federal courts would examine policies that may be linked to the past de jure system but cannot be practically eliminated. Finally, the federal courts had to evaluate higher education policies to determine whether some of them could be practically eliminated. If they could, and the state failed to comply, then it had not satisfied the burden of proving that it removed all vestiges of prior discrimination.

The standards, set forth by the Supreme Court, created a myriad of complex legal and educational issues for the lower federal courts to resolve. However, these constitutionally rooted equal protection standards were at odds with the testimony of former and current African American students at the University of Mississippi and the NAFEO-National Bar Association *amicus curae* briefs submitted to the U.S. Court of Appeals for the 5th Circuit in 1990. The students filed their brief to present evidence to the court concerning the hostile climate on the TWIs toward African American students and desegregation issues in general. The personal testimonies of these students demonstrated their fear and mistrust of the University of Mississippi (Ole Miss), and the racial harassment and discrimination that occurred there. One student, James Gilleylen, who attended undergraduate and graduate school at Ole Miss in the 1970s and the early 1980s, recalled how the faculty routinely berated him in his classes. When he inquired about his grade in one of his English classes, the faculty member told him that

> Black people have an inherent problem in terms of their mastering the English language. You have problems in terms of being able to write and speak. Problems with the spoken language as well as the written language. (Motion of former Black students, 1990, p. 7)

Furthermore, as soon as the professor looked at his assignment, which was a discussion of past educational experiences, he initially got a D and then a grade of F. In one of his graduate school classes, the professor told Gilleylen and the rest of the students to "not place too much credence in the census data because it was collected by a bunch of unemployed illiterate black folk" (p. 8). This same professor would also open the class when Gilleylen arrived by saying "well I guess we can start, the nigger has arrived." Another African American student recalled her experience of being told by a professor to either choose a major other than speech pathology or enroll in speech therapy sessions herself because Black people couldn't talk (p. 9). One of the current African American students described an incident where she was slapped in the face with a confederate flag by White students in plain view of the university police—yet nothing was done to stop it, as the White students continued to harass her both verbally and physically (p. 11). In short, African American students argued that when they exercised their "free choice," the TWI made no effort to stop the racial discrimination and harassment at institutions such as Ole Miss. Therefore, it should have been little wonder that some African American students continued to shun these places in favor of the HBCUs.

Critical Race Theory is an important tool with which to view the African American student's personal testimonies on their experiences at the TWIs. According to Delgado (1989), one could view these incidents as "cultural lag" or isolated events. However, these stories can also be the description of the minority critique of the ideology of racism manifested as White institutional control (Delgado, 1989, p. 2413). Wendy Brown (1992) argued in favor of a critical race legal theory approach to *Fordice* in order to ferret out the

> contextual analysis of history and the political realities of race: Critical race scholars have convincingly critiqued the tendency of Courts to disengage law from the political and cultural realities of our multicultural society and create the illusion either that racial discrimination against blacks and other racial minorities no longer exists, or that it is no longer influenced by state conduct. (p. 80)

The role of Critical Race Theory in *Fordice* and other higher education cases is important because it serves as a way for members of the majority to enrich their own reality (Delgado, 1989). Critical Race Theory serves an important role because storytelling comprises an integral part of historical and current legal evidence in the higher education desegregation cases. The federal courts and the White European American majority should be interested in these "stories," because, as Delgado asserts, it is only through listening that "one can acquire the ability to see the world through others eyes" (Delgado, 1989; p. 2439). Finally, Critical

Race Theory also exposes the flaws in the color-blind position in that it documents how African American students have to compromise their race and culture in order to fit into the TWIs campus experience.

For instance, in the 1995 *Fordice* ruling, Federal District Court Judge Biggers noted the high percentage of African American students graduating from the TWIs since the 1960s. Therefore, he surmised that these institutions must be successful. However, the judge failed to consider a different understanding of this success; that is, how African American students have had to tolerate a hostile racial climate in order to survive in TWIs. A critical race educational policy perspective presents testimonial evidence showing how much these students have had to adapt to survive and graduate from the TWIs. This notion of success through resiliency is not the case for White students. Furthermore, the judicial decisions demonstrates that the federal courts are willing to tolerate inequality between public HBCUs and TWIs and willing to support affirmative action measures to increase White European American enrollment at the public HBCUs. However, Judge Biggers has denied support for the public HBCUs to enhance programs that will attract students of all races to further the mission of these institutions.

The critical race legal position takes the explicit mission of HBCUs, as well as the voices of African American students, and makes them central categories in desegregation issues in higher education. Moreover, TWIs should be called upon to develop and implement plans that truly address the educational, social, financial, and political issues of desegregation in higher education. This indeed happened recently with the $503 million *Fordice* tentative settlement in Mississippi between state and federal officials. However, Federal District Judge Neal Biggers invalidated the intent of this agreement by, once again, placing the burden of desegregation on the public HBCUs. By arguing that the historically White universities in "the state averaged twenty-six percent African American students on their campuses" (*Ayers*, 2001, p. 6)—a number that did not parallel the White student enrollment at HBCUs—he emphasized that the *Fordice* mandate should have aimed at increasing White student enrollment at HBCUs. Furthermore, he implied in this ruling that as more resources were given to institutions in general, and public HBCUs in particular, it merely increased the racial segregation because African American students would choose to go to public HBCUs (*Ayers*, 2001, p. 6). Therefore, one of the policy consequences was that public

TWIs were allowed to continue to gain relatively more in state appropriations per student. In fact, the average per student appropriation in 1997 for the state of Mississippi was $3,143 for students attending public TWIs, as opposed to $2,618 for students at public HBCUs (Sav, 1997; Brady, Eatman, & Parker, 2000, p. 313). The *Fordice* mandate only guaranteed that this financial gap would widen.

The U.S. Supreme Court and the federal district courts should not have placed the disproportionate burden on the HBCUs to dismantle the previous de jure system. According to the summary by the *Harvard Law Review Board* (1992) the mere existence of HBCUs under *Fordice* was now constitutionally suspect. This legal burden would fall disproportionately on HBCUs because most states would pursue the option of closing and/or reshaping these institutions, rather than improving their resources. The *Law Review* summary argued that the freedom of choice rights of African American students were ignored by the U.S. Supreme Court in that they already had the option of attending one of the TWIs. Instead, it would have been advisable for the Court to carefully examine the historical evidence of legally segregated higher education to see if that past discrimination had a direct impact on the lack of integration in higher education as well as a disproportionate share of resources going to the TWIs and take remedial steps to correct this imbalance.

If African American concerns were placed first in a remedy for desegregation in higher education, then further restructuring should occur by improving the status of the public HBCUs. There can be little argument about a caste system of public higher education in the U.S., where the flagship research institutions garner the lion's share of resources, followed by comprehensive institutions and community colleges. A critical race educational policy analysis in higher education desegregation posits that if minority student concerns centered at the forefront of the attempts to change higher education, then the HBCUs can be viewed as flagship institutions because they provide a supportive environment for student learning. Furthermore, they serve the needs of minority and majority students particularly in the professional schools, whose graduates provide services for the citizens of the state.

If the primary purpose of public higher education is broadened to emphasize the importance of providing a supportive environment for student learning and service to the state, then the missions of institutions may need to be revised as well. The perceptions of racial inferiority still

linger in higher education and the literature is ripe with examples of this
at both the macro and micro levels. One of the ways this impression can
be overcome is through judicially mandated program enhancement at the
public HBCUs. Indeed this was a part of the *Knight* (1995) ruling to provide support for high-quality engineering programs in order to change
the general perception of the public HBCUs in the state. This improvement in turn would potentially increase White student enrollment, provide more resources for the public HBCU, and put them more in an
institutional position of strength as opposed to the punitive policy orientation of *Fordice* as articulated in this most recent ruling. From a CRT
policy perspective, the Court rulings in higher education desegregation
should provide remedies to assist higher education institutions in addressing the obstacles minority students face during their undergraduate
careers. These difficulties undermine their ability to persist, succeed, and
graduate. The goal should be to yield permanent changes in institutional
policies that will eliminate academic and social barriers. Qualitative research in this area can inform the courts and institutions as to the context
and needs of the students, provide history regarding previous targeted
programs for African American students and other students of color, and
develop new implementation efforts to increase minority student success.

Conclusion

Critical Race Theory and its tenets of storytelling have emerged as
an important part of the legal proceedings in the recent higher education
desegregation decisions. Critical Race Theory positions itself against the
objective neutrality of the law to argue that the law is not color-blind.
Rather, American jurisprudence has historically been used against African Americans and other people of color, and continues to do so in the
present day. The critical race theorists have posited that these marginalized views should be heard, especially with respect to the evidence of
discrimination against the HBCUs and African Americans at the TWIs.

The previous court rulings called for the higher education institutions
to dismantle the legal vestiges of segregation. Desegregation was indeed
seen as the goal. However, the stories of discrimination against HBCUs
and African American students who attended TWIs were entirely ignored, painting a portrait of continued resistance to desegregation. To be

sure, African Americans *are* asserting their freedom of choice to attend TWIs, but HBCUs should not be forced to bear the burden of these desegregation efforts, nor should TWIs be let off the proverbial hook so easily for condoning racist practices.

As the details of higher education unfold in this anti-affirmative action/post-*Fordice* era, critical race educational policy analysis must be developed, articulated, and heard in order to have an effect in preserving the public HBCU presence and addressing indifference to racial diversity at TWIs. In other words, Critical Race Theory has to be connected more to critical policy analysis and critical qualitative research on race in education. Given the growing political conservatism in the U.S. Congress and state governments, Critical Race Theory in educational policy will be an essential legal voice for racial social justice in higher education.

References

Adams v. Califano, 480 F. 2nd 1159 (D. D. C. Cir. 1977).

Anderson, J. A. (1994, September 9). *United States remand findings of fact and conclusions of law in Ayers U.S. v. Fordice*. Civil Action No. GC75–9–NB. [Testimony as expert historian witness].

Ayers, D., Jr. (1995, February 16). Conservatives forge new strategy to challenge affirmative action. *New York Times*, pp. A1, A22.

Ayers v. Allain, 674 F. Supp. 1523 (N.D. Miss. 1987).

Ayers v. Allain, 893 F. 2nd 732 (5th Cir. 1990).

Ayers v. Fordice, 879 F. Supp. 1419 (1995).

Ayers and U.S. v. Musgrove and State of Mississippi. (2001, May 8). Civil Action No. 4:75cv9–B–D in the U.S. District Court for the Northern District of Mississippi Greenville division.

Ball, S. (1990). *Politics and policy making in education*. London: Routledge.

Banning, M. (1999). Race, class, gender, and classroom discourse. In L. Parker, D. Deyhle, & S. Villenas (Eds.), *Race is...race isn't: Critical race theory and qualitative studies in education* (pp. 155–180). Boulder, CO: Westview Press.

Bazemore v. Friday, 478 U.S. 385 (1986).

Bell, D. A. (1979). Black colleges and the desegregation dilemma. *Emory Law Journal 28*, 949–984.

Bell, D. A. (1988). White superiority in America: Its legal legacy, its economic costs. *Villanova Law Review, 33*, 767–779.

Blake, E., Jr. (1991). Is higher education desegregation a remedy for segregation but not educational inequality? A study of the *Ayers v. Mabus* desegregation case. *Journal of Negro Education, 60*, 538–566.

Brady, K., Eatman, T., & Parker, L. (2000). To have or not to have? A preliminary analysis of higher education funding disparities in the post-*Ayers v. Fordice* era: Evidence from critical race theory. *Journal of Education Finance, 25*, 297–323.

Brown v. Board of Education, 347 U.S. 483 (1954).

Brown, M. C., II. (1999). *The quest to define collegiate desegregation: Black colleges, Title VI and post-Adams litigation*. Westport, CT: Bergin & Garvey.

Brown, W. R. (1992). The convergence of neutrality and choice: The limits of the state's affirmative duty to provide equal educational opportunity. *Tennessee Law Review, 60*, 65–131.

Carbado, D. W. (2000). Black rights, gay rights, civil rights. *UCLA Law Review, 47*, 1467–1520.

Chambliss, A. O. (1991, November 13). *Opening statement of final oral arguments before the U.S. Supreme Court in U.S. v. Fordice*. Washington, DC: Anderson Reporting Company.

Chang, R. (1993). Toward an Asian American legal scholarship: Critical race theory, post-structuralism, and narrative space. *California Law Review, 81*, 1241–1323.

Cizek, G. J. (Ed.). (1999). *Handbook of educational policy*. San Diego, CA: Academic Press.

Crenshaw, K. W. (1988). Race, reform and retrenchment: Transformation and legitimation in anti-discrimination law. *Harvard Law Review, 101*, 1331–1387.

Crenshaw, K., Gotanda, N., Peller, G., Thomas, K. (Eds.). (1995). *Critical race theory: The key writings that formed the movement*. New York: The New Press.

Davis, R. N. (1993). The quest for equal education in Mississippi: Implications of *U.S. v. Fordice. Mississippi Law Journal, 62*, 406–501.

Delgado, R. (1989). Storytelling for oppositionists and others: A plea for narrative. *Michigan Law Review, 87*, 2411–2441.

Delgado, R., & Stefancic, J. (2000). *Critical race theory: The cutting edge* (2nd ed.). Philadelphia: Temple University Press.

Delgado Bernal, D. (1998). Using a Chicana feminist epistemology in educational research. *Harvard Educational Review, 68*, 555–582.

Essed, P. (1991). *Understanding everyday racism: An interdisciplinary theory.* Thousand Oaks, CA: Sage.

Feagin, J. R. (1992). The continuing significance of racism: Discrimination against black students in white colleges. *Journal of Black Studies, 22*, 46–78.

Feagin, J. R. (2000). *Racist America: Roots, current realities, and future reparations.* New York: Routledge.

Freeman, K. (Ed.). (1998). *African American culture and heritage in higher education research and practice.* Westport, CT: Prager.

Goldberg, D. T. (1993). Racist culture: Philosophy and the politics of meaning. Cambridge, MA: Blackwell Press.

Gonzalez, F. E. (1998). Formations of Mexicananess/Growing up Mexicana: Trenzas de identidades multiples/Braids of multiple identities. *International Journal of Qualitative Studies in Education, 11*, 81–102.

Gotanda, N. (1991). A critique of our constitution is color-blind. *Stanford Law Review, 44*, 1–68.

Green v. New Kent County School Bd. 391 U.S. 430 (1968).

Halpern, S. C. (1992). Deciding *Ayers v. Mabus*: Documenting the disparities in state funding for public higher education in Mississippi: 1960–1990. *Black Issues in Higher Education, 27*, 20–23.

Halpern, S. C. (1995). *On the limits of the law: The ironic legacy of Title VI of the 1964 Civil Rights Act.* Baltimore: Johns Hopkins University Press.

Haney-López, I. F. (1997). Race, ethnicity, and erasure: The salience of race to LatCrit theory. *La Raza Law Journal, 10*, 57–125.

Harris, C. (1993). Whiteness as property. *Harvard Law Review, 106*, 1701–1791.

Harvard Law Review Board. (1992). Supreme Court leading cases. *Harvard Law Review, 106*, 163–240.

Hayman, R. (1995). The color of tradition: Critical race theory and postmodern constitutional traditionalism. *Harvard Civil Rights-Civil Liberties Law Review, 30*, 57–108.

Healy, P. (1994, November 16). Louisiana proposes 10-year plan to desegregate its public colleges. *The Chronicle of Higher Education*, pp. 32–34.

Hebel, S. (2000, October 27). A pivotal moment for desegregation. *The Chronicle of Higher Education*, pp. 26–29.

Hebel, S. (2001a, June 8). A new push to integrate public Black colleges. *The Chronicle of Higher Education*, p. 22.

Hebel, S. (2001b, May 4). A settlement and more division in Mississippi. *The Chronicle of Higher Education*, pp. A23–24.

Hidalgo, N. M. (1998). Toward a definition of a Latino family research paradigm. *International Journal of Qualitative Studies in Education, 11*, 103–120.

Hood, S. (1984). *The caste system of higher education: Title III and legislative intent.* Unpublished doctoral dissertation. University of Illinois at Urbana-Champaign.

House, E. R. (1999). Race and policy. *Educational Policy Analysis Archives, 7*(16). [Available online: http://epaa.asu.edu/epaa/v7n16.html].

Iglesias, E. M., & Valdes, F. (Eds.). (1999). Special issue on LatCrit: Beyond/between colors: Deconstructing insider/outsider positions in LatCrit theory. *University of Miami Law Review, 53*, (4).

Jaschik, S. (1991, July 8). High-court ruling transforms battles over desegregation at colleges in 19 States. *The Chronicle of Higher Education*, pp. A16, A18.

Jaschik, S. (1994, March 9). Victory for black colleges. *The Chronicle of Higher Education*, pp. 20–21.

Jaschik, S. (1995, March 17). Ruling in Mississippi: Latest decision in 20-year old college desegregation case gets mixed reviews. *The Chronicle of Higher Education*, pp. 23–25.

Johnson, A. M. (1993). Bid whist, tonk, and *U. S. v. Fordice*: Why integrationism fails African-Americans again. *California Law Review, 81*, 1401–1470.

Johnson, A. M. (1994). Defending the use of narrative and giving content to the voice of color: Rejecting the imposition of process theory in legal scholarship. *Iowa Law Review, 79,* 803–852.

Kairys, D. (Ed.). (1990). *The politics of law: A progressive critique.* New York: Pantheon.

Katz, I., Glass, D. C., & Cohen, S. (1973). Ambivalence, guilt, and the scapegoating of minority group victims. *Journal of Experimental Social Psychology, 9,* 423–436.

Knight v. State of Alabama, 787 F. Supp. 1030 (N.D. Ala. 1991).

Knight v. State of Alabama, 14 F.3rd 1534 (11th Cir. 1994).

Knight v. State of Alabama, 900 F. Supp. 272 (N.D. Ala. 1995).

Kujovich, G. (1987). Equal opportunity in higher education and the Black public college: The era of separate but equal. *Minnesota Law Review, 72,* 30–164.

Ladson-Billings, G. (1998). Just what is critical race theory and what is it doing in a field like education? *International Journal of Qualitative Studies in Education, 11,* 7–24.

Ladson-Billings, G. & Tate, W. F., IV (1995). Toward a critical race theory of education. *Teachers College Record, 97,* 47–68.

Lee, W. Y. (1998). Policy, practice, and performance: Strategies to foster the meaningful involvement of African Americans in higher education decision-making processes. In K. Freeman (Ed.), *African American culture and heritage in higher education research and practice* (pp. 157–172). Westport, CT: Prager.

López, G. R. (2001). Re-visiting white racism in educational research: Critical race theory and the problem of method. *Educational Researcher, 30,* 29–33.

Lugg, C. A. (1996). *For God and country: Conservatism and American school policy.* New York: Peter Lang.

Matsuda, M. J. (1987). Looking to the bottom: Critical legal studies and reparations. *Harvard Civil Rights-Civil Liberties Law Review, 22,* 323–400.

McCarthy, C., & Crichlow, W. (Eds.). (1993). *Race, identity, and representation in education.* New York: Routledge.

Mercer, J. (1992, October 28). Black college would be closed in Mississippi plan to comply with court ruling on desegregation. *The Chronicle of Higher Education,* p. A29.

178 Laurence Parker

Mercer, J. (1993, November 17). Praise and fury pursue chief of state's public university system. *The Chronicle of Higher Education*, 31–32.

Meyers v. Board. of Education of San Juan School District (1995), 905 F. Supp. 1544n (D. Utah 1995).

Motion of former black students of the University of Mississippi for leave to file brief amicus curiae in support of Ayers petitioners (1990, October). No. 90–6588 and No. 90–1205, Greenwood, MS: Willie J. Perkins, Counsel of record.

Natriello, G. (Ed.). (1999). Special theme issue: Education and race. *Teachers College Record, 100* (4).

Parker, L., Hood, S., & Anderson, J. A. (in press). *Racial desegregation in higher education: History, power and social justice*. New York: Teachers College Press.

Parker, L., & Lynn, M. (in press). Critical race theory and qualitative inquiry: An introduction to its utility and problematics for research. *Qualitative Inquiry*.

Pillow, W. S. (1997). Decentering silences/troubling irony: Teen pregnancy's challenge to policy analysis. In C. Marshall (Ed.), *Feminist critical policy analysis: A perspective from primary and secondary schooling* (pp. 134–152). Bristol, PA: Falmer Press.

Pizarro, M. (1998). Chicana/o power! Epistemology and methodology for social justice and empowerment in Chicana/o educational communities. *International Journal of Qualitative Studies in Education, 11*, 57–80.

Post-trial proposed findings of facts and conclusions of law. (1990). Jointly submitted by the *Knight* and *Sims* plaintiffs and defendants to the board of trustees for Alabama A & M University and Alabama State University. Civil Action No. V83–M–1676–S. Birmingham, AL.

Preer, J. L. (1982). Lawyers v. Educators: *Black colleges and desegregation in public higher education*. Westport, CT: Greenwood.

Regents of the University of California v. Bakke, 438 U.S. 265 (1978).

Roithmayr, D. (1999). Introduction to critical race theory in educational research and praxis. In L. Parker, D. Deyhle, & S. Villenas (Eds.), *Race is...race isn't: Critical race theory and qualitative studies in education* (pp. 1–6). Boulder, CO: Westview Press.

Sav, G. T. (1997). Separate and unequal: State financing of historically black colleges and universities. *Journal of Blacks in Higher Education, 15*, 101–104.

Scheurich, J. J. (1994). Policy archeology: A new policy studies methodology. *Journal of Education Policy, 9*, 297–316.

Schiff, M. (1985). Reverse discrimination re-defined as equal protection: The Orwellian nightmare in the enforcement of civil rights laws. *Harvard Journal of Law and Public Policy, 8*, 627–687.

Schmidt, P. (2001, May 25). U of California ends affirmative action ban. *The Chronicle of Higher Education*, pp. 23–25.

Smedley, A. (1999). *Race in North America: Origin and evolution of a world view* (2nd ed.). Boulder, CO: Westview Press.

Solorzano, D. G. (1997). Images and words that wound: Critical race theory, racial stereotyping and teacher education. *Teacher Education Quarterly, 24*, 5–19.

Solorzano, D. G. (1998). Critical race theory, racial and gender micro aggressions, and the experiences of Chicana and Chicano scholars. *International Journal of Qualitative Studies in Education, 11*, 121–136.

Solorzano, D. G., & Yosso, T. J. (in press). Critical race methodology: Counter storytelling as an analytical framework for education research. *Qualitative Inquiry*.

Special issue on LatCrit theory. (1996). *La Raza Law Journal, 9*, 1–101.

Stanfield, J. H., II. (1999). Slipping through the front door: Relevant social scientific evaluation in the people of color century. *American Journal of Evaluation, 20*, 415–431.

Stefkovich, J. A., & Leas, T. (1994). A legal history of desegregation in higher education. *Journal of Negro Education, 63*, 406–420.

Tanaka, G., & Cruz, C. (1998). The locker room: Eroticism and exoticism in a polyphonic text. *International Journal of Qualitative Studies in Education, 11*, 137–154.

Tate, W. F., IV. (1997). Critical race theory in education: History, theory, and implications. In M. Apple (Ed.), *Review of Research in Education* (pp. 195–250). Washington, DC: American Educational Research Association.

Taylor, E. (2000). Critical race theory and interest convergence in the backlash against affirmative action: Washington State and Initiative 200. *Teachers College Record, 102*, 539–560.

Taylor, S., Rizvi, F., Lingard, B., & Henry, M. (1997). *Educational policy and the politics of change*. New York: Routledge.

Thornton, J. M. (1991, December 27). *Testimony for the* Knight *plaintiffs on history of desegregation in Alabama as expert witness.* U.S. District Court, Northern District of Alabama Southern Division, Civil Action CV83–M–1676–S.

Tolett, K. S. (1973). Black institutions of higher learning: Inadvertent victims or necessary sacrifices? *The Black Law Journal, 3,* 162–175.

U.S. v. Fordice, 112 S. Ct. 2727 (1992).

Villalpando, O. (2000, November). *Self-segregation or self-preservation? A critical race theory and Latina/o critical theory analysis of a study of Chicana/o college students.* Paper presented for session symposium on critical race perspectives, interdisciplinary implications and teaching concerns, at the annual meeting of the American Educational Studies Association, Vancouver, BC, Canada.

Villenas, S., Deyhle, D., & Parker, L. (1999). Critical race theory and praxis: Chicano(a)/Latino(a), and Navajo struggles for dignity, educational equity and social justice. In L. Parker, D. Deyhle, & S. Villenas (Eds.), *Race is...race isn't: Critical race theory and qualitative studies in education* (pp. 31–52). Boulder, CO: Westview Press.

Vinovskis, M. V. (1999). *History and educational policymaking.* New Haven, CT: Yale University Press.

Ware, L. (1994). The most visible vestige: Black colleges after Fordice. *Boston College Law Review, 35,* 633–680.

Williams, J. B. (1997). *Race discrimination in public higher education: Interpreting Federal civil rights enforcement, 1964–1996.* Westport, CT: Prager.

Wing, A. (1997). *Critical race feminism: A reader.* New York: New York University Press.

Young, M. D. (1999). Multifocal educational policy research: Toward a method for enhancing traditional educational policy studies. *American Educational Research Journal, 36,* 677–714.

8

Race-Based Methodologies: Multicultural Methods or Epistemological Shifts?

Wanda Pillow

We, the natives of this continent, are the storiers of presence.
—Gerald Vizenor, 1998

As the circle of who has a say over what we know and how we come to know has expanded, so have our discussions of research methodologies and epistemologies. Indeed, it may even feel to some that we are now in a state of proliferating epistemologies as attention to varying epistemological frameworks for research—including Black Feminist (Collins, 1991), Chicana (Delgado Bernal, 1998; Trujillo, 1998; Villenas, 1996), Critical Race Theory (Crenshaw et al., 1995; Ladson-Billings & Tate, 1995; Parker, Dehyle, & Villenas, 1999; Solorzano, 1998; Solorzano & Villalpando, 1998; Tate, 1997), First Nations and Indigenous (Bishop, 1998; Hermes, 1998; Rains, Archibald, & Dehyle, 2000), Queer (Britzman, 1995; Tierney, 1999), and Borderlands (Anzaldúa, 1987; Elenes, 1997)—has been growing. However, the emergence of what I will here term "race-based" research methodologies[1] has been questioned, and at times dismissed as ideological and political rather than given serious attention as real or legitimate research methods, methodologies, and epistemologies.

For example, an American Educational Research Association (AERA) conference panel (Donmoyer, 2000) witnessed poststructural theorists voicing concern over a proliferation of epistemologies, questioning whether these new race-based research examples really should be counted as epistemolgical and methodological shifts. Aside from the irony of poststructuralists speaking against the proliferating of anything, what is most interesting to ask is why this concern was voiced, why it was raised at this particular point in time, and as Cynthia Tyson (1998) asked, "who benefits" from such discussions? While some (e.g., Miller, 1998) characterize the proliferation of epistemologies as relativistic, meaningless, and methodologically flawed, and others (e.g., Seale, 1999) feel it is leaving researchers in an abyss of methods talk, Denzin and Lincoln (1994) remind us that proliferation is often a marker—a "moment" in qualitative methods—of paradigm shifts and responses to crises of representation and legitimation. However, as Cynthia Dillard (2000b) on the above AERA panel challenged, "who is this [proliferating epistemologies] a concern for?"

Given Dillard's challenge to unpack the discourse of paradigm proliferation and think about who was talking (or not talking) about race-based methodological work and how this work was situated, I attended qualitative research sessions at this conference and observed three distinct treatments of this moment of crisis and proliferation in educational research. One approach to a proliferation of race-based methodologies is an absolute silence—an absence and an exclusion of any shifts in thinking brought about by race-based methodology. In these sessions, the broad depth of history, literature, and research in race theory and race-based methodology and the many challenges such work has made to the field of educational research did not even register a mention. *Race* in these sessions operated as a privileged absence—absent because these researchers saw no need to address processes of racism and racialization in their research, and privileged because approaching theory and research as if they are raceless perpetuates a reproduction of Eurocentric privilege reinforcing its own assumed neutrality.[2]

A second trend I observed operates under an inclusion type model, a multicultural model for panel sessions. Under this framework, sessions typically had one person—usually of color—who was invited into a broader discussion on research methodology. This person was situated as the spokesperson for race and race-based methodology—making a space for race-talk to occur in this space—while the other panelists usually did not speak to this work, except to perhaps critique it. In these sessions, because the person who spoke about race-based methodologies was often a raced person among a sea of others (e.g., White), the work of race-based methodology was easily discussed and dismissed by other panelists and audience members as not theoretical or methodological work but as racial identity politics. For example, after going to multiple sessions with many repeat audience members, I noted that it was assumed that the Black female would speak about race from a Black female perspective, not because there is a theoretical challenge from her work, but because of her ethnic background. While audience and panel members were often receptive to this work, acceptance occurred through a liberal inclusiveness that assumed they knew what this person would say. This process of racialized hearing always already delimited how the raced person would be heard.

The third trend I observed, although few in number, was discussion exclusively focused on the work of race theorizing and/or race-based methodology. These sessions did not make space for race talk or seek to authorize or legitimize the work of race. Rather, they claimed space for this work by utilizing and speaking to and from a rich history of race-theory work embedded into specific discussions of research methodology, epistemology, or relating of research results. Presenters in these sessions worked out of entirely different and differing epistemological positions and experiences and often incorporated research work that was educative and activist.

What the above depictions make apparent about this new moment in educational research is that while the new or alternative race-based methodologies have been questioned or included as part of a multicultural moment in educational research, there continues to be surprisingly little attention paid to the critique and challenges these methodologies and epistemologies offer to all educational researchers. Such absence of engagement allows and perpetuates a categorization of race-based research work as simply identity work, standpoint theories, or counter-stances. However, race-based methodologies offer much more than that. They offer a larger critique of the epistemological and methodological foundations of social science research, i.e., a powerful critique that is of considerable significance to all researchers. Race-based methodologies do not offer an "add race and stir" approach, but offer an epistemological shift in how we know what we know, how we come to believe such knowledge, and how we use it in our daily lives. This shift impacts and raises questions that are central to educational research including who can be a "knower," what counts as knowledge, and what the purposes of research and knowledge production are or should/could be.

In this discussion, I pay close attention to the different kinds of knowledge produced through race-based methodologies. After detailing the work of race-based methodologies, I briefly challenge some of the most common misconceptions currently circulating about race-based methodologies. Specifically I explore the limits of characterizing race-based methodologies as new and proliferating, as simply offering a counterstance, or situated as identity work, and how the relationship between poststructural theory and race-based methodologies has been characterized. Exploration of these points raises further questions about who can, does, and should do race-based research, and with what tools.

Distinguishing Methods from Methodology and Epistemology: A Dance Lesson

Before continuing it is important to distinguish between what is meant by method, methodology, and epistemology. Are we talking about a new way of doing data collection (i.e., methods), a new lens (i.e., methodology), or a new way of seeing and producing knowledge (i.e., epistemology)? An example here may be helpful. Building from Sandra Harding's (1987) description of the differences between method, methodology, and epistemology,[3] I extend her example to the dance floor. A few years ago, with many students, friends, and colleagues, I began going to salsa dance nights. A novice to the movement of salsa and merengue, I was dependent on help from my friends. Thinking about this chapter, I realized that some taught me salsa as a method, others as methodology, and still others as an epistemology. For example, two friends attempted to teach me salsa dance as a method—literally breaking the movements down step by step—first step forward, shift, rock, lift, back, and again, other side. I tried this, but as I looked around I realized that while what I had learned in terms of the basic step was necessary, it was not looking or feeling sufficient. At this point, some other close friends, grabbed my hands and led me through their methodology—watch me and learn, feel the music how I feel it, move how I move, see you move like this and you feel it. This helped, but it left me dancing a copy of anyone I danced with. To make matters worse, if my friends danced away I was lost without their model, schizophrenically adopting various dance styles of anyone around me. So later, self-conscious about what I was doing and still wanting to "get it," I asked a dear friend, who moved uniquely and smoothly, to show me how to dance, and as she danced she replied, "I can't tell you how to do it, I just know how to do it; you just have to feel it. It just happens and you know it." Ah, epistemology.

I take the time to tell this story because perhaps like many other non-Latinas who started salsaing either as part of the Latin dance craze in the U.S., or as in my case, with Latina/o friends who included me in their dance nights out, I do not think that until my friend said to me those words was I thinking about the cultural meanings of this dance. What is even more important is that I was intrinsically aware of the cultural signification of salsa dancing; but that night, I was so intent on learning how to do the dance, I forgot the meaning, significance, power, and pleasure of the dance I was trying to learn. My friend's words, although kind, told me to stop trying to learn how to do the steps, and instead to watch and feel how the dance is done, and to accept that I may not ever get it.

This experience has affected how I think about and use race-based methodologies. Just as I dance many different kinds of dances, I need—personally, politically, and theoretically—to utilize different feminist and race-based methodologies. If I approach each methodology as simply made up of methods that I can learn to do, I miss the depth and critique of the epistemological foundations of each. Likewise, Harding (1987) in response to the question, "Is there a unique feminist method?" replies "no," and further suggests that such a focus upon methods masks the most interesting aspects of "doing" feminist research. To avoid this methodological trap, Harding (1987) shifts the question from, "Is there a feminist method?" to one of, what is it that makes, in her example, feminist research so powerful? Here I ask the same question of race-based methodologies: "What is it that make race-based methodological research so powerful?"

The Powerful Work of
Race-Based Methodologies

Important to the discussion of the work of race-based methodologies is an acknowledgment that most often those who are producing this theory and knowledge were and are constructed as racialized subjects, as the

Other, and thus have experienced the position of "being said." Race-based methodology thus shifts the locus of power in the research process by situating subjects as knowers. Race-based methodology work describes and provides a way for the "raced" academic to think about our unique roles as researchers and theorists. These are roles that exist in both/and relationships including insider/outsider (Brayboy, 2000; Delgado-Gaitán, 1993; Johnson-Bailey, 1999; Ladner, 1987), outsider/within (Collins, 1991), and colonizer/colonized (Villenas, 1996) and, roles that offer alternative ways of survival such as border crosser (Anzaldúa, 1987), trickster (Buendía, Chapter 3 in this volume; Vizenor, 1998), *la conciencia de la mestiza* (Sandoval, 1998), and *mestizaje* (Moraga & Anzaldúa, 1981).

These works push the edges of the boundaries of what is acceptable to do and talk about in research and disrupt the idea that one should not study one's own community. Indeed, Harding (1998) argues that work from those on the margins of institutions or discourse structures can "lead to a more objective account" (p. 155) of these institutions, discourses, and epistemological frameworks. More importantly, this work lays a groundwork for acknowledgment that there is something uniquely different that is produced when power relationships in research are redefined.[4]

Equally important to acknowledge is that race-based methodologies arise because existing theoretical models and methodological discussions are insufficient to explain the complexity of racialized histories, lives, and communities. Furthermore, as Stanfield (1999) and others argue, it is not only that existing paradigms are insufficient, but also that they are inherently Eurocentric and thereby perpetuate White privilege and reproduce racism. Scheurich and Young (1997) refer to this as epistemological racism—racism that, as Stanfield (1999) notes, is "more than negative attitudes and behaviors towards racialized out-groups. It involves the very way this society is organized, and significantly influences our views and treatments of self and others" (p. 420).

Thus, race-based methodologies repeatedly challenge the belief that our scientific practices and theories are somehow neutral and lay a foundation for examining the epistemological foundations of research and for developing alternative epistemological frameworks. This work is vital to race-based methodologies, for as Gloria Ladson-Billings (2000) notes, "the claim of an epistemological ground is a crucial legitimating force"

(p. 258). Beyond legitimation, however, when race-based methodologies work from a race-based epistemology, they raise an "epistemological challenge" for researchers, a challenge that critiques not only racism but also questions the "nature of truth and reality" (p. 259).

Only when this questioning is initiated is it possible to examine, challenge, and change existing models for techniques and processes of doing research. Race-based methodologies acknowledge and understand that how we conduct research is intimately connected to the kinds of questions we ask, how we ask them, and for what purpose, and that the processes of doing research cannot be disconnected from epistemologies that guide our research. As Mary Hermes (1998) states for herself, "the 'way' of doing research was inextricable from the research and its context and cultural locations" (p. 155). In other words, where we practice our research, with whom, and why cannot be artificially separated from each other. This leads to a blurring of lines between methods, methodology, and epistemology.

Thus, race-based methodologies shift not only what kinds of questions are asked, what Stanfield (1999) refers to as the "substance of questions," but also change the "process, the form in which questions are asked and analyzed" (p. 421). In this way, race-based methodologies focus on different questions, add new information, and shift our thinking not only about research issues or subjects, but also challenge normative, hegemonic frameworks. Additionally, as is evident from the above, a shift in thinking about race correlates to a shift in thinking about the purposes of research. Prevalent in race-based methodologies is research "for"—that is, research that is useful and accountable to research subjects as opposed to providing or answering to our institutions (e.g., see Carter's chapter 2 in this volume). Race-based methodologies address what Stanfield (1999) names a "relevance gap"—a gap between how much social science research data speak to, and work for, the experiences of people.

Race-based methodologies and epistemologies including Critical Race Theory, LatCrit, Border theory, Black Feminism, Chicana feminism, and indigenous methodologies not only work to expose racism and processes of racialization but also work to give voice to differing discourses that seek social change. While this work may differ in styles of writing and trace different historical foundations, race-based methodologies do share several traits in common. Dolores Delgado Bernal (in press) combines Solorzano's (1998) defining characteristics of CRT with LatCrit theory as the basis of support for an "endarkened feminist epistemology" (Dillard, 2000b). These characteristics include: the importance of transdisciplinary approaches; an emphasis on experiential knowledge; a challenge to dominant ideologies; the centrality of race and racism and their intersectionality with other forms of subordination; and a commitment to social justice. These traits are evident in the chapters in this book and in other race-based methodological works.

An additional point that is important to forefront is how race-based methodology necessitates thinking about—and using—language differently. If language has been one of the "master's tools" used to reproduce oppression and racism, then language also needs to be rethought. For example, Dillard (2000b) notes the importance of this in her work, explaining that the use of the term *endarkened* feminist epistemology, in contrast to the term *enlightened,* argues for a "shift in our research metaphors and an uncovering of the ideologies that we have taken for granted, those that have traditionally left unproblematized our goals, purposes, and practice in educational research" (p. 662). Working within and against the limits of our language structures is one way race-based methodologies push us to rethink our categories and to rethink how we think we know what we know, providing a new ethics for approaching research.

Race-based methodology has also sought to identify and describe the different methods, processes, and epistemologies that are utilized in this work. For example, Delgado Bernal (1998) describes four sources of "cultural intuition" in her description of Chicana feminist epistemology, which incorporate "collective experience and community memory" (p. 563). A focus on collective memory, re-historicizing, as well as the use of narratives and storytelling in CRT and other race-based methodologies works to put race at the center of research, theoretically and in practice. This work then engages its methods, methodologies, and epistemologies in telling stories that have gone untold or need to be retold from the perspective of the raced voice.[5] There is power in this work as Vizenor (1998) states, "Native stories create a sense of presence, a tease of memories, and a resistance to pictures of victimry" (p. 154). Filling in the gaps and also retelling histories and stories is necessary work because of the dual existence of race as an absence[6] and as an *overrepresentation* in social science theory and research. In these dual ways, raced subjects are overburdened with the weight of representations and misrepresentations, resulting in a process of racialization and racism that race-based methodologies seek to deconstruct and relieve.

Thus, race-based methodology develops and traces an additional historical, foundational body of experience, knowledge, and voice from which to work. In this way, race-based methodology contributes to a decentralization of Eurocentric thought. Similarly, Kris Gutiérrez (1995) speaking about the development of ethnic studies notes:

> One of central aims of ethnic studies, for example, has been to make visible the essential philosophies, culture, and histories of ethnic peoples and, thus, to produce a complete scholarship that necessarily challenges prevailing Euro-centric thoughts and methods. From this perspective, then, ethnic studies is not the inclusion or integration of new themes or experiences into the existing curriculum; that would simply require studying new subjects through the same Eurocentric lens, rather [it is] a process by which students, teachers, and researchers develop new forms of agency. Instead, ethnic studies seeks to locate itself in a much broader sociocultural terrain in which groups of color and women of color are integral to the understanding of everyday life in American context. (p. 362)

Similarly, race-based methodologies exemplify how issues of race are critical factors in our research methods, theories, and practices. Race in this way cannot be situated as on the side, as an add-on category, or as a package of diverse research methods. Rather, race in this work is central to the theorizing and asking of critical questions about a range of epistemological, social, cultural, and political practices, discourses, structures, and institutions. Race-based methodologies make visible what is often invisible, taken for granted, or assumed in our knowledge and practice[7] and do this work out of necessity.

Common Misconceptions of Race-Based Methodologies

Although there is a rich history and depth to the development of race theory and race-based epistemologies and methodologies (e.g., see Goldberg, 1993), there are many common misconceptions of this work. In some cases, these misconceptions are themselves proliferated and proliferative—that is, they are prevalent in our discourse and are very difficult to change. By discrediting or dismissing race-based methodologies, these misconceptions also work to perpetuate Eurocentric privilege and reproduce epistemological racism. Thus, I specifically expose them here in order to challenge their dominance.

Misconception #1: Race-Based Methodologies Are "New" and Are "Proliferating"

While race-based theory and methodology may appear to be new to mainstream academic journals and researchers—where this work has not been cited, utilized, or published—it does have a long, rich history (e.g., see Guy-Sheftall, 1995; hooks, 1989; Outlaw, 1996). Indeed, the invisibility and masking of this history is one example of how epistemological racism occurs.

The choice of the term proliferation, in response to race-based methodology, is certainly not neutral, and like Dillard (2000a), I think it is important to ask for whom this proliferation is a problem. On the one hand, such a label is comical because a review of educational journals will make apparent that such work has not proliferated to any significant extent (Foster, 1999). On the other hand, the fact that race-based research is labeled as proliferate is indicative of the suspicion, skepticism, and mistrust toward this work in the field of qualitative research (López, 2001). Indeed, a disciplining of boundaries, voiced through concern over methodological soundness or proliferating epistemologies, works to protect White, Eurocentric privilege in the academy by continuing to situate some research and theory work as real and the rest as weak.

For example, Margolis and Romero's (1998) research demonstrates how this hidden curriculum in graduate programs "maintains an implicit hierarchy of knowledge" (p. 19) that not only maintains current practices of privilege, but also validates such practices. Furthermore, Margolis and Romero point out the paradox for female minority students, who when studying race, were seen as being "too close" to their work and thus not engaged in serious scholarship, whereas White males were reinforced and supported for taking up gender and race work. As Margolis and Romero state, "students of color pursuing topics directly tied to their ethnic communities must establish a delicate balance to avoid exclusion from mainstream sociology and 'banishment' to ethnic studies" (p. 23).

Thus, a discourse of proliferation around race-based epistemologies contributes to a disciplining of boundaries that works for those already privileged in the academy. Moreover, this discourse highlights the need for surveillance and containment of raced work. It must be surveilled because it exposes race-based methodology to a type of scrutiny not put on other work; it must be contained because proliferation encourages feelings of an epidemic and/or crisis within the academy. Perhaps race-based epistemologies feel proliferative because unlike most academic race talk, this work is occurring not only through a Black/White lens, but encompasses a range of multiplicity of identities and epistemologies, including indigenous, Indian, Black feminist, Chicana, Queer, CRT, and LatCrit.

Indeed, Dillard (2000a) asserts that the questions arising around proliferating paradigms are not due to the proliferation of different paradigms, but rather, the fact that different people are now using these paradigms. Additionally, race-based methodologies may feel proliferative because this work does not make apparent how a White academic can engage in, or use these approaches: "Here is something new and I cannot use it!"—a situation that can cause much apprehension to the theoretically progressive researcher.[8] Because race-based methodologies necessarily engage in foundational critiques of all theoretical work, paradigms that are typically viewed as progressive and liberating in their methods, methodologies, and epistemologies (e.g., critical theory, feminism, Marxism) have not been able to claim an innocent space from participation in the (re)production of exclusion or of misinformation about people of color. In this way, a discourse of proliferation speaks more to the fear, anger, or alarm felt by scholars who do not see a place for themselves or their theories in a race-based future than it does about the state of race-based methodologies.

Misconception #2: Race-Based Methodologies Are Simply Counterstances

I have often heard race-based methodologies described as a trend, a present day historical shift, or a counterstance. These phrases all seek to suggest that race-based methodologies are temporal and temporary, and thus, short-lived. Whereas race-based methodologies do offer counterstances and countervoices that challenge dominant perceptions and conceptions of racialized and subjected individuals, they also challenge us to produce different kinds of knowledge and to produce that knowledge differently. Racialized persons and race-based methodologies experience and have to account for the need to both tell the untold story and the counterstory and to have this oppositionist story be heard. While working against inclusion as a remedy (Gutierrez-Jones, 1998), race-based methodologies recognize that hierarchical inversions of power, for example, will not be enough. Race-based methodologies work beyond a counterstance toward a dismantling of Eurocentric and racist theories and practices.

As Anzaldúa (1987) notes, "it is not enough to stand on the opposite river bank, shouting questions, challenging patriarchal, white conventions" (p. 78). This would, as she further explains, "lock one into a duel of oppressor and oppressed" making "all reaction limited by, and dependent on, what it is reacting against" (p. 78). Anzaldúa acknowledges that a counterstance is necessary as "a step towards liberation from cultural domination," but "it is not a way of life" (p. 78). She suggests that once we let go of reacting to dominance, "the possibilities are numerous," including existing "on both shores at once" or to "disengage from the dominant culture…and cross the border into a wholly new and separate territory" or "another route" that we may not know yet (pp. 78–79). The race-based methodologies discussed in this book chose differing possibilities, but they all work toward possibilities beyond counterstances and need to be read and understood as such.

Misconception #3: Race-Based Methodologies Are Simply Identity Politics

Because race-based methodologies place race central to theory and practice, they are often accused of being politically motivated. That is, this work is largely seen as ideological work for a certain group of individuals and thus is not real research or theory work, or is methodologically flawed (e.g., see López, 2001, for tracing of this concept, and Miller, 1998, as an example of this critique). Conflation of the author's identity with identity politics dismisses and ignores the epistemological insights of race-based methodologies.

As presented above, race-based methodologies engage in work that engages the politics of identity as necessity, but also work to further question the structures, language, and practices that construct identity politics. Ladson-Billings (2000) argues "the point of working in racialized discourses and ethnic epistemologies is not merely to 'color' the scholarship. It is to challenge the hegemonic structures (and symbols) that keep injustice and inequity in place. The work also is not about dismissing the work of European and Euro-American scholars. Rather, it is about defining the limits of such scholarship" (p. 271). Working at the limits of existing paradigms raises questions and challenges that cannot simply be dismissed as identity politics.

Delgado Bernal (in press) argues that "endarkened feminist epistemologies are not just a darker shade of the same old popular research paradigms, rather they offer unique ways of knowing and understanding the world based on the raced and gendered experiences of women of color."

Race-based methodology necessarily engages in work that simultaneously creates spaces to (re)claim identities while also working to keep fluid these identities in order to interrupt an essentialization of identity that has often been so harmful for racialized persons historically. For example, racial minority women have always had to negotiate borders and intersections of their identities working within and against theories that do not account for the multiplicity of their lives. Race-based methodologies offer a way to speak to the complexity of lived experiences across multiplicity—to speak for cultural identities while also speaking against essentialistic discourses that have made these identities problematic. For example, Anzaldúa's (1987) work leads toward an understanding of Chicana identity and subjectivity that recognizes class, race, nationality, and sexual discontinuities within the Chicana/o communities and recognizes the relations between past and present oppression. Such work leads to more in-depth understandings of the histories, processes, structures, and discourses of racialization, racism, colonialism, and post-colonialism—identity work that is political and theoretical, but certainly not simplistic.

Misconception #4: Race-Based Methodologies Arise out of Poststructuralism or a Postmodern Moment

The emergence of race-based epistemologies is often linked with or characterized as arising out of a crisis of representation brought on by critical theory and poststructuralism. For example, Derek Jinks (1997) notes how "CRT is often characterized—usually as a precursor to criticism—as postmodern" (p. 502). This is an odd linkage to make given that there are various and ambivalent responses by CRT scholars and race-based theorists on the usefulness of poststructuralism (Collins, 2000; Jinks, 1997; Stanfield, 1999). While poststructural theory certainly has challenged epistemological and methodological foundations of social science research (St. Pierre & Pillow, 2000), situating race-based methodologies, which do similar work, as under poststructuralism creates an unequal relationship between these two paradigms, one in which race-based methodologies are beholden and indebted to poststructuralism (Pillow, 2001).

This misconception is even more striking when considering the paucity of poststructural education research that addresses race as an issue or that includes even a mention of how race-theory and race-based methodologies could aid in a poststructural analysis (Felski, 1992; Pillow, 2001). A lack of acknowledgment of the epistemological challenges raised by race-based methodologies affords theoretical primacy to poststructural theories and delimits the possibilities of exploring potential relationships between these paradigms (Perez-Torres, 1997). Such a linear tracing, which puts race-based theories in debt to poststructural discourse, masks other readings—other long traditions of *different* ways of knowing, being, learning, and seeing (Anzaldúa, 1987; Collins, 1991; Vizenor, 1998), which only works to continue a Eurocentric privileging of poststructural theory. A desire to place race in poststructural theory is as misguided as previous attempts to simply add race to critical theory, or feminism to Marxism. Race-based methodologies should not be subsumed under poststructural theory but should be read and used for the critique and insight they provide to poststructurally informed research.

In Conclusion:
Who Will Lead the Dance?

I have made a case for understanding and utilizing race-based methodologies as not simply new methods, but work that raises consciousness of, and asks critical questions about, our most fundamental epistemological practices. Such an understanding of race-based methodologies would make unsatisfactory easy incorporations of this work into qualitative research curricula as an add-on or as multicultural examples of doing research. Instead this work should be read, studied, and used for the methodological and epistemological challenges these theories raise for all educational researchers. Race-based methodologies are not a new tool or solution to simply add in, and thus take care of, oppressive privilege and racism in our research paradigms. Rather, they request something much more difficult than integration; they work to destabilize the very foundations for thinking about, doing, and writing up social science research. However, as Norma Alarcón (1999) notes, alternative epistemologies will certainly not make Eurocentric epistemology disappear. On the contrary, the biggest threat of the proliferation of this work may be that race-based methodologies and epistemologies will be subsumed by and under Eurocentric theory and practices.

Publications like this volume attempt to work against a too easy consumption and repackaging of race-theory work. However, a question remains, one that has haunted qualitative research for some time. That is, what do race-based methodologies tell us about who should study whom? Who can or should use these theories? What do I do if I need to work out of and with several differing race-based epistemologies at once? Echoing Guillermo Gomez-Pena (in Fusco, 1995) who notes that in the U.S. pragmatic society, "intellectuals and artists have to look the way they think. They have to look like what they believe" (p. 165), I wonder if we have to *look* like our theory?

This question is best addressed by returning to my earlier salsa example. Who should do salsa? Should Latinas/os be able to claim this dance as their own? What if you look like someone who should know how to salsa but you cannot—are you really who you seem to be? What if you are a Latina/o but still cannot dance salsa, does this make you any less Latina/o? These questions raise issues about the politics of identity, representation, and performance—questions that all racialized persons find themselves subjected to on a daily basis—and they also speak to embedded epistemological stances on race.

It is context, both theoretical and practical, that is important here. That is, it matters who is asking the questions and who is being asked. To be certain, where we are doing salsa and with whom we are doing it will change the context, meaning, and performance of the dance. While one can learn the mechanics of the dance and perhaps master the steps, many will argue that salsa is also a movement, sway, and a history that cannot be taught. It has to be experienced, felt, observed, shared, and practiced. Here I find Cynthia Tyson's (1998) response to the question of, "what is it that makes a race-based epistemology different?" particularly powerful. She states that what is shared and unique is a "specificity of oppression, one not based solely on victimization, but also on struggle and survival" (p. 22).

Race-based methodologies and epistemologies thus are different cultural intuitions (Delgado Bernal, 1998) and cannot be taught. They are learned and experienced from within. Perhaps this is what is most upsetting to many White colleagues—the fact that here is something new that cannot be easily replicated. To those theorists, researchers, and scholars who are serious about joining our efforts, I suggest they engage in the difficult process of "unlearning your privilege as a loss" (Spivak, 1993). This suggests that you dance with us—not as the leader of the dance or to master the dance and repackage it in some better form—but to simply listen, learn, and shift, both personally and epistemologically.

Notes

1. I am using the phrase "race-based methodologies" to refer to a broad body of work that has challenged and continues to challenge Eurocentrism and racism in existing frameworks and epistemologies for doing and thinking about social science research.

2. As Stanfield (1999) and Scheurich and Young (1997) point out, a privileged absence of race in theory and research not only perpetuates Eurocentric privilege but it is also a form of epistemological racism.

3. Harding (1987) asserts "a research method is a technique for (or way of proceeding in) gathering evidence" (p. 2) while "methodology is a theory and analysis of how

research does or should proceed" (p. 3) and "an epistemology is a theory of knowledge" (p. 3).

4. It is helpful here to look at feminist theory's impact on qualitative research as a comparative example because feminist research shares several common points of critique with race-based methodologies in fundamentally challenging traditional social science research. For example, feminist epistemology impacted methodological discussions about the processes of doing research, including what is studied, how, why, and to what purpose. Feminist epistemology acknowledges and affirms women's experiences and authorizes research that focuses upon the daily lived realities of women and exploration of issues unique to women that have not been considered to be important or legitimate to study. Feminist epistemology also leads to discussion about how to do research, questioning and interrupting standard assumptions about issues of objectivity, validity, and generalizability as goals in social science research and establishing new guidelines for how to collect data from women and for purposes of social change. Such emphases include work that seeks to recover women's voices, challenge what has previously been said and assumed about women, identify sites of oppression, and establish a place for new voices to be heard. While these practices led to new methodological and theoretical insights, feminist theory and research often excluded work that critically incorporated and examined the intersections of oppression across gender, race, ethnicity, and class in women's lives, thereby perpetuating a form of colonial thinking and Eurocentric privilege in this work (Anzaldúa, 1987; Collins, 1991). However, there is a rich and important history by women of color feminists that is vital to acknowledge and that has pertinence for race-based methodologies (Dillard, 2000a, 2000b; Sandoval, 1998; Trujillo, 1998).

5. Delgado (1989) notes the importance of this for CRT because history, collective memory, and storytelling shape identity, and identity shapes collective status, and from status rights are derived.

6. While issues related to over- and misrepresentations of raced persons in social science research, discourses, and cultural media may be more easily identified, the work of absence, not only as missing, but as a *theme*, is as debilitating. Vizenor (1998) notes "the absence of natives as an *indian* presence is a simulation that serves the spurious histories of dominance" (p. 25).

7. This is likely what makes many uncomfortable with race-based methodologies, that is, there is no innocent space for Eurocentric, White, colonial privilege and practice to exist unnamed. This critique raises questions and challenges about who can/should do race-based methodology work and how this work should be done, a point I discuss at the end of this chapter.

8. Derrick Bell's (1980) interest convergence theory is useful here to examine this response. Interest convergence theory suggests that White scholars will promote ad-

vances to standpoints by persons of color, such as race-based methodologies, only when White interest is promoted as well.

References

Alarcón, N. (1999). *Postmodern malinches: The making of a Chicana political imaginary*. Inaugural address of U.S. Latina/Latino Perspectives on La Malinche. University of Illinois Latina/Latino Studies Program, Second Biannual Conference.

Anzaldúa, G. (1987). *Borderlands/La Frontera/The New Mestiza*. San Francisco: Aunt Lute Books.

Bell, D. (1980). *Brown v. Board of Education* and the interest convergence dilemma. *Harvard Law Review*, 93, 518–533.

Bishop, R. (1998). Freeing ourselves from neo-colonial domination in research: A Maori approach to creating knowledge. *International Journal of Qualitative Studies in Education, 11*(2), 199–219.

Brayboy, B. (2000). The Indian and the researcher: Tales from the field. *International Journal of Qualitative Studies in Education, 13*(4), 415–426.

Britzman, D. (1995). Is there a queer pedagogy? Or, Stop reading straight. *Educational Theory, 45*(2), 151–165.

Collins, P. H. (1991). *Black feminist thought: Knowledge, consciousness and the politics of empowerment*. London: Harper Collins Academic.

Collins, P. H. (2000). What's going on? Black feminist thought and the politics of postmodernism. In E. St. Pierre & W. S. Pillow (Eds.). *Working the ruins: Feminist poststructural research and practice in education* (pp. 41–73). New York: Routledge.

Crenshaw, K., Gotanda, N., Peller, G., & Thomas, K. (Eds). (1995). *Critical race theory: The key writings that formed the movement*. New York: The New Press.

Delgado, R. (1989). Legal storytelling: Storytelling for oppositionists and others: A plea for narrative. *Michigan Law Review, 87*, 2411–2441.

Delgado Bernal, D. (1998). Using a Chicana feminist epistemology in educational research. *Harvard Educational Review, 68*(4), 555–579.

Delgado Bernal, D. (in press). Toward an endarkened feminist epistemology: Recognizing students of color as holders and creators of knowledge. *Qualitative Inquiry*.

Delgado-Gaitán, C. (1993). Researching change and changing the researcher. *Harvard Educational Review, 63*(4), 389–411.

Denzin, N. K., & Lincoln, Y. S. (1994). Introduction: Entering the field of qualitative research. In N. K. Denzin & Y. S. Lincoln (Eds.), *Handbook of qualitative research* (pp. 1–17). Thousand Oaks, CA: Sage.

Dillard, C. (2000a). Cultural paradigms revisited. Panelist on: *Paradigm talk revisited: How else might we characterize the proliferation of research perspectives within our field?* Interactive symposium at American Educational Research Association Annual Meeting. New Orleans, LA.

Dillard, C. (2000b). The substance of things hoped for, the evidence of things not seen: Examining an endarkened feminist epistemology in educational research and leadership. *International Journal of Qualitative Studies in Education, 13*(6), 661–681.

Donmoyer, R. (2000). Chair. *Paradigm talk revisited: How else might we characterize the proliferation of research perspectives within our field?* Interactive symposium at American Educational Research Association Annual Meeting. New Orleans, LA.

Elenes, A. C. (1997). Reclaiming the borderlands: Chicana/o identity, difference, and critical pedagogy. *Educational Theory, 47*(3), 359–375.

Felski, R. (1992). Whose postmodernism? *Thesis Eleven, 32,* 129–140.

Foster, M. (1999). Race, class, and gender in education research: Surveying the political terrain. *Educational Policy, 13*(1), 77–85.

Fusco, C. (1995). *English is broken here: Notes on cultural fusion in the Americas.* New York: The New Press.

Goldberg, D. T. (1993). *Racist culture/philosophy and the politics of meaning.* Oxford, UK: Blackwell.

Gutiérrez, K. (1995). Pedagogies of dissent and transformation: A dialogue with Kris Gutiérrez. In P. McLaren (Ed.), *Critical pedagogy and predatory culture: Oppositional politics in a postmodern era* (pp. 161–162). New York: Routledge.

Gutierrez-Jones, C. (1998). Injury by design. *Cultural Critique, 40,* 73–103.

Guy-Sheftall, B. (Ed.), (1995). *Words of fire: An anthology of African-American feminist thought.* New York: The New Press.

Harding, S. (1987). Introduction: Is there a feminist method? In S. Harding (Ed.), *Feminism & methodology* (pp. 1–14). Bloomington, IN: Indiana University Press.

Harding, S. (1998). *Is science multicultural? Postcolonialism, feminisms, and epistemologies.* Bloomington, IN: Indiana University Press.

Hermes, M. (1998). Research methods as a situated response: Towards a First Nations methodology. *International Journal of Qualitative Studies in Education, 13*(4), 155–168.

hooks, b. (1989). *Talking back: Thinking feminist, thinking black.* Boston: South End Press.

Jinks, D. P. (1997). Essays in refusal: Pre-theoretical commitments in postmodern anthropology and Critical Race Theory. *Yale Law Journal, 107*(499), 499–528.

Johnson-Bailey, J. (1999). The ties that bind and the shackles that separate: Race, gender, class, and color in a research process. *International Journal of Qualitative Studies in Education, 12*(6), 659–670.

Ladner, J. (1987). Introduction to tomorrow's tomorrow: The Black woman. In S. Harding (Ed.). *Feminism & Methodology* (pp. 74–83). Bloomington: Indiana University Press.

Ladson-Billings, G. (2000). Racialized discourses and ethnic epistemologies. In N. Denzin & Y. Lincoln (Eds.), *Handbook of qualitative research* (2nd ed) (pp. 257–278). Thousand Oaks, CA: Sage.

Ladson-Billings, G., & Tate, W. F., IV. (1995). Toward a critical race theory of education. *Teachers College Record, 97*, 47–63.

López, G. R. (2001). Re-visiting white racism in educational research: Critical race theory and the problem of method. *Educational Researcher, 30*(1), 29–33.

Margolis, E., & Romero, M. (1998). The department is very male, very white, very old, and very conservative: The functioning of the hidden curriculum in graduate sociology departments. *Harvard Educational Review, 68*(1), 1–32.

Miller, S. I. (1998). Response: Coloring within and outside the lines: Some comments on Scheurich and Young's "Coloring epistemologies: Are our research epistemologies racially biased?" *Educational Researcher, 27*(9), 23–26.

Moraga, C., & Anzaldúa, G. (Eds.). (1981). *This bridge called my back: Writings by radical women of color.* New York: Kitchen Table/Women of Color Press.

Outlaw, L. T., Jr. (1996). *On race and philosophy.* New York: Routledge.

Parker, L., Deyhle, D., & Villenas, S. (Eds). (1999). *Race is...race isn't: Critical race theory and qualitative studies in education*. Boulder, CO: Westview Press.

Perez-Torres, R. (1997). Nomads and migrants: Negotiating a multicultural postmodern-ism. In A. Darder, R. D. Torres, & H. Guttierrez (Eds.), *Latinos and education* (pp. 239–258). New York: Routledge.

Pillow, W. S. (2001). *Why Foucault? Thinking about race, colonial desire, and poststruc-tural responsibility*. Invited paper presented at AERA Annual Meeting: Seattle, WA.

Rains, F. V., Archibald, J. A., & Deyhle, D. (Eds.). (2000). Through our eyes and in our own words: The voices of indigenous scholars [Special Issue]. *International Journal of Qualitative Studies in Education, 13*(4).

Sandoval, C. (1998). Mestizaje as method: Feminists-of-color challenge the canon. In C. Trujillo (Ed.), *Living Chicana theory* (pp. 352–370). Berkeley, CA: Third Woman Press.

Scheurich, J. J., & Young, M. D. (1997). Coloring epistemologies: Are our research epis-temologies racially biased? *Educational Researcher, 26*(4), 4–16.

Seale, C. (1999). Quality in qualitative research. *Qualitative Inquiry, 5*(4), 465–478.

Solorzano, D. (1998). Critical race theory, race and gender microaggressions, and the experience of Chicana and Chicano scholars. *International Journal of Qualitative Studies in Education, 11*(1), 121–136.

Solorzano, D., & Villalpando, O. (1998). Critical race theory, marginality, and the ex-perience of minority students in higher education. In C. Torres & T. Mitchell (Eds.), *Emerging issues in the sociology of education: Comparative perspectives* (pp. 211–224). Albany: State University of New York Press.

Spivak, G. C. (1993). *Outside in the teaching machine*. New York: Routledge.

Stanfield, J. H., II. (1993). Epistemological considerations. In J. H. Stanfield II & R. M. Dennis (Eds.), *Race and ethnicity in research methods* (pp. 16–36). Newbury Park, CA: Sage.

Stanfield, J. H., II. (1999). Slipping through the front door: Relevant social scientific evaluation in the people of color century. *American Journal of Evaluation, 20*(3), 415–431.

St. Pierre, E., & Pillow, W. S. (Eds.). (2000). *Working the ruins: Feminist poststructural research and practice in education*. New York: Routledge.

Tate, W. F., IV. (1997). Critical race theory and education: History, theory and implications. In M. Apple (Ed.), *Review of research in education* (pp. 191–243). Washington, DC: American Educational Research Association.

Tierney, W. G. (Ed.). (1999). Special issue on Queer Frontiers: Qualitative research and queer theory. *International Journal of Qualitative Studies in Education, 12*(5).

Trujillo, C. (Ed.). (1998). *Living Chicana theory*. Berkeley, CA: Third Woman Press.

Tyson, C. A. (1998). A response to "Coloring epistemologies: Are our qualitative research epistemologies racially biased?" *Educational Researcher, 27*(9), 21–22.

Villenas, S. (1996). The colonizer/colonized Chicana ethnographer: Identity marginalization, and co-optation in the field. *Harvard Educational Review, 66*, 711–731.

Vizenor, G. (1998). *Fugitive poses: Native American Indian scenes of absence and presence*. Lincoln, NE: University of Nebraska Press.

Conclusion

Gerardo R. López &
Laurence Parker

Most qualitative research method texts aim to provide readers with de-
scriptive and useful tools for designing, conducting, and evaluating
qualitative research studies. By discussing concrete issues such as research paradigms, subject sampling, document analysis, fieldnotes, interview techniques, observation methods, and data analyses, these texts
effectively describe the terrain of good qualitative research. While some
authors are better than others in describing particular qualitative approaches, most individuals who "do" qualitative research—both novices
and experts alike—rarely question the validity, credibility, or trustworthiness of these approaches. In other words, the qualitative research
methods adopted by the larger community of scholars are seen as universal tools of human inquiry.

Conspicuously absent from these texts, however, is a critical discussion of race and racism—especially a cogent analysis of how race mediates and/or intersects with the research process. While some of these
texts may provide readers with a general introduction to "alternative"
perspectives and research paradigms, it is relatively safe to assume that
the vast majority of qualitative method texts tend to relegate race to theoretical footnotes and/or the occasional token chapter or special journal
issue. As Wanda Pillow cogently observes in her discussion in this volume, these "add race and stir" approaches fail to probe critical questions
that need to be raised about the biases inherent in traditional qualitative
pursuits.

Although a number of books, essays, and journal articles have
emerged in recent years to provide readers with a multitude of race-based
alternatives to staple methodological offerings (e.g., Collins, 1991;
Gordon, 1990; Parker, Deyhle, & Villenas, 1999; Stanfield, 1985; Tyson,
1998), the vast majority of this scholarship is not well received within

the larger academic community (López, 2001). In fact, as Pillow's chapter points out, critiques of this work typically take many forms:

- the work is quickly labeled as "identity politics" and is dismissed as mere ideological and political propaganda;
- the work is criticized for failing to distinguish itself from other qualitative methods and/or research paradigms;
- the work is identified and/or associated with postmodernism and other "new wave" theories and is summarily rejected as being unscientific; and
- the work is questioned for failing to provide "hard data" to certify its claims.

Collectively, these criticisms suggest the topic of race is not largely viewed as a legitimate arena for "doing" good qualitative research.

In contrast to traditional qualitative methodologies that are largely perceived as being racially neutral, qualitative methods that place issues of race at the center of their analysis are automatically viewed with suspicion. Because of this a priori categorization, the validity, credibility, and trustworthiness of race-based methlogies are constantly questioned within the academy.

Such criticisms not only reinforce racism by relegating race-based scholarship to a secondary position, but they also place those of us who write about them in a methodological bind: The more we write about the salience of race and racism in the academy, the more criticism we get; the more criticism we get, the more it confirms our beliefs. As a result, scholars who write in this tradition constantly find themselves searching for a way out of this methodological trap.

Out of this frustration and schizophrenic vacillation emerged the origins of this book. Born out of an incessant and disturbing need to unapologetically situate ourselves and our work within the larger academic discussion surrounding qualitative research, we started a conversation several years ago about the need to do something to shake up the academy. The idea for the book was further solidified when James J. Scheurich and Michelle D. Young published an article titled *"Coloring epistemologies: Are our research epistemologies racially biased?"* in the May 1997 issue of *Educational Researcher*.

Coloring (Our Own) Epistemology

The Scheurich and Young article not only echoed recent critiques made by scholars of color surrounding civilizational and epistemological racism in our research methodologies (e.g., Banks 1993; Bishop, 1998; Collins, 1991; Delgado Bernal, 1998; Gordon, 1990; Ladson-Billings & Tate, 1995; Stanfield, 1993), but it was one of the first to move this discussion to a national level by virtue of the forum in which it was published. Indeed, the race and racism allegations raised by Scheurich and Young ignited a debate in many intellectual circles—including AERA-sponsored internet discussion groups—about the nature of knowing and the possibility (or impossibility) of knowledge being grounded in different racial and cultural realities.

Admittedly, our initial reaction to "Coloring" was one of agitation, cynicism, and disbelief. The fact that two White scholars could garner enough attention from the research community about salient issues that have been discussed by people of color for many years was overwhelming. Indeed, we were simultaneously both shocked and annoyed. What started as an e-mail message between us, soon turned into an extended "electronic discussion" between several contributors of this book. Part of this discussion thread is reproduced below:

> Gerardo López: I think Jim [Scheurich] and Michelle [Young's] contribution is certainly "valid." However people of color have been saying exactly what they've said for years. Why is it that a prestigious journal privileges their voices over ours? Is it that their voices are less threatening? Would the reception be the same if two black people wrote the paper? It makes me wonder....Isn't our scholarship valid on its own terms? Does it need to be "approved" or legitimated by two White people before it is seen as legitimate within the academy?

> Larry Parker: My problem with this piece is not so much what Scheurich and Young said, but what [*Educational Researcher* Features Editor] Bob Donmoyer said at the opening of his editorial page. He basically said "...it is not always clear how the methodologies of color differ from some other qualitative methods, in particular, some of the methods emerging out of White feminist theory." Besides the overall tone of the introduction, which I found to be offensive, Donmoyer placed the burden on scholars of color to "prove" their case to the White publisher.

Gerardo López: I was also offended by Donmoyer's introduction. It was interesting to note how Bob "invited" scholars of color to prove their case. This reminds me of Gloria Anzaldúa's introduction to [her book] *Haciendo Caras* where White women asked women of Color to "teach" them about racism. After reading Bob's introduction, I felt as if the burden was placed on us (once again) to "validate" or "invalidate" what Jim and Michelle had raised.

Marjorie Davis: The issue I have is that he [Bob Donmoyer] gives too much credit to Jim and Michelle for "starting" the debate on racist epistemologies. Perhaps he doesn't know these issues have been around for a long time. On the other hand, perhaps he does know, but they just didn't make sense to him until two White people wrote about them.

Melanie Carter: I agree that the Scheurich and Young piece is troublesome on a number of levels. However, what is most troublesome, and actually dangerous, is that its presence in *Educational Researcher* and the aura surrounding it, positions two White researchers as representatives of the academy's "postmodern" take on cultured/raced epistemologies....Despite the nasty comments [circulating on the AERA Division D Listserv], or perhaps because of the nasty comments, attention (i.e., credit) will be given to Scheurich and Young for starting this debate when this conversation has been going on for a very long time. The difference is that people of color were always seen as "bitching" rather than "theorizing." (Personal e-mail communication, May 13, 1997–May 15, 1997)

To be certain, Bob Donmoyer was very sympathetic and understanding of our position—especially when we brought these issues to his attention. In fact, on more than one occasion, he encouraged us to individually and collectively submit our ideas and work to *Educational Researcher* for consideration.

However, we felt that writing a response to "Coloring" was not where we wanted to focus our collective energies. It was our belief that the focus of our writing should not center around Scheurich and Young but should emerge from our own situated realities. In effect, we did not want to further privilege the work of two White scholars; doing so would only substantiate Melanie Carter's claim that too much attention and credit was given to Scheurich and Young for bringing these issues to the fore. Rather, we wanted to re-focus, and re-center, the larger academic discussion on the various ways in which race mediates, influences, and "colors" the work we do.

After several years of discussing and "working through" these issues, the chapters in this volume are the cumulative result of our efforts to craft our own arguments and begin the process of coloring our own epistemology.

Individual and Collective Insights

The chapters in this book provide a broad foundation for understanding the various ways in which race colors our research. Rather than merely accept at face value the "stock stories" that circulate every day about the "real," each chapter in this book suggests that the real is itself a manifestation of a highly racialized discourse (Delgado, 1995). Similar to Critical Race Theorists who write about these issues in the legal arena, the authors in this book challenge our most fundamental assumptions about knowledge and truth through the process of counterstorytelling—stories that demonstrate and reveal different understandings of reality.

As Melanie Carter's chapter cogently points out, our fate, as scholars of color, is the fate of our stories. As such, we have an ethical obligation to challenge racialized misunderstandings and tell our version of reality in a more contextualized fashion. Rather than accept "stock stories" at face value, Carter suggests we must offer a variety of "counterstories" that accurately detail the role of White racism in the larger social order. While such a move undoubtedly places scholars of color and their stories "at risk" within the academy, Carter questions the legitimacy of academia as the validating site for our research. Instead, Carter believes our work ought to be legitimized and driven by the voices of those we research—its value, purpose, and significance driven by communities of color. By taking control of our stories—i.e., by asking "Who tells the story?" "How are those stories told?" and "Who is the intended audience?"—we take control of our fate, both inside and outside of the academy.

In like fashion, Cynthia Tyson questions the overall purpose of qualitative research and concludes that race-based scholarship is fundamentally influenced and driven by a different set of values. The knowledge we generate not only emerges from the specificity of oppression, but this basis influences the epistemological and ontological purposes of our research. Rather than generate knowledge for "knowledge sake," Tyson suggests our research should be driven by emancipatory purposes. This call for social change is fundamentally different from the call made by critical theorists—since people of color are the ones directly affected by systems of oppression. Although Whites can, and do, have a responsibility for joining our struggle, the specificity of oppression offers a uniquely different vantage point for understanding the negative effects of racism—offering an epistemology of struggle and survival that provides unique insights and opportunities for social change.

As the chapter by Buendía suggests, this unique insight carries with it different metaphorical structures for viewing the world. In essence, Buendía is suggesting the social imaginary of people of color is uniquely different from those of mainstream populations, offering alternative metaphorical systems that often "speak against" dominant renderings. These counternarratives not only provide a different understanding of reality but open up possibilities for understanding this reality in new and fundamentally different ways.

López continues this dialogue by probing the counternarratives of parent involvement in migrant households. Not only does his chapter substantiate theoretical claims that people of color have uniquely different epistemologies, but such understandings provide critical insights into our most fundamental assumptions surrounding educational policies and practices. In this case, these understandings not only disrupt the hegemonic discourse surrounding parental involvement but open up new possibilities, knowledges, and understandings of involvement that have largely been ignored in the mainstream academic literature. In other words, these counternarratives not only force researchers, practitioners, and policy makers to rethink their most fundamental assumptions, but they force them to resist facile explanations of school failure for students of color.

Similarly, the chapter by Parker suggests these "subjugated standpoints" (Haraway, 1996) engender situated knowledge that offer different values, perspectives, and understandings of reality. The legal and policy making process in education desegregation cases not only fails to take these perspectives into account, but it further exacerbates the problem by ignoring or downplaying the historical role of White racism in social relations. The net results are policies and legal mandates that have a deleterious impact on communities of color. Parker's analysis provides a provocative historical account of the concerted legal attack against HBCUs—an attack that not only ignored their historical mission but thoroughly disregarded the role of racism in society by equating "race conscious" recruitment efforts with "discrimination" against Whites. In this regard, Parker's critique effectively echoes the voices of Critical Race Theorists who consistently point out the various ways in which the U.S. legal system works in the interests of White individuals.

The concluding chapter by Wanda Pillow not only effectively summarizes the "myths" associated with race-based scholarship but communicates to White audiences those very same issues that we have been wresting with all along: That our contribution, both individually and collectively, is not to provide audiences with a new multicultural methodology, but to allow them to see a different way of doing research altogether. In other words, our hope is not to merely tinker with the "master's tools" (Lorde, 1984) of human inquiry in order to make them more user-friendly, but to offer fundamentally different ideas that have serious implications for how we view, understand, and come to know the real (López, 1997).

Promises and Possibilities: Where Do We Go From Here?

In *Black feminist thought: Knowledge, consciousness, and the politics of empowerment*, Patricia Hill Collins (1991) cogently summarizes the educational importance of introducing and privileging historically marginalized perspectives in the research process:

> If the epistemology used to validate knowledge comes into question, then all prior knowledge claims validated under the dominant model become suspect. An alternate epistemology challenges all certified knowledge and opens up the question of whether what has been taken to be true can stand the test of alternative ways of validating truth. (p. 219)

In other words, subaltern epistemologies, methodologies, value-orientations, and perspectives not only challenge our most fundamental assumptions about reality and truth but challenge the very process of arriving at truth claims. They not only question the normality and presumed apoliticality of the knowledge production process, but clear a space for further dialogue on how race can—and invariably does—mediate the research process.

Challenging racial orthodoxy in academic research is not new, despite the fact that it has received increased attention in the post-Scheurich and Young years. Some scholars (e.g., Bell, 1992; Delgado, 1995) would argue that the racial problem in this society is not only intractable but insoluble. This notion is supported by other scholars who, like ourselves, claim that our research traditions emerge from racism deeply ingrained in society. Given this history, an overhaul in our research paradigms may not drastically alter racial relations in the larger social order to any significant extent. However, this reason alone should not stop us from thinking differently about the salience and permanence of race and racism in society—and the promises and possibilities that can be made given these circumstances. As Lazos so eloquently states in her introduction, this book is but a mere starting point in the larger educational conversation surrounding issues of race and racism.

As educational scholars, and as scholars of color, we have a duty to raise these questions about epistemological racism, interrogate frameworks and positions that privilege certain perspectives over others and challenge the truths we all take for granted. We have a duty to create our own theories and transform the "theorizing space" from which we and our theories have historically been excluded. As Gloria Anzaldúa (1990) reminds us:

> Theory produces effects that change people and the way they perceive the world. Thus we need *teorías* that will enable us to interpret what happens in the world, that will explain how and why we relate to people in specific ways, that will reflect what goes on between inner, outer, and peripheral "Is" within a person and between the personal "Is" and the collective "we" of our ethnic communities. *Necesitamos teorías* that will rewrite history using race, class, gender, and ethnicity as categories of analysis, theories that cross borders, that blur boundaries—new kinds of theories with new theorizing methods. We need theories that will point out ways to maneuver between our particular experiences and the necessity of forming our own categories and theoretical models for the patterns we uncover. (pp. xxv–xxvi)

Indeed, we may not drastically change research methods and epistemologies privileged in academia overnight, but we can—and we should—be at the forefront of social, educational, political, and epistemological change. Our theories, our fate, and our futures are dependent on this critical work.

References

Anzaldúa, G. (Ed). (1990). *Making face, making soul/Haciendo caras: Creative and critical perspectives by feminists of color*. San Francisco: Aunt Lute Books.

Banks, J. A. (1993). The canon debate, knowledge construction, and multicultural education. *Educational Researcher, 22*(5), 4–14.

Bell, D. (1992). *Faces at the bottom of the well: The permanence of racism*. New York: Basic Books.

Bishop, R. (1998). Freeing ourselves from neo-colonial domination in research: A Maori approach to creating knowledge. *International Journal of Qualitative Studies in Education, 11*(2), 199–219.

Collins, P. H. (1991). *Black feminist thought: Knowledge, consciousness and the politics of empowerment*. New York: Routledge.

Delgado, R. (1995). Legal storytelling/Storytelling for oppositionists and others: A plea for narrative. In R. Delgado (Ed.), *Critical race theory: The cutting edge* (pp. 64–74). Philadelphia: Temple University Press.

Delgado Bernal, D. (1998). Using a Chicana feminist epistemology in educational research. *Harvard Educational Review, 68*(4), 555–582.

Gordon, E. W. (1990). The necessity of African American epistemology for educational theory and practice. *Journal of Education, 172*, 88–106.

Haraway, D. (1996). Situated knowledges: The science question in feminism and the privilege of partial perspective. In E. F. Keller & H. E. Longino (Eds.), *Feminism and Science* (pp. 249–263). Oxford: Oxford University Press.

Ladson-Billings, G., & Tate, W. F. (1995). Toward a critical race theory of education. *Teachers College Record, 97*, 47–68.

López, G. R. (1997). Reflections on epistemology and standpoint theories: A response to "An indigenous approach to creating knowledge." *International Journal of Qualitative Studies in Education, 11*(2), 225–231.

López, G. R. (2001) Re-visiting white racism in educational research: Critical race theory and the problem of method. *Educational Researcher, 30*(1), 29–33.

Lorde, A. (1984). The master's tools will never dismantle the master's house. *Sister outsider: Essays & speeches*. Freedom, CA: Crossing Press.

Parker, L., Deyhle, D., & Villenas, S. (Eds.). (1999). *Race is...race isn't: Critical race theory and qualitative studies in education.* Boulder, CO: Westview Press.

Scheurich, J. J., & Young, M. (1997). Coloring epistemologies: Are our research epistemologies racially biased? *Educational Researcher, 26*(4), 4–16.

Stanfield, J. H. (1985). The ethnocentric bias of social science knowledge production. *Review of Research in Education, 12,* 387–415.

Stanfield, J. H. (1993). Methodological reflections: An introduction. In R. M. Dennis & J. H. Stanfield (Eds.), *Race and ethnicity in research methods* (pp. 3–15). Newbury Park CA: Sage.

Tyson, C. A. (1998). Coloring epistemologies: A response. *Educational Researcher, 27*(9), 21–22.

Contributors

Edward Buendía is an assistant professor in the Department of Education, Culture, and Society at the University of Utah. His areas of research inquiry include the formation of school curricula and school practices as they pertain to immigrant students and students of color, and the possibilities and limitations of alternative research frameworks for engaging in Qualitative Research. He has articles in periodicals such as *Teaching and Teacher Education, American Educational Research Journal, Teachers College Record*, and *Cultural Studies*.

Melanie Carter is an assistant professor of Educational Leadership at Clark Atlanta University where she teaches courses in Educational Foundations, Educational Policy, and Qualitative Research. Her research focus is the historical agency of African Americans in accessing and creating educational institutions. Her publications include: "Race, Jacks and Jump Ropes: Theorizing School Through Personal Narratives" (2001) in *Sisters of the Academy: Emergent Black Women Scholars in Higher Education* and "Keeping a Close Watch: A Cultural Philosophy of School Change" (2001) in the *National Association of Secondary School Principals* (NASSP) *Bulletin*.

Arisve Esquivel is a doctoral student at the University of Illinois at Urbana-Champaign, Department of Educational Policy Studies, History Division. Her research focuses on Latinas/os in higher education, with particular emphasis on issues of recruitment and access. She is also interested in Latina/o Studies and the intersection of race/ethnicity, class, and gender. She completed her master's degree in Education at the University of Illinois.

Sylvia R. Lazos Vargas is an associate professor at the University of Missouri-Columbia School of Law. She is a race relations expert and Latino/a critical (LatCrit) theorist. Her numerous articles in the areas of citizenship, race, and equality advocate that U.S. courts recognize the role of interracial conflict in resolving constitutional equal protection claims. Her approach to Critical Race Theory is to concentrate on opportunities for positive interventions in resolving racial conflicts. She is co-director of the Multi-Disciplinary and International Project for the Study of Inter-group, Ethnic, and Racial Conflicts, at the Center for the Study of Dispute Resolution at University of Missouri-Columbia, and she is the co-chair of an interdisciplinary project examining the impact of Latino/as in rural Missouri.

Gerardo R. López is an assistant professor in the Department of Educational Leadership and Policy Studies at Indiana University. His specializations are educational policy, parental involvement, and school-community relations. He has published in the *American Educational Research Journal, Harvard Educational Review, Educational Administration Quarterly, International Journal of Qualitative Studies in Education*, and *Educational Researcher.*

Jennifer Ng is a doctoral student in Educational Policy Studies at the University of Illinois at Urbana-Champaign. She is a former middle school English teacher, and her research interests include issues of race, class, and gender on teacher preparation for education in urban contexts.

Laurence Parker is an associate professor in the Department of Educational Policy Studies at the University of Illinois at Urbana-Champaign. His research and teaching interests are in the area of critical race theory and educational policy, urban education leadership, and higher education desegregation. He is currently working on a book addressing African American community of interest related to desegregation and affirmative action in higher education.

Wanda Pillow is an assistant professor in the Department of Educational Policy Studies at the University of Illinois Urbana-Champaign. Her research and teaching interests cross policy studies, qualitative methodology, and feminist poststructural theory. She is completing a book on teen pregnancy educational policy and is continuing her research on the uses of present and past representations and writings about Sacajawea.

Cynthia Tyson is an assistant professor in the School of Teaching and Learning at the Ohio State University where she teaches courses in social studies/global and multicultural education. Her research interest include the examination of race/racism in qualitative research, the development of sociopolitical identity in civic education, and how literature written for children and young adults impacts student social activism. She has published articles in *Educational Researcher, International Journal of Qualitative Studies in Education, Journal of Literacy Research,* and other books and journals.

Index

Studies in the Postmodern Theory of Education

General Editors
Joe L. Kincheloe & Shirley R. Steinberg

Counterpoints publishes the most compelling and imaginative books being written in education today. Grounded on the theoretical advances in criticalism, feminism, and postmodernism in the last two decades of the twentieth century, Counterpoints engages the meaning of these innovations in various forms of educational expression. Committed to the proposition that theoretical literature should be accessible to a variety of audiences, the series insists that its authors avoid esoteric and jargonistic languages that transform educational scholarship into an elite discourse for the initiated. Scholarly work matters only to the degree it affects consciousness and practice at multiple sites. Counterpoints' editorial policy is based on these principles and the ability of scholars to break new ground, to open new conversations, to go where educators have never gone before.

For additional information about this series or for the submission of manuscripts, please contact:

Joe L. Kincheloe & Shirley R. Steinberg
c/o Peter Lang Publishing, Inc.
275 Seventh Avenue, 28th floor
New York, New York 10001

To order other books in this series, please contact our Customer Service Department:

(800) 770-LANG (within the U.S.)
(212) 647-7706 (outside the U.S.)
(212) 647-7707 FAX

Or browse online by series:
www.peterlangusa.com